Securing an IT Organization through Governance, Risk Management, and Audit

T0382820

Internal Audit and IT Audit

Series Editor: Dan Swanson

PUBLISHED

Leading the Internal Audit Function
by Lynn Fountain
ISBN: 978-1-4987-3042-6

Securing an IT Organization through Governance, Risk Management, and Audit
by Kenneth Sigler and James L. Rainey, III
ISBN: 978-1-4987-3731-9

CyberSecurity: A Guide to the National Initiative for Cybersecurity Education (NICE) Framework (2.0)
by Dan Shoemaker, Anne Kohnke, and Ken Sigler
ISBN: 978-1-4987-3996-2

Operational Assessment of IT
by Steve Katzman
ISBN: 978-1-4987-3768-5

FORTHCOMING

Practical Techniques for Effective Risk-Based Process Auditing
by Ann Butera
ISBN: 978-1-4987-3849-1

The Complete Guide to CyberSecurity Risks and Controls
by Anne Kohnke, Daniel Shoemaker, and Ken E. Sigler
ISBN: 978-1-4987-4054-8

Software Quality Assurance: Integrating Testing, Security, and Audit
by Abu Sayed Mahfuz
ISBN: 978-1-4987-3553-7

Internal Audit Practice from A to Z
by Patrick Onwura Nzechukwu
ISBN: 978-1-4987-4205-4

Securing an IT Organization through Governance, Risk Management, and Audit

Ken Sigler • Dr. James L. Rainey, III

CRC Press
Taylor & Francis Group
Boca Raton London New York

CRC Press is an imprint of the
Taylor & Francis Group, an **informa** business
AN AUERBACH BOOK

CRC Press
Taylor & Francis Group
6000 Broken Sound Parkway NW, Suite 300
Boca Raton, FL 33487-2742

First issued in paperback 2020

© 2016 by Taylor & Francis Group, LLC
CRC Press is an imprint of Taylor & Francis Group, an Informa business

No claim to original U.S. Government works

ISBN-13: 978-1-4987-3731-9 (hbk)
ISBN-13: 978-0-367-65865-6 (pbk)

This book contains information obtained from authentic and highly regarded sources. Reasonable efforts have been made to publish reliable data and information, but the author and publisher cannot assume responsibility for the validity of all materials or the consequences of their use. The authors and publishers have attempted to trace the copyright holders of all material reproduced in this publication and apologize to copyright holders if permission to publish in this form has not been obtained. If any copyright material has not been acknowledged please write and let us know so we may rectify in any future reprint.

Except as permitted under U.S. Copyright Law, no part of this book may be reprinted, reproduced, transmitted, or utilized in any form by any electronic, mechanical, or other means, now known or hereafter invented, including photocopying, microfilming, and recording, or in any information storage or retrieval system, without written permission from the publishers.

For permission to photocopy or use material electronically from this work, please access www.copyright.com (http://www.copyright.com/) or contact the Copyright Clearance Center, Inc. (CCC), 222 Rosewood Drive, Danvers, MA 01923, 978-750-8400. CCC is a not-for-profit organization that provides licenses and registration for a variety of users. For organizations that have been granted a photocopy license by the CCC, a separate system of payment has been arranged.

Trademark Notice: Product or corporate names may be trademarks or registered trademarks, and are used only for identification and explanation without intent to infringe.

Visit the Taylor & Francis Web site at
http://www.taylorandfrancis.com

and the CRC Press Web site at
http://www.crcpress.com

Contents

V

Foreword

I am both honored and humbled to have been selected to write the foreword to *Securing an IT Organization through Governance, Risk Management, and Audit.*

This seminal work is long overdue. It offers practical solutions to a complex and expensive challenge facing our nation's critical infrastructure in both the public and private sectors. I do not say this lightly.

I have been actively involved professionally in the cybersecurity discipline for almost 20 years. My first big success was as the legal architect of the chairman of the Joint Chiefs of Staff–directed military exercise Eligible Receiver 97.

It was my first opportunity to brief the Department of Defense General Counsel and subsequently the Attorney General of the United States on the legal and policy implications and the technological challenges implicated in cybersecurity. It was also their first introduction to, and appreciation of, the proper role of technical means of verification via system penetration testing in order to evaluate the efficacy of the Department of Defense's cybersecurity defenses.

Eligible Receiver 97 was a watershed event. The "white hat" hackers, referred to ironically as the Red Team, successfully gained complete access to mission-critical computer systems at highly sensitive although unclassified levels. What was even more remarkable was that the tools and techniques used were downloaded from the Internet. In other words, these were tools that your common hacker could and did use to attack government and commercial systems connected to the Internet.

The success of Eligible Receiver 97 changed the way senior military and civilian leadership viewed the emerging discipline of cybersecurity. Resources were redirected from more traditional military programs to cybersecurity but the necessary sense of urgency never gained a lasting foothold. The cyberalarms went off but we all too often simply hit the reset button, hoping the problem would simply go away. Hope is not a strategy. It is not even a plan to make a plan!

I am of the strong view that the key individual in helping our nation appreciate the seriousness of the growing cyberthreat to our critical infrastructures was Richard A. Clarke. He was the National Coordinator for Security, Infrastructure Protection, and Counterterrorism under President Bill Clinton and subsequently served President Bush as the Special Advisor to the President on Cybersecurity. Many of the programs he advocated during his tenure, had they not suffered from being "over-coordinated," would have resulted in our national cybersecurity programs being more robust. I must say the same about Melissa Hathaway's efforts with the Comprehensive National Cybersecurity Initiative.

Where does that leave us today? I take little comfort in recalling the history of the Internet. The architects designing this information railroad of Internet commerce were "connections"—the engineer was "features"—and riding in the caboose that was left at the station was the flagman—"security."

Threat actors of the 1970s were largely mischief makers and pranksters. They transitioned a decade later from individual brigands with destructive intent to present-day brigades of hackers working in concert for profit. All too often, we learn that they are acting at the behest and under the protection of nation states.

We also are challenged by malicious insiders. They are like vicious rapacious moths gulping gaping holes in the thin fabric of security that was installed like a decorative curtain as a clever afterthought.

As a result, every day we learn of some new computer security failure brought about by known and unknown computer exploits. What can we do to reduce the risk?

I suggest that risk has three elements: threat actors operating in the threat environment; uncorrected system vulnerabilities; and unexpected consequences. Each leg of the risk triad must be reduced to more manageable levels. There are no silver bullet solutions but there are intelligent choices that can be implemented.

One such intelligent choice is *Securing an IT Organization through Governance, Risk Management, and Audit*. This book offers an implementable, realistic, cost-effective, and workable methodology to help mitigate the risk triad previously mentioned.

This is not a textbook, although it could certainly be used as one. The real value of this commendable work is to reduce the knowledge fog that frequently engulfs senior business management and results in the false conclusion that overseeing security controls for information systems is not a leadership role or responsibility but a technical management task. This is an example of arrogant hubris.

This book is better described as a manual that identifies and describes successful and reproducible business practices and processes directly related to governance, risk management, and audit. Drawing on the Cybersecurity Framework called for in Executive Order 13636 and developed by the National Institutes of Standards and Technology through a collaborative effort between industry and government, the framework identifies and describes standards, guidelines, and best practices designed to help mitigate cybersecurity risk.

The authors, recognizing that it is not enough to identify the most efficient standard from among the many from which we have to choose, take their scholarship to the next level by mapping the framework standards to a proven implementation methodology.

That methodology is described in detail in Control Objectives for Information and Related Technology, generally referred to as COBIT 5. The COBIT publications resulted from a series of studies done by the Information Systems Audit and Control Association, a nonprofit, independent association that advocates information security, assurance, risk management, and governance.

I encourage cybersecurity practitioners at all levels, as well as those in senior management, to carefully read, implement, and practice the techniques and methodologies set forth so clearly in this notable contribution to the field of cybersecurity. It is a book to read, study, and implement. The return on your investment of time, human, and financial resources will benefit your organization ten times over.

Richard HL Marshall, Esq.
Former Director of Global Cyber Security Management
Department of Homeland Security
Former Associate General Counsel for Information Assurance
National Security Agency
Chief Executive Officer, X-SES Consultants, LLC

Preface

The implementation of appropriate security controls for an information system is an important task that can have major implications for the operations and assets of an organization. Security controls are the management, operational, and technical safeguards or countermeasures prescribed for an information system to protect the confidentiality, integrity, and availability of the system and its information. There are several important questions that should be answered by organizational officials when addressing the security considerations for their information systems:

- What security controls are needed to adequately protect the information systems that support the operations and assets of the organization in order to accomplish its assigned mission, protect its assets, fulfill its legal responsibilities, maintain its day-to-day functions, and protect individuals?
- Have the selected security controls been implemented or is there a realistic plan for their implementation?
- What is the desired or required level of assurance (i.e., grounds for confidence) that the selected security controls, as implemented, are effective in their application?

An effective IT security program should include

- Periodic assessments of risk, including the magnitude of harm that could result from the unauthorized access, use, disclosure, disruption, modification, or destruction of information and information systems that support the operations and assets of the organization;
- Policies and procedures that are based on risk assessments, cost-effectively reduce information security risks to an acceptable level, and ensure that information security is addressed throughout the life cycle of each organizational information system;
- Subordinate plans for providing adequate information security for networks, facilities, information systems, or groups of information systems, as appropriate;
- Security awareness training to inform personnel (including contractors and other users of information systems that support the operations and assets of the organization) of the information security risks associated with their activities and their responsibilities in complying with organizational policies and procedures designed to reduce these risks;
- Periodic testing and evaluation of the effectiveness of information security policies, procedures, practices, and security controls to be performed with a frequency depending on risk, but no less than annually;
- A process for planning, implementing, evaluating, and documenting remedial actions to address any deficiencies in the information security policies, procedures, and practices of the organization;
- Procedures for detecting, reporting, and responding to security incidents; and
- Plans and procedures to ensure continuity of operations for information systems that support the operations and assets of the organization.

It is of paramount importance that responsible individuals within the organization understand the risks and other factors that could adversely affect their operations and assets. Moreover, these officials must understand the current status of their security programs and the security controls planned or in place to protect their information systems in order to make informed judgments and investments that appropriately mitigate risks to an acceptable level. The ultimate objective is to conduct the day-to-day operations of the organization and to accomplish the organization's stated missions using defined processes of governance, risk management, and audits.

Information is a key resource for all organizations. The information and communications technologies (ICTs) that support information continue to advance at a rapid pace. They are also under increasing attack. Destructive security breaches against financial, retail, and energy providers indicate a need for defined management frameworks that address technology-related risk at an acceptable level. Many organizations recognize this challenge but need help charting a road map to protect valuable business assets. They need an approach that draws on the success of others through manageable processes and measurable improvement. This book describes proven practices to exploit opportunity through a better understanding of organizational risk and active management processes. This book enables the reader to implement Control Objectives for Information and Related Technology (COBIT) methods as an effective way to use the Cybersecurity Framework (described in the following paragraph). Application of these components enables communication about priorities and activities in business terms, turning potential organizational risk into competitive advantage.

In 2013, U.S. President Obama issued Executive Order (EO) 13636, Improving Critical Infrastructure Cybersecurity. The EO called for the development of a voluntary risk-based cybersecurity framework (the Cybersecurity Framework, or CSF) that is "prioritized, flexible, repeatable, performance-based, and cost-effective." The CSF was developed through an international partnership of small and large organizations, including owners and operators of the nation's critical infrastructure, with leadership by the National Institute of Standards and Technology (NIST). The CSF provides a risk-based approach that enables rapid success and steps to increasingly improve cybersecurity maturity. Because these values closely mirror the governance and management principles provided in COBIT, those practices were used in the CSF as an implementation road map.

This book provides details of the CSF with emphasis on the processes directly related to governance, risk management, and audit. Additionally, the book maps to each of the CSF steps and activities the methods defined in COBIT 5, which resulted in an extension of the CSF objectives with practical and measurable activities. Achieving CSF objectives using COBIT 5 methods helps to leverage operational risk understanding in a business context, allowing the ICT organization to be proactive and competitive. This approach, in turn, enables proactive value to the ICT organization's stakeholders, converting high-level enterprise goals into manageable, specific goals rather than an unintegrated checklist model.

While the CSF was originally intended to support critical infrastructure providers, it is applicable to any organization that wishes to better manage and reduce cybersecurity risk. Nearly all organizations, in some way, are part of critical infrastructure. Each is connected to critical functions as a consumer through the global economy, through telecommunication services and in many other ways. Improved risk management by each member of this ecosystem will, ultimately, reduce cybersecurity risk globally.

Acknowledgments

A book of this magnitude could not have come to successful completion without the assistance of many people. First and foremost, we would like to thank our family and friends for their continued patience and support. In particular, much thanks to Ken's wife Tricia, who once again demonstrated the admirable qualities of the usual rock upon which his efforts are founded.

The months when this book was written were challenging times for James. During that period, he lost his grandfather. Three months later his grandmother passed. A short time after that, one of his brightest students lost his life to senseless violence. Each of these individuals played an instrumental role in molding James into the professional that he has become today.

Additional gratitude goes out to the originator of this effort, Dan Swanson, whose tremendous ideas helped bring the book to reality. We would also like to thank our acquisition editor, Rich O'Hanley, who has provided tremendous patience and understanding. Much thanks also go out to Bernadette McAllister, PhD, for the time and effort she put into providing content expert review and feedback. Finally, heartfelt thanks to our project team: project coordinator Hayley Ruggieri, copy editor Adel Rosario from MTC Publishing, and project editor Rachael Panthier. With the help of those three individuals, you are assured a quality reading experience.

Authors

Ken Sigler is a faculty member, since 2001, of the Computer Information Systems (CIS) program at the Auburn Hills, Michigan, campus of Oakland Community College and the chair of the Campus Senate. His primary research are in the areas of software management, software assurance, and cybersecurity. He has authored several books on the topic of cybersecurity ICT management, and to his credit, he developed the college's CIS program option Information Technologies for Homeland Security, which has a recognized relationship with the Committee on National Security Systems. Sigler serves as the liaison for the college as one of three founding members of the International Cybersecurity Education Coalition (ICSEC), which is now the Midwest chapter for CISSE. Throughout his entire tenure at the college, he has also served as postsecondary liaison to the articulations program with Oakland County, Michigan, secondary school districts. Through that role, he developed a 2 + 2 + 2 Information Security Education process leading students through information security coursework at the secondary level into a four-year articulated program leading to a career in information security at a federal agency. Sigler is a member of the Institute of Electrical and Electronics Engineers, the Distributed Management Task Force, and the Association for Information Systems.

James L. Rainey, III, DMIT, is an IT specialist with the U.S. government, where he works with a group of developers on modernizing systems. Dr. Rainey earned a BA degree from the University of Detroit Mercy in 1995 and an MS degree in computer and information systems in 1997 (where he studied under Dr. Daniel Shoemaker). He did a tour with the National Security Agency (Fort Meade, Maryland) in 1998 where he earned a citation for his work with one of their internal groups. Dr. Rainey also worked at GM's Tech Center in Warren, Michigan, while working for Electronic Data Systems (EDS) as a developer. Following his job with EDS, he worked at Comerica Bank's Data Center in Auburn Hills, Michigan, as a developer. He taught at the University of Detroit Mercy's Computer and Information Systems Department for 10 years as an adjunct professor. Prior to accepting this position, Dr. Rainey worked on a large-scale enterprise resource planning implementation as both a Systems Applications and Products (SAP) basis administrator and eventually being promoted as infrastructure architect. Dr. Rainey has been published in refereed IT security journals. In April of 2010, he successfully defended his dissertation at Lawrence Technological University, where Dr. Annette Lerine Steenkamp chaired his committee and Dr. Richard Bush served as a committee member. The research topic was "A Process Improvement Model for Improving Problem Resolution Tracking in Data Centers."

Organization of the Text

This book is divided into two parts. The first part is organized around the Framework for Improving Critical Infrastructure Cybersecurity. The framework is focused on using business drivers as a basis for guiding cybersecurity activities and emphasizing cybersecurity risk as a core component to an ICT organization's risk management processes. The framework is made up of three parts: the core, the profile, and the implementation tiers. Within the core is a set of cybersecurity activities, outcomes, and references that the framework prescribes as being common across all critical infrastructure sectors. At the profile level, the framework provides guidelines for an ICT organization to use in developing profiles. Through the individual profiles, the framework assists in aligning cybersecurity activities with business requirements, risk tolerance, and resources. The information resource level provides the link between the framework's defined processes to private and public sector standards that further define each process. It is through this linkage that COBIT serves as a primary resource for most of the processes defined in the framework. In general, the framework defines what needs to be done, and the provided resources (COBIT in the context of this book) detail how to do it. As a result, the goal of the first part of this book is to provide a comprehensive survey of all of the elements of the framework and how they work together to provide a mechanism for ICT organizations to clearly understand the characteristics of their approach to managing cybersecurity risk to ensure defect-free software products. In addition, this part presents and discusses three new elements that are necessary to ensure a secure software process: risk understanding, secure coding, and security testing.

The second part of the book presents the COBIT Framework in detail, addressing the following components: assumptions, IT governance, audit guidelines, framework principles, and the framework model. The framework is then decomposed to examine its content at a granular level, focusing on its practical aspects. Next, the control objectives from COBIT are evaluated from a high level and also eventually decomposed to further address the framework's practical elements.

The second part of the book also examines the IT manager's perspective on how the framework should be used to factor in strategic IT decisions from the perspective of what questions are addressed through the framework itself. The Capability Maturity Model and its maturity levels are also compared to qualitative maturity descriptions which are embedded in COBIT.

Finally, the second part of the book provides a demonstration of the concept by showing how to accurately build an audit plan following COBIT.

Because the intent is to provide comprehensive advice about how to structure and improve secure system development through defined processes of governance, risk management, and audit, these two parts are designed to cross-reference each other. The first part presents the commonly agreed-on elements of the critical infrastructure cybersecurity and the second presents the COBIT standard from the perspective of managing cybersecurity governance, risk, and audit. To ensure a successful learning experience, the authors provide

- Insights—Supplemental material inserted directly within the chapters to provide further understanding of presented chapter content.
- Chapter Summary—A bulleted list providing a brief but complete summary of the chapter.
- Case Projects—Hypothetical scenarios designed to put the learner into the role of management or other organization decision makers. The projects are designed to reinforce one or more of the major topics presented in each chapter.

PART I

Cybersecurity Risk Management and the Framework for Improving Critical Infrastructure Cybersecurity

1

CYBERSECURITY RISK MANAGEMENT

After reading this chapter and completing the case project, you will

- Understand the definition of *cybersecurity* and how it fits into the overall scope of information and communications technology (ICT) organization management;
- Understand the importance of cybersecurity risk management as it relates to managing ICT life cycle processes;
- Understand the relationships between managing ICT governance, risk, and audit;
- Understand the best practices for using standards and frameworks to foster productivity in managing ICT governance, risk, and audit; and
- Understand the benefits of using standards and frameworks within ICT life cycle processes.

Cybersecurity

This book is based on a simple reality. The failure to include governance, risk management, and audit within the management structure of an information and communications technology (ICT) operation leads to unreliable and insecure products. Accordingly, this book describes an approach that lets ICT managers establish and sustain a logical and secure management process. The advice shared in the book is supported by a well-defined and standard set of management practices that have been proved to ensure trustworthy products.

A common cliché used by many ICT managers is, "if it isn't broke, why fix it?" The answer lies in the growing number of harmful effects of exploitation. As ICT systems continue to take advantage of the Internet and cloud computing technologies, those systems continue to grow exponentially, connecting layer of software made up of trillions of lines of code. Those layers impact every aspect of the general public's way of life, from social networking and other forms of personal entertainment to national defense. A security attack in any of those layers could lead to personal tragedy or national disaster. How serious is the problem? Veracode, a major ICT security firm found that "58 percent of all software applications across supplier types [failed] to meet acceptable levels of security" (Veracode 2012).

Cybersecurity: A Definition

The field of cybersecurity has taken on a number of definitions over the years. However, the common body of knowledge throughout the ICT industry agrees that cybersecurity is concerned with creating and implementing processes that identify emerging threats in addition to providing cost-effective countermeasures to address those threats. The National Initiative for Cybersecurity Careers and Studies more formally defines *cybersecurity* as "strategy, policy, and standards regarding the security of and operations in cyberspace, and encompass[ing] the full range of threat reduction, vulnerability reduction, deterrence, international engagement, incident response, resiliency, and recovery policies and activities, including computer network operations, information assurance, law enforcement, diplomacy, military, and intelligence missions as they relate to the security and stability of the global information and communications infrastructure" (National Initiative for Cybersecurity Careers and Studies 2014). Cybersecurity as a discipline has grown quickly, most notably since the 9/11 attacks. Since that time, given the critical role that the Internet plays in our lives, a formalized discipline to study effective ways to ensure confidentiality, integrity, availability, authentication, and nonrepudiation of digital information has moved to the front of our national priority list.

Despite the national attention the field of cybersecurity has received since the beginning of the 21st century, there is still much debate about what mechanism provides the right set of actions to eliminate, or at least minimize, security attacks. Part of the reason for this debate is that the field of cybersecurity consists of contributions from a number of different disciplines. These disciplines include the following:

- Traditional computer security and computer science studies, which provide the knowledge for safeguarding electronic information
- Networking studies, which supply the knowledge necessary to secure storage and transmission of data and information
- Software engineering, which adds process considerations, such as verification, validation, configuration management, and other forms of life cycle process security
- Business management, which provides the knowledge necessary to conduct project management, create and sustain security policy, and enforce contract and regulation compliance
- Legal studies, which contribute consideration of intellectual property, privacy rights, copyright protection, cyberlaw, and cyberlitigation

All of these disciplines provide a distinct contribution to the underlying effort of protecting an organization's data and information infrastructures. It is only through collaboration between all of these areas, working together toward goal, that significant organizational effectiveness can be achieved toward establishing best practices for cybersecurity. There is still an issue to resolve, however. Many ICT organizations still struggle with managing "who does what." There remains a lack of clear understanding regarding the scope of contribution each discipline serves within the cybersecurity initiative. Regardless of the management structure, common sense tells us that there are three vital components that need to exist within an organization in order for cybersecurity to be achieved: ICT governance, controls, and audit. In a later section of this chapter you will learn how implementing a framework based on those practices is vital to the success of cybersecurity initiatives in an organization.

INSIGHT   CYBERSECURITY MYTHS
THAT SMALL COMPANIES STILL BELIEVE

High-profile breaches at Target (TGT), Home Depot (HD), and JPMorgan Chase (JPM) have put cybersecurity on the agenda for companies large and small. But despite the ongoing media commentary and "best practices" memos, consultant Adam Epstein of Third Creek Advisors notes that board members of small-cap companies and those considering or preparing initial public offerings are still befuddled by persistent myths on this topic.

The confused companies include many in Silicon Valley, where one would expect to find more tech savvy, he says. I asked Epstein, the author of a how-to book for corporate boards, to bang out a primer on what directors think they know about cyber threats but really don't. Herewith, his free advice:

1. **Cyber breaches are preventable.** No, they're not. Breaches are a matter of when, not if. As security guru Tom Ridge recently noted in my interview with him in *Directorship* magazine, your networks have likely already been breached. If Fortune 50 companies with nine-digit annual cybersecurity budgets can't prevent breaches, neither can you. Effective cybersecurity is more about identifying corporate "crown jewels," making it as difficult as possible for them to leave the building, and having a thoughtful plan for post-breach resilience.

2. **The information technology (IT) team is on it.** No, probably not. Boardroom cybersecurity oversight generally consists of inviting the head of IT to make a periodic presentation on the company's firewalls and antivirus software. Lacking security experts, most boards collectively exhale on hearing the IT update. Unfortunately, cybersecurity is only partially an IT issue. It's also a matter of corporate culture, employee training, and physical security. You need to worry about disgruntled employees and your supply chain, not to mention that little company you just acquired. That's way beyond IT.

3. **Cyber theft is about credit cards.** In the past several months, I've consulted with several boards whose members said that because their businesses don't store or process credit card data, this area isn't a cause for concern. Wrong. Cyber thieves have disparate goals, ranging from semi-benign mayhem, to espionage, to misappropriation, to terrorism. Credit card information is certainly a target, but so is personal info, intellectual

property, strategy memos, customer lists, and other nonpublic information.

4. **Always disclose cyber incursions immediately.** While it's admirable to want to get out in front of breach incidents and voluntarily disclose them, this can sometimes put a board at a disadvantage. Consider the Target breach, where the size and nature of the crisis expanded substantively with each press release. Malware can morph after being detected and wreak further havoc. It's often unlikely that the first information received by the board about a breach will be accurate and comprehensive, so exercise caution not to complicate a crisis by voluntarily misrepresenting it.

5. **No worries, we've got insurance for this.** A lot of so-called cyber coverage results from a three-page application that barely addresses the quality and extent of your company's computer-network architecture, physical and data security protocols, and corporate risk culture. The resulting coverage usually comes up short. Scores of cyber policies exclude more than they cover. Make sure the policy is underwritten after extensive, informed security assessments of your company—not just a standardized form sent via e-mail.

Good luck. You'll need that, too. (Barrett 2014)

Cybersecurity Risk Management

Simply put, risk management is the practice of looking at what could go wrong and then deciding on ways to prevent or minimize potential problems. It encompasses four components: frame, assess respond, and monitor. We all carry out informal risk management numerous times in the course of a day without even realizing it. Every time we cross a street, we stop to weigh the risk of rushing in front of oncoming traffic, waiting for the light to change, using the crosswalk, etc. Our ability to analyze the consequences of each decision is risk assessment. What we decide to do after performing that quick analysis is risk response based on proper early training and our experience of crossing a road. We may decide to wait for the traffic light and use the crosswalk, which greatly reduces the potential risk; we may follow someone else across the street, allowing them to make the decision for us; or we may simply choose not to cross the street. These decisions are a result of our risk assessment of the situation. If you make it across the street, you remember what worked. If anything went wrong, such as a honked horn or brakes squealing, you should evaluate (or monitor) whether another choice would have been better.

For a manager the issues of risk assessment may seem difficult and the right decisions for risk management may seem challenging; but the principles remain the same. It is the responsibility of management to make the best decision based on the information at hand. A well-structured risk management process, when used effectively, can help. In the case of a local government, for example, a citizen may report a pothole on a local road and you are obligated to determine an appropriate response. There are many factors to consider: what if a car gets damaged driving on the pothole? Is the cost to fix the pothole justified by the potential consequences? What if a citizen sues or seeks restitutions for the damage caused by the pothole? You have to analyze the risk and then decide how to manage the problem. Is it best to put signs around the pothole warning citizens? Should you pay overtime to send a road crew out to fix it? Do you ignore the problem? Risk assessment allows managers to evaluate what needs to be protected relative to operational needs and financial resources. This is an ongoing process of evaluating threats and vulnerabilities and then establishing an appropriate risk management process to mitigate potential monetary losses and harm to an organization's reputation. For cybersecurity, the program should be appropriate for the degree of risk associated with the organization's systems, networks, and information assets. For example, organizations accepting online payments are exposed to more risks compared to websites with only static information.

Risk Management Components

Risk management and a risk management framework seem to be the same thing, but it is important to understand the distinction between the two. The risk management process is specifically detailed by the National Institute of Standards and Technology (NIST) in three different volumes. NIST SP 800-30, "Guide for Conducting Risk Assessments," provides an overview of how risk management fits into the system development life cycle and describes how to conduct risk assessments in addition to how to mitigate risks. NIST SP 800-37 discusses the risk management framework defined by NIST. Finally, NIST SP 800-39, "Managing Information Security Risk," defines the multitiered, organization-wide approach to risk management that is discussed in this chapter.

Managing risks is a difficult, multidimensional activity that requires contributions from everyone within the ICT organization. The management at the top tier has the responsibility of providing the strategic vision and ensuring that the goals and objectives for the organization are met. The middle management plans, executes, and manages projects. Individuals that middle managers oversee have roles that require them to operate the information systems supporting the organization's missions/business functions. NIST characterizes risk management as "a comprehensive process that requires organizations to: (i) frame risk (i.e., establish the context for risk-based decisions); (ii) assess risk; (iii) respond to risk once determined; and (iv) monitor risk on an ongoing basis using effective organizational communications and a feedback loop for continuous improvement in the risk-related activities of organizations. Risk management is carried out as a holistic, organization-wide activity that addresses risk from the strategic level to the tactical level, ensuring that risk-based decision making is integrated into every aspect of the organization" (Ross 2011). Figure 1.1 shows the correlation between the components of

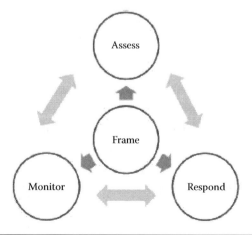

Figure 1.1 Risk management components.

risk management. Each of them interrelated with one another and lines of communication go between them. The output from one component becomes the input to another component. It should be noted that not every organization or periodical will use the same terminology for the four components. However, the criteria from which the components are based, and are described in the rest of this section, tend to remain consistent regardless of the terminology used for each component.

The first component of risk management addresses how ICT organizations frame risk. The senior management within the organization establishes the risk framework that will be used to define risk assumptions, risk constraints, risk tolerances, and risk priorities. Defining risk assumptions includes determining the likelihood that a vulnerability, threat, or occurrence could impact the organization and what the consequences or impact would be if it were to occur. Issues in the enterprise that restrict or slow risk assessments, risk response, or risk monitoring are categorized as risk constraints. Risk tolerances are those possible events or occurrences whose impacts on the organization are acceptable; often these risks are deemed acceptable because of the excessive cost of countering them. Finally, risk priorities are those events that must be protected against and systems that have a reduced risk tolerance. Many organizations prioritize system risk acceptance based on whether or not the systems support critical business or mission functions, as these systems have the lowest risk tolerance and highest risk priority.

The second component puts into context the organization's practices to assess risk based on the organizational risk frame. Before the organization commits resources to cybersecurity and ICT controls, it must know which assets have protection and the extent to which those assets are vulnerable. Risk assessment helps to answer those questions and determine the most cost-effective set of controls for protecting assets. Important to note is that not all risks can be anticipated and measured, but most organizations are able to gain understanding of the risks they face. Through risk assessment, managers try to determine the value of information assets, points of vulnerability, the likely frequency of the problem, and the potential for damage. For example, if some form of cybersecurity event is likely to occur no more than once a year, with a maximum of a $1000 loss to the organization, it might not be justifiable to spend $20,000 on the design and maintenance of a control to protect against that event. However, that same event could be found to occur once a day, with a potential loss of $300,000 a year. In that case, $100,000 spent on a control might be appropriate. Once the risks have been assessed, ICT management can concentrate on the organizational hardware and software assets (or control points) with the greatest vulnerability and potential for loss.

The third component provides practices related to how organizations respond to risk once it is identified. This identification normally is an input to the risk response from the risk assessment component in the form of the determination of risk, but it can also come from the risk frame in the form of the risk management strategy. The risk response serves to provide an organization-wide, consistent response that addresses the risk frame. This includes developing courses of action, evaluating alternative courses of action, determining the appropriate course or courses of action, and implementing the risk response based on the selection. These steps are illustrated in Figure 1.2. The selection made has the potential to change the organization's risk procedure and, once made, the other components of the risk management process need to be evaluated for necessary changes.

The fourth and final component of risk management is concerned with how organizations monitor risk over time. This component validates that the risk program has implemented the planned risk response and that information security plans are derived from traceable mission/business functions. It also determines the effectiveness of ongoing risk response plans and determines and identifies changes

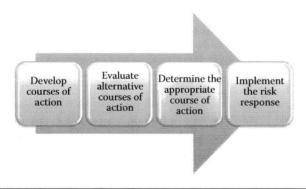

Figure 1.2 Steps of risk response.

in the environment that will impact the risk profile of the organization. The risk program can be modified as needed to respond to changes identified in the monitoring process. These changes initiate updates to the organization's risk assessment, risk response, and risk frame components.

As indicated in the four components of risk management that have been described, organizations must also consider external risk relationships when necessary. These external entities include those in which there is an actual or potential risk relationship. For example, consideration needs to be given to organizations that could impose risks on, transfer risks to, or communicate risks to other organizations, as well as those to which organizations could impose, transfer, or communicate risks. Depending on the type of business being assessed, external risk relationships could include suppliers, the customer's business partners, and service providers. For those organizations that have already identified persistent threats, specific attention should be given to the risk posed by suppliers within the organizations supply chain. Although management has control over the risks only within the boundaries of their organization, the more that an organization is aware of external risks, the easier it will be to implement internal practices to safeguard the potential for unexpected event caused by information sharing.

Risk Management Tiered Approach

In order to implement the risk management process throughout the organization, a three-tiered approach can be is used to manage risk at the

1. Organization level;
2. Mission/business process level; and
3. Information system level.

The risk management process is carried out through the three tiers with an underlying objective of continuous risk-related process improvement throughout the organization and effective communication between the tiers and among all stakeholders with a shared interest in the mission/business success of the organization. Figure 1.3 shows the three-tiered approach to risk management along with some of its key characteristics.

Strategic risk

Tier 1
Organization

Tier 2
Mission/business process

Tier 3
Information systems

Tactical risk

Figure 1.3 Three-tiered risk management approach.

Tier 1: Organizational Level

A risk management program is not going to be successful unless strategies are implemented and properly managed. Tier 1 is focused on risk from an organizational perspective by establishing and implementing governance structures that are consistent with the strategic goals and objectives of organizations and the requirements defined by federal laws, directives, policies, regulations, standards, and missions/business functions. The Control Objectives for Information and Related Technology (COBIT 5), a leading framework for ICT governance and management, and introduced in detail in Chapter 8, defines governance as follows: "Governance ensures that stakeholder needs, conditions and options are evaluated to determine balanced, agreed-on enterprise objectives to be achieved; setting direction through prioritization and decision making; and monitoring performance and compliance against agreed-on direction and objectives" (Information Systems Audit and Control Association 2012). Essentially, tier 1 implements the first component of risk management, risk framing, by providing the governance for all risk management activities performed through the organization. Tier 1 risk management activities directly affect and serve as a basis for the success of the activities performed at tier 2 and tier 3. For example, tier 1 defines the missions and business functions of the organization that, in turn, influence the design and development of the mission/business processes created at tier 2 to accomplish those missions/business functions. Tier 1 also provides a prioritization of missions/business functions, which, in turn, drives investment strategies and funding decisions, which, in turn, affect the development of ICT system (including cloud computing infrastructures and embedded cybersecurity architecture) at tier 2 and the allocations and deployment of management, operational, and technical security controls at tier 3. Trails of feedback such as these could, and often does, result in changes to the organizations risk framework.

Tier 2: Mission/Business Process Level
Tier 2 addresses risk from a mission/business process perspective. The input to this level is the risk context, decisions, and output of the activities at tier 1. This level in the organization has specific goals to ensure that the organization remains viable. Human resources is a good example of a mission or business process level function of an organization. Activities typical at tier 2 include the following:

- Defining the mission of business need
- Prioritizing the mission or business processes
- Defining the type of information required to carry out the mission or business processes
- Incorporating and establishing ICT solutions with required security components

Enterprise architecture decisions made at tier 2 determine the acceptable technology solutions that can be implemented at tier 3. Additionally, decisions made by management at tier 2 influence the allocation of certain security controls to specific components or information systems once they are implemented at tier 3, based on the organization's established information needs. Managers at this level may determine what technologies are acceptable for processing the information created from a specific business function. To achieve success, the selection of approved and prohibited technologies should be well documented and distributed to the business function area and all stakeholders (including ICT developers and administrators) who support the business function.

Tier 3: Information System Level

Tier 3 contains the activities associated with risk from an information system perspective and is guided by the risk context, risk decisions, and risk activities at tier 1 and tier 2. Activities at this level include categorizing the information system; implementing security controls, and managing the selection of the implemented controls, including continuous monitoring. The information system in this tier is at the core of the risk assessment process and dependent on the accurate implementation of security controls, including common controls across all three tiers in order to operate as effectively as possible. Controls not allocated to tier 1 or tier 2 are levied to the information system at tier 3.

INSIGHT   OBSERVATIONS ON THE RISK MANAGEMENT OF MEDICAL DEVICE AND SOFTWARE CYBERSECURITY

People don't do what we expect, but what we inspect.

Lou Gerstner
Former chief executive officer (CEO) of IBM

Many healthcare organizations have worked hard to reduce cybersecurity risks in recent years. Annual risk assessments have been completed, often by third-party security professionals. New technology has been implemented. Security-related processes have been improved. Additional staff with cybersecurity skills have been hired. Progress has been made. Unfortunately however, there is still much to be done before patients can have the level of confidence in the cybersecurity of healthcare organizations that they deserve.

One area of potential weakness is the supply chain and those vendors who provide applications and medical devices to healthcare organizations. Do they measure up to healthcare security requirements? It is not an easy question to answer, but it is an important one.

In recent years, the cybersecurity risks related to medical devices have captured much attention. Recently, a *Reuters* article stated, "The U.S. Department of Homeland Security is investigating about two dozen cases of suspected cybersecurity flaws in medical devices and hospital equipment that officials fear could be exploited by hackers." The devices under investigation include infusion pumps and implantable heart devices. None of this is new. In 2012, Jerome "Jay" Radcliffe described how he made the troubling discovery that he could hack the insulin pump which he wears and on which his life depends. In addition to the risk that life-sustaining medical devices may be hacked, and their settings altered to cause injury, there is the risk that medical devices may become infected by malware or be attacked in some other manner that exploits a cyber-vulnerability. This may cause the medical device to malfunction or result in the device being used by cybercriminals for their nefarious purposes.

How are we to respond to these cybersecurity risks in medical devices?

1. Know what the Food and Drug Administration (FDA) requires of manufacturers and healthcare organizations with respect to cybersecurity:
   - "Manufacturers are responsible for remaining vigilant about identifying risks and hazards associated with their medical devices, including risks related to cybersecurity, and are responsible for putting appropriate mitigations in place to address patient safety and assure proper device performance. Hospitals and healthcare facilities should evaluate their network security and protect the hospital system."

2. Don't purchase medical devices that can store electronic protected health information (ePHI) without examining the Manufacturer's Disclosure Statement for Medical Device Security (MDS²). This form discloses the cybersecurity safeguards supported or not supported by the device. This information can be used to evaluate whether a medical device has sufficient security safeguards. Do you, for example, want to purchase a medical device if the manufacturer states that they do not test and approve operating system security patches or allow antivirus software to be installed?

3. Ensure that medical devices are installed and operated as per organizational security policy. Important considerations may include vendor remote support processes, secure network configuration, installation and updates of antivirus software, installation of security patches as approved by the manufacturer, and back up of data.

Healthcare organizations need to be informed of the cybersecurity risks in medical devices and should make it clear to the manufacturers that purchases will not be made without evidence that cybersecurity risks are being adequately addressed.

Like medical devices, applications such as electronic health records (EHRs) and patient portals have similar risks. How do healthcare organizations know that an application is secure enough to protect ePHI? Cybersecurity weaknesses in applications have led to numerous security breaches. During risk assessments, hospitals should ask their application vendors for evidence of third-party security assessments of each application.

One recent response from a major healthcare IT vendor states that they have conducted an internal security risk assessment, the results of which are confidential, and that they did implement and verify risk control measures, but that there has not been any third-party security review. The vendor also states that the product has received meaningful use certification. Unfortunately, this is a pretty typical response. While it is reassuring to know that this vendor performed a risk assessment and implemented improved security measures as a result of the assessment, it is not too much to expect third-party validation of the application security and greater transparency about the results. The stakes are just too high to accept less.

If you are wondering if the EHR certification criteria dealing with security controls are sufficient, unfortunately the answer is no. While the application security controls addressed in the certification criteria are important, application security risks go far beyond what is addressed in the certification criteria.

The financial industry is ahead of the healthcare industry with respect to cybersecurity. The Financial Services Information Sharing and Analysis Center (FS-ISAC) recently published a white paper dealing with concerns about the security of software from third party service and product providers. The paper makes the following observations:

1. "It is the responsibility of the financial services industry to make software security requirements explicit rather than implicit.
2. If a vendor controls the development and build process, then they also are responsible for applying appropriate security controls."

The paper from FS-ISAC recommends three security controls. While all three controls are relevant to healthcare, I will describe just one. It is that financial services industry members should require their software vendors to utilize a software security testing methodology known as binary static scanning and that the scans be conducted by a third-party. The scans can expose security vulnerabilities in software and can be used by the vendor to fix security vulnerabilities before the software is released. A scan report summary can be provided by the vendor to the financial organization to demonstrate that third-party security reviews have been conducted and to communicate the findings.

The financial services industry has developed an effective approach to assure application security in its third-party developed applications. In healthcare, there is clearly a similar need since virtually all healthcare applications are developed and purchased from third parties. We need to communicate similar expectations. I encourage your feedback and suggestions on this important matter. (Bell 2014)

Managing ICT Security Risk through Governance, Control, and Audit

Earlier in the chapter you learned that confusion about managing specific roles within the organization to establish cybersecurity and risk management best practices frequently leads to compromise of information. Often, information will exist in two different areas of the organization and modifications made, in turn, lead to inconsistencies that make cybersecurity difficult if not impossible.

The best way to ensure that the compromise does not happen is to implement and sustain ICT governance program within the organization. Such a program should include strategies and policies that put technical and behavioral controls in place to safeguard all of the hardware and software that need to be protected. Security controls are technical or administrative safeguards or countermeasures for avoiding, counteracting, or minimizing loss or unavailability due to threats acting on their matching vulnerability, i.e., security risk. Controls are referenced all the time in security, but they are rarely defined. Further, mechanisms should be in place to ensure the employment and efficient use of controls throughout the ICT process. This can be achieved through performing audit functions that have been clearly defined in an audit plan. The purpose of this section is to take a detailed look at governance, controls, and audits in order to further understand their role within the scope of risk management as a vital component of cybersecurity. The remaining chapters of this book look at each in terms of their roles within the NIST Framework for Improving Critical Infrastructure Cybersecurity and the COBIT 5 framework.

Governance

You have already read that protecting data is priority within most organizations in light of the recent problems at the National Security Agency, Target, and other organizations. Developing policies represents the first step for any effective risk management and compliance program. Where do we start? Policies help align the organization to management's vision, effectively communicating how leaders wish the organization to operate and providing important guidance to management. Most managers welcome these guidelines when determining their course of action. While many policies appear to be obvious, most organizations implement governance based on established frameworks (such as the NIST framework and COBIT 5). Frameworks help guide the development of a set of policies concerning a particular area of risk or compliance. Other examples include well-known documents such as the International Organization for Standardization (ISO) standards ISO 9000; the Project Management Institute's Project Management Body of Knowledge; and Committee of Sponsoring Organizations (COSO), the framework that supports all Sarbanes–Oxley compliance programs. Some may view these documents as standards, which is true, but policymakers use them as frameworks to develop a set of comprehensive policies.

Most organizations share similar risks and objectives. Industry groups establish frameworks to try to address the same types of concerns. ISO 9000 became popular when many companies were attempting to improve the quality of their processes and products. This framework represented a proven approach, and thousands of companies became certified as a result. Likewise, the COSO framework has become the internationally recognized standard for financial reporting.

Developing an effective set of policies is a top–down effort based on an established framework, sensitivity to the objectives of the organization, the risks management faces, and regulatory compliance. Developing policies to protect sensitive data led us to several frameworks: We have already mentioned several NIST special publications. ISO 27001 has become the international de facto standard for information security management. Another widely used standard is the Payment Card Industry Data Security Standard. Since the early 2000s the management within the healthcare industry has had to become familiar with the Health Insurance Portability and Accountability Act, which provides privacy and confidentiality of all patient health data and information. A final example is Internal Revenue Service Publication 1075, *Tax Information Security Guidelines for Federal, State and Local Agencies*. All of these documents describe a series of recommended controls designed to address data security risks. Thankfully, they include the same types of controls and follow similar strategies.

The cornerstone of any effective risk management and compliance project is the risk assessment and strategic business plan. Policies support the organization's governance by meeting stakeholder needs and addressing risk. The upper-level management communicates their strategy through a collection of policies provided to the management. The risk assessment highlights the most important areas of concern and allows management to construct policies that address these areas, and most policies follow established frameworks.

The next thing we need to consider is implementation. Many ICT organization approaches borrow from change management strategies utilized during any significant organizational change. These strategies include education, management support, communicating the need to change and the benefits of the future state, and encouraging ownership of the new policies.

As is the case in all ICT strategy implementation, chances of success are much higher when the key members of management are involved during the entire process. Involving managers early helps them overcome fears about changes, and they view the new set of policies as partly theirs. Well-publicized security breaches can help them understand the overwhelming risks of not changing.

Documenting and implementing policies require significant effort and investment. Ensuring that the policies adequately address the organization's needs is also critical. Frameworks assure management that it is on the right track and that the result will address the most critical areas of concern.

Controls

According to the Government Accountability Office, "The control environment sets the tone of an organization, influencing the control consciousness of its people. It is the foundation for all other components of internal control, providing discipline and structure. Control environment factors include the integrity, ethical values, and competence of the entity's people; management's philosophy and operating style; and the way management assigns authority and organizes and develops its people" (United States Government Accountability Office 2009).

Often, controls are grouped into one of two categories: general controls or application controls. General controls govern the design processes, security procedures, and use of the software and security of the data files throughout an organization's ICT infrastructure. From this we can derive that general controls apply to all computerized applications and consist of the combination of hardware, software, and manual procedures that create an overall control environment.

General controls include software controls, physical hardware controls, computer operation controls, data security controls, controls over implementation of system processes, and administrative controls. Table 1.1 describes the functions of each of these controls.

Application controls are unique to each individual application within the system, such as payroll or order processing. They include both automated and manual procedures that ensure only authorized data are processed by the application. Application controls are often further classified as follows:

- Input controls
- Processing controls
- Output controls

Input controls ensure data accuracy and completeness. Such controls include input authorization, data conversion, data editing, and error handling. Processing controls ensure the data completeness and accuracy during processing. Output controls ensure that the results of the processing are accurate, complete, and properly disseminated.

Table 1.1   General Controls

TYPE OF GENERAL CONTROL	DESCRIPTION
Software controls	Monitor the use of system software and provide unauthorized access to application and system software.
Hardware controls	Ensure that system hardware is physically secure, and check for equipment malfunction.
Computer operation controls	Oversee the work of the ICT organization or function to ensure that defined procedures are consistently and correctly applied to the storage and processing of data. They include controls over the setup of batch processing, as well as backup and recovery procedures for processing that ends abnormally.
Data security controls	Ensure that business asset data on disk or tape are not subject to unauthorized access, change, or destruction while they are in use or in storage.
Implementation controls	Audit the ICT development process according to an adopted framework, to ensure that the process is properly controlled and managed.
Administrative controls	Formalize standards, frameworks, rules, procedures, and control disciplines to ensure that general and application controls are properly executed and enforced.

Notice the correlation between application control categories and the generic definition of a computer as being any electronic device designed to accept input, perform processing, and produce output. The generic definition typically also includes a feedback loop. In this context the feedback to the organization regarding appropriate design and implementation of the controls comes from audits, which are discussed in the next section.

Audits

Putting controls in place based on a framework supported by strategies and policies defined through an ICT governance program is a good first step toward fulfilling the requisites of cybersecurity risk management. However, management needs to know that ICT security and controls are effective. This is achieved through conducting complete and systematic audits. An ICT audit examines the organizations over all security environments in addition to the controls that govern individual information systems. COBIT 5 provides a comprehensive set of audit process definitions that an organization can implement that allows an ICT auditor to trace the flow of sample transactions through the system and perform tests using, if appropriate, automated audit software. The ICT audit may also examine data quality.

Security audits review technologies, procedures, documentation, training, and personnel. A thorough audit plan is created and may also include a simulated attack or disaster to test the response of technology, ICT staff, and individuals from other business units.

The audit lists and ranks the control weaknesses and estimates the probability of their occurrence. Next, it performs an assessment of the financial and organizational impact of each threat. This information can then be used as feedback into the process, for management to be advised of the weaknesses and enable them to respond through a planning effort devised to counter significant weaknesses in controls.

INSIGHT   A WALK THROUGH 3 STAGES OF AN SAP SECURITY AUDIT

Tracy Levine, a Systems, Applications, and Products in data processing (SAP) application consultant at itelligence, fields some questions about various stages of preparing for an SAP security audit.

In her blog post, "How to Survive an SAP Security Audit," Tracy Levine, an SAP application consultant at itelligence, writes about three stages of an SAP security audit and uses political terms to describe them: state of the union, political reform, and ongoing legislation. Using her model, I asked Tracy to respond to a few questions related to preparing for an SAP audit.

In the first stage, the state of the union, an organization asks itself the following questions: "Where are we now? How did we get here? What challenges do we face?" Could you cite some examples of challenges organizations may face when preparing for an SAP security audit?

The primary concern when preparing for an SAP audit is gaining a clear understanding of client-specific security requirements and being able to articulate these requirements in terms of business processes. Oftentimes, SAP security requirements remain undocumented, what we refer to as "tribal knowledge," as in there is no central repository that clearly defines the SAP landscape and tracks and monitors changes. As the SAP landscape matures, scalability efforts prove more difficult with increased requirements and a lack of correspondence between functional silos. Changes done by one functional team may override requirements that were purposely implemented for another, driven by a lack of visibility with regard to change management. Furthermore, clients may be concerned with underlying segregation of duties (SoD) violations and the need for a Sarbanes–Oxley (SOX)–compliant deployable role design.

In his video from Governance, Risk and Compliance (GRC) *2013, Steve Biskie refers to thinking about risk in terms of "what can go wrong." He uses an example of "inadequate mapping of business processes to role design" as an example of something that can go wrong. Can you cite some other examples of what can go wrong in relation to managing the security of an SAP environment?*

To piggyback on Steve Biskie, suboptimal role designs, which are not task based, may lead to the provisioning of roles with too much access or inherent SoD violations. By utilizing a task-based role design, organizations are more inclined to adhere to the principle of least privilege, defined as a system in which users are only able to access the information and resources that are necessary for legitimate business purposes. Position-based or user-based role designs do not take into account scalability for business solutions and the opportunity for avoidable SoD conflicts.

Another example of mismanagement of security in the SAP environment involves inefficiencies surrounding the user provisioning process. A lack of automation with workflow capabilities and an embedded risk analysis can decrease visibility, and increase the risk of SoD conflicts. Furthermore, manual provisioning processes can lead to long cycle times from the time of request to the time access is granted or denied.

How has the emergence of mobile and cloud technologies posed new challenges to organizations that are preparing for an SAP security audit?

With the expansion of mobile and cloud technologies comes an increased risk for cyber attacks to SAP systems. This leads us to the question, how secure is the cloud and is there a way to mitigate any associated risks? One of the benefits of the SAP HANA Cloud Platform, as highlighted at the 2013 SAPPHIRE Now conference, is the ability to leverage multiple deployment options—whether in a customer's data center, the public cloud, the managed cloud, or a hybrid environment—to help meet the changing needs of any organization. SAP has also released SAP Mobile Secure, an enterprise mobility management tool that provides organizations with increased security for apps and mobile devices. Furthermore, the cloud edition of SAP Afaria addresses the need for a convenient, reliable, and low-cost solution that provides a way to manage security risk with or without any prior SAP infrastructure.

In the second stage, political reform, one of the questions you cite that an organization asks is "How will this change the way we do business?" Could you provide an example of a business-changing issue pertaining to security of an SAP environment?

Political reform refers to the need to make modifications to the current role design, role management methodologies, or user provisioning process. This can lead to a need for clearer definition of jobs and responsibilities in the SAP landscape. Additionally, it may require previously grouped tasks to be separated across individuals within an organization to avoid inherent SoD conflicts. For some companies, the greatest challenge in prioritizing SAP security is the need for increased collaboration between the business and IT. This collaboration can lead to more defined requirements regarding ownership of SAP roles and critical permissions across functional areas within the organization.

In the third stage, ongoing legislation, one of your questions is "What risks do we still have and how are we going to monitor them?" Could you provide an example of changes an organization has made to the methods it uses to monitor risk?

There are many automated and manual options when it comes to monitoring and assessing risks. SAP Access Control and Risk Management offer tools to meet this demand. The Risk Management tool enables organizations to quantify risks based on impact and probability. Owners can be assigned to risks, and notifications can be activated to bring awareness to controls that have or have not been performed. Those who are fearful of an upcoming SAP audit need not worry. Most organizations have unavoidable risks associated with some aspect of their security design. However, it is essential that companies are able to demonstrate the steps they have taken to mitigate these risks. Leveraging automated or manual mitigating controls as part of SAP Access Control is one method for taking a proactive approach to known risks.

For organizations that do not deploy GRC, it is essential to have a central repository to manage approvals and changes that have been executed in the SAP landscape. A repository can be used as an in-house audit tool to track change logs or actions that have been taken against mitigating controls. However, risk-monitoring methods are only valuable if companies have been able to appropriately assess not only risk priority levels but also the effectiveness of controls that are in place.

When you speak with clients about preparing for an SAP security audit, what do they seem most concerned about? What's turning them into insomniacs?

First of all, no one should be losing sleep over an SAP security audit, but a lack of transparency can lead to uncertainties surrounding the business. The greatest concern, understandably, is a need for increased visibility into the cumulative nature of a user's access in business terms. This lack of visibility also leads to risks with regard to critical access and permissions. Many organizations are concerned that they aren't following industry standards and best practices when it comes to SAP security, which will evoke wariness in auditors. Has everything been secured as it should be? Are we following a streamlined process when it comes to making critical program and configuration changes and have the necessary authorization checks been implemented and tested? Who requested the change, who approved it, and who tested it? This again is where the need for a central repository or GRC landscape comes to fruition. It is not enough to have the processes in place. Monitoring efforts need to be performed to ensure that controls have been executed.

Another growing concern for savvy organizations is the need for information in real time. Many companies have employed detective controls, which do not allow for a proactive approach to SAP security risks. Detective controls are valuable with regard to reporting and analytics, but with the onset of competition in the environment via cloud and mobility comes an increased need for preventive measures and risk-monitoring efforts. By gaining a better understanding of the organization's SAP landscape, organizations often see decreased administrative and testing efforts to maintain the security environment, an increased ease of scalability, and a minimization of SoD conflicts as well as data integrity issues due to a misuse of users' authorizations. (Byrne 2013)

Implementing Best Practices Using a Single Cybersecurity Framework

Formal standards are meant to embody the model for the "common body of knowledge and accepted state of industry best practice" (NIST Framework for Improving Critical Infrastructure Cybersecurity and COBIT 5). Logic should support the correctness of that assumption without much additional proof, as it would be impossible to build a common cybersecurity governance, risk management, and audit process without adopting some sort of standard, accepted model. Given the amount of activities embodied in ICT work, such a model has to be broad and comprehensive. As a result, such all-embracing models are commonly called umbrella frameworks.

Umbrella frameworks are named after their intent, which is to cover the entire scope of ICT that they define. In that respect, umbrella frameworks specify an ideal model at a level sufficient to allow any organization to tailor processes to fit within its structure. Theoretically, a single umbrella framework can describe a competent technology or management process in any level of detail.

Many of the umbrella frameworks utilized in the ICT industry provide specifications for the activities performed in software and system life cycle processes. Noticeably absent in those frameworks are specifications for activities related to governance, risk management, and audit of cybersecurity processes. You will learn in the next several chapters that, as much as there is a life cycle for activities performed to develop ICT systems and software, there exists an umbrella framework providing specifications for cybersecurity life cycle processes. Further, you will learn that many of the defined cybersecurity activities can and should be performed in parallel with the activities of the other industry frameworks.

Nonetheless, you should keep two important caveats in mind when considering the application of umbrella frameworks. First, no two organizations operate in the same way, so each individual cybersecurity life cycle process has to be considered differently in terms of its particulars. These differences may be large or small, but because they exist, every organization must decide how to explicitly array the processes it adopts within the larger concepts and principles of a cybersecurity life cycle model represented by an umbrella framework. In other words, although organizations can use a standardized framework to guide the creation of a coherent set of defined governance, risk management, and audit processes and activities, they must tailor the implementation in a way that makes the most sense for them.

Second, an organization should not rely on just the process definitions of the umbrella framework. All umbrella frameworks reference, in one way or another, other industry standards to further define the activities and documentation required of each life cycle process. Our discussion of the Framework for Improving Critical Infrastructure Cybersecurity

is no different. That framework provides the foundation for the defini-
tion of cybersecurity life cycle processes, and relies on COBIT 5; the
Council on CyberSecurity's Top 20 Critical Security Controls; ANSI/
ISA-62443-2-1 (99.02.01-2009), Security for Industrial Automation
and Control Systems: Establishing an Industrial Automation and
Control Systems Security Program; ANSI/ISA-62443-3-3 (99.03.03-
2013), Security for Industrial Automation and Control Systems: System
Security Requirements and Security Levels; the ISO/International
Electrotechnical Commission (IEC) standard ISO/IEC 27001,
Information Technology—Security Techniques—Information Security
Management Systems—Requirements; and NIST Special Publication
800-53 Revision 4: Security and Privacy Controls for Federal Information
Systems and Organizations to further define each activity.

Chapter Summary

- An organization's digital data are vulnerable to destruction, misuse, error, fraud, and hardware or software failures.
  Managers must be aware of which data and information
  assets are most vulnerable and valuable in order to implement
  the appropriate safeguards.
- Lack of strategies and policies developed through an adopted
  cybersecurity governance program, and controls that support
  those strategies and policies, can cause organizations relying
  on business functions to lose sales and productivity. Data and
  information assets, such as confidential employee records,
  trade secrets, or business plans, lose much of their value if
  they are revealed to outsiders or they expose the organization
  to legal liability.
- Organizations need to establish a good set of general and
  application controls for their information infrastructure.
  Processes associated with risk management are defined to
  evaluate information assets, identify control weaknesses, and
  determine the most cost-effective set of controls.
- The ICT cybersecurity life cycle is composed of a coherent set
  of best practices based on a framework that defines the activities and tasks that should be performed.

Case Project

On Christmas Eve 2014, an unwanted Christmas present was delivered to Suny Corp. That afternoon Suny's network was attacked, attracting numerous phone calls from customers angered at an error message they were receiving when they attempted to access the network. An independent hacker group called "Lizard Squad" took responsibility of that attack and claimed that it was in retaliation of a recently released movie. This attack has generated concern by Suny management about the security of not only their networks but all of their data and information assets. They would like an assessment of their existing risk management procedures and ask that the NIST Framework for Improving Critical Infrastructure Cybersecurity be used to redefine their cybersecurity life cycle process.

As a first step, your task is to help Suny assess their existing governance, controls, and audit procedures. Since this situation is real, but you do not have access to the internal management and existing ICT infrastructures, your results will be hypothetical. However, you should provide a statement detailing what exists currently, so that you can accurately develop a plan for the implementation of the framework once you become better acquainted with risk management frameworks in the next chapter.

2

INTRODUCTION TO THE FRAMEWORK FOR IMPROVING CRITICAL INFRASTRUCTURE CYBERSECURITY

After reading this chapter and completing the case project, you will

- Have an overview understanding of the Framework for Improving Critical Infrastructure Cybersecurity including its history, purpose, and benefits;
- Be able to identify and describe each component of the framework core;
- Understand the implementation tier model of the framework and be able to compare that model to similar models used in the ICT industry;
- Understand the how the framework uses profiles to aid organizations in creating and assessing their cybersecurity program; and
- Be able to develop a plan for implementing the framework.

Understanding risk management and security frameworks is not a simple accomplishment. With cyberthreats changing on nearly a daily basis, and with them, an organization's business environment and ability to meet new changing requirements, the ability to apply new risk strategies is critical. Strategies that are well planned, developed, and documented are applied to the vast array of levels of security needed in order to evolve and support business operations and risk, not simply as an effort in compliance of local, state, and federal regulations.

The Framework for Improving Critical Infrastructure Cybersecurity, a set of guidelines and practices created by the U.S. NIST, provides government and nongovernment organizations with a vital first step toward managing cybersecurity risk. Moving forward, organizations need solutions that not only satisfy the NIST Cybersecurity Framework (CSF) at the time of deployment but that also enable continued security as threats and business needs change and evolve.

It is noteworthy to mention that at the time of this writing, the implementation of the CSF is voluntary. However, while some organizations and government agencies may feel that the framework does not constitute a foolproof formula for cybersecurity, its benefits may be missed by those who choose to skip or postpone implementation of the guideline, in part or in whole. That is because the framework comprises best practices from various standards bodies that have proved to be successful when implemented, and it also may deliver regulatory and legal advantages that extend well beyond improved cybersecurity for organizations that adopt it early. In reality, while the framework targets organizations that own or operate critical infrastructure, adoption may prove advantageous for businesses across virtually all industries.

The CSF, which was drafted by the Commerce Department's NIST, contains no surprises. The majority of what is presented is common sense material. Bob Gourley states in his article "Initial Assessment on NIST Coordinated Framework for Improving Critical Infrastructure" that, ". . . experienced cyber security professionals will find this framework is very basic. Think of it as a high school level introduction to cyber security challenges" (Gourley 2015). However, what is not mentioned in his article is that the framework does not introduce new standards or concepts; rather, it leverages and integrates industry-leading cybersecurity practices that have been developed by organizations such as NIST and the ISO. The framework is basic. If not presented at a basic level, the framework risked the likelihood that it would not gain the attention of the ICT industry. As mentioned above, the framework is not intended to be an all-in-one guide. Therefore, ICT managers need to be familiar with the standards the framework references, in order to implement the cybersecurity practices defined within each category.

Overview of the Framework

The framework is the result of a February 2013 executive order titled "Improving Critical Infrastructure Cybersecurity." The order emphasized that "[i]t is the Policy of the United States to enhance the security and resilience of the Nation's critical infrastructure and to maintain a cyber-environment that encourages efficiency, innovation, and economic prosperity while promoting safety, security, business confidentiality, privacy, and civil liberties" (Executive Order no. 13636 2013). That order resulted in 10 months of collaborative discussions with more than 3000 security professionals to develop a risk-based compilation of guidelines that can help organizations identify, implement, and improve cybersecurity practices, and create a common language for internal and external communication of cybersecurity issues.

The executive order defines critical infrastructure as "systems and assets, whether physical or virtual, so vital to the United States that the incapacity or destruction of such systems and assets would have a debilitating impact on security, national economic security, national public health or safety, or any combination of those matters" (Executive Order no. 13636 2013). The key point to be made is that cybersecurity external and internal threats to the private and public sector are on the rise. It is becoming increasingly important for organizations and federal agencies responsible for critical infrastructure to have a defined reiterative approach to identifying, assessing, and managing cybersecurity risk.

The resulting CSF is a reiterative process designed to evolve in sync with changes in cybersecurity threats, processes, and technologies. At the time of this writing the framework was in its inaugural version. It will be revised periodically to incorporate lessons learned and industry feedback. In effect, the framework envisions effective cybersecurity as a dynamic, continuous loop of response to both threats and solutions.

The framework provides an assessment mechanism that enables organizations to determine their current cybersecurity capabilities, set individual goals for a target state, and establish a plan for improving and maintaining cybersecurity programs. It comprises three primary components: core, profile, and implementation tiers.

"The Core presents industry standards, guidelines, and practices in a manner that allows for communication of cybersecurity activities and outcomes across the organization from the executive level to the implementation/operations level" (National Institute of Standards and Technology 2014). The core is a hierarchical structure that consists of five cybersecurity risk functions. Each function is further broken down into categories and subcategories. These categories include processes, procedures, and technologies such as asset management, alignment with business strategy, risk assessment, access control, employee training, data security, event logging and analysis, and incident response plans. Together, they provide ICT management a high-level strategic view of the activities performed in life cycle cybersecurity risk management. Each subcategory is further matched to information resources. The information resources are industry standards and guidelines that in combination provide a set of cybersecurity risk management best practices.

The profile component gives organizations the ability to align and improve cybersecurity practices based on their individual business needs, tolerance to risk, and resource availability. To do so, organizations create a current profile by measuring their existing programs against the recommended practices in the framework core.

To identify a target profile, organizations employ the same core criteria to determine the outcomes necessary to improve their overall cybersecurity program. Unique requirements by industry, customers, and business partners can be factored into the target profile. Once completed, a comparison of the current and target profiles will identify the gaps that should be closed to enhance cybersecurity and provide the basis for a prioritized road map to help make improvements.

Implementation tiers help create a context that enables organizations to understand how their current cybersecurity risk management capabilities rate against the characteristics described by the framework. Tiers range from partial (Tier 1) to adaptive (Tier 4). NIST recommends that organizations seeking to achieve an effective, defensible cybersecurity program progress to tier 3 or tier 4.

Benefits of Adopting the Framework

For many organizations, regardless of whether they are owners, operators, or suppliers of critical infrastructure, the CSF may be well worth adopting merely for its stated goal of improving risk-based security. But it also can provide additional benefits that include effective collaboration and communication of security initiatives with upper-level management and industry organizations, as well as potential future improvements in legal implications and even assistance with regulatory compliance.

An important goal in the development of the framework was collaboration to share information and improve cybersecurity practices and threat intelligence within and between industry organizations.

Effective collaboration is dependent upon open and meaningful discussions. To that extent, the framework has created a common language to facilitate conversation about cybersecurity processes, policies, and technologies, both internally and with external entities such as third-party service providers and partners. The federal government, though NIST, encourages organizations to share current intelligence on vulnerabilities, threat information, and response strategies. The potential benefits of a common language and definition of life cycle cybersecurity activities together with increased collaboration are abundant. If, for example, an organization's entire supply chain adopts the framework, risks to the supply chain can be better communicated, understood, and potentially lessened.

It is important to note that the framework presents the discussion of cybersecurity in the vocabulary of risk management. This is with good reason: Executive leaders and board members typically are well versed in risk management, and framing cybersecurity in this context will enable security leaders to more effectively articulate the importance and goals of cybersecurity. It can also help organizations prioritize and validate investments based on risk management.

A common framework for cybersecurity will also enable ICT managers to effectively communicate practices, goals, and compliance requirements with third-party partners, service providers, and regulators. In particular, there should be a more meaningful, structured dialogue of cybersecurity priorities with third parties.

INSIGHT   CIOs IGNORE THE NIST CYBERSECURITY FRAMEWORK AT THEIR OWN PERIL

On December 5, 2014, the National Institute of Standards and Technology (NIST, part of the Commerce Department) issued an update to its "Framework for Improving Critical Infrastructure Cybersecurity." Since its issuance earlier this year, there seems to be a growing consensus that the Framework is fast becoming the *de facto* standard for private sector cybersecurity as viewed by regulators and U.S. lawyers. The Dec. 5 update was a progress report on implementation of the Framework in the United States and indicated that NIST intends to continue to collaborate with stakeholders to drive its adoption.

The Framework was developed as a result of a Presidential Executive Order for improving critical infrastructure cybersecurity. One would expect that critical infrastructure would refer to items like power plants, dams and defense facilities. However, as defined by the Department of Homeland Security, critical infrastructure includes all of these and also covers just about every industry in the U.S., including commercial facilities such as arenas, casinos, shopping malls and, of current relevance, motion picture studios. Thus, a position can be taken that the Framework applies to virtually every company in the United States.

If the Framework is eventually considered the standard for cybersecurity, and a company suffers a breach, the CIO [chief information officer] (and ultimately the CEO and Directors) may have to explain to regulators, or to plaintiffs in any lawsuit, why they had not previously implemented and documented compliance with the Framework. Companies that are not in compliance with the Framework's standards, may be at increased risk of liability for security breaches.

Global cybersecurity spending is expected to exceed $50 billion in 2014. Cyber executives do not need the government to tell them how to prevent cyber attacks—they do that on a daily basis. The Framework provides a methodology to think through and develop a cybersecurity program within an organization—it is not the solution itself.

Simplistically, the Framework is almost like a GAP analysis. A company sets up its "Framework Profile." The current company status is the Current Profile, where the company wants to end up is the Target Profile, and the company establishes a plan to get itself from one to the other. For example, the Cornerstone Bank in Lexington, Virginia is using the Framework to measure its security technology against the Framework's various tiers. The process anticipates, and successful compliance requires, discussions between an organization's IT people and its business people.

A CIO who uses the Framework could point to that use to demonstrate compliance with best practices in the event of a cyber breach. This could provide a meritorious defense in any post-breach investigation by regulators. Actions taken now to comply with the Framework will enable a CIO to argue later that the company followed the recommendations of NIST and that, therefore, any cyber breach should not be attributed to corporate or individual negligence.

Richard Raysman and Francesca Morris are partners in the New York office of Holland & Knight.

Richard Raysman
Wall Street Journal, 2014

Framework Core

The main thrust of the framework is described in the framework core, which provides a set of activities and references that are outcome based and focused on specific actions at all levels of the organization. These functions and categories are not new but instead have roots in existing information security standards. In this section you will learn about the underlying structure of the framework, how it defines each of its functions, the categories within each function, and the standard information resources used to match each subcategory. Figure 2.1 depicts the hierarchical structure of the frame core.

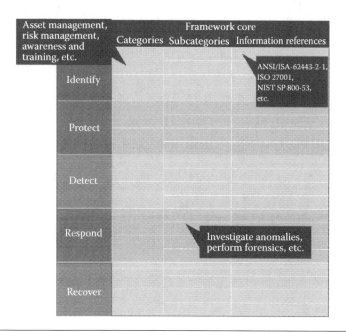

Figure 2.1   Framework core hierarchical structure.

Functions

Notice that five separate functions organize cybersecurity activities at their highest level. The framework functions include the following:

- Identify: activities that provide an understanding of how to manage cybersecurity risks to systems, assets, data, and capabilities
- Protect: the controls and safeguards necessary to protect or deter cybersecurity threats
- Detect: continuous monitoring to provide proactive and real-time alerts of cybersecurity-related events
- Respond: incident-response activities
- Recover: business continuity plans to maintain resilience and recover capabilities after a cyberattack

The functions provide the mechanism for ICT management to organize cybersecurity risk information. Through an organized approach supported by appropriate internal and external data and information, the organization is in a better position to make risk management decisions, address cybersecurity threats, and provide the resources necessary for process improvement. The functions also align with existing methodologies for incident management and help show the impact of investments in cybersecurity. Within the framework core, each function can easily be mapped to individual categories and subcategories by using the function's unique identifier. Table 2.1 provides a list of the identifiers and their associated functions.

Categories

At the next level of the hierarchy, the framework core identifies a desired set of common outcomes for each function. In every area

Table 2.1   Framework Core Function Unique Identifiers

FUNCTION UNIQUE IDENTIFIER	FUNCTION
ID	Identify
PR	Protect
DE	Detect
RS	Respond
RC	Recover

of business, organizations need a clear set of agreed-upon goals to help drive the decisions that managers make on a day-to-day basis. Likewise, goals need to be established to help measure the quality and completeness of each of the activities performed within each business area. The framework core provides leverage for each organization to determine how to perform the cybersecurity activities within each function. To that extent, it provides a clear set of outcomes for each function at a lower level of abstraction in order to present a clear set of criteria that can easily be managed and measured. The framework takes a unique approach in defining the outcomes. At the category level, each function is broken into three to six general categories that define outcomes for that function. As will be explained in the next section, those categories are further broken down into subcategories that provide greater support for cybersecurity managerial decision making and process improvement. Similar to functions, each category can be mapped back to its associated functions and activities using a unique identifier containing the function identifier and an alphabetic code classifying each category. Table 2.2 provides a list of the category identifiers and categories for each function.

Subcategories

The framework core further divides each category into three to six subcategories that provide specific outcomes of technical and/or management activities. Mapping through the framework core is again extended into each subcategory; each containing a label that includes the category identifier combined with a successive numbering sequence. It is important to note that the framework uses the term *results* to describe what is provided by each subcategory. Remember that the key to effective management decision making and process quality measurement is accomplished through assessment of the provided results. Caution should be taken that the subcategories define what the activities of that category should accomplish. They do not provide, however, detail about how they should be completed. The decision of how activities are completed is largely dependent on an organization's environment. To that extent, the framework provides information resources for each subcategory that an organization can use to further define how an activity should be performed.

Table 2.2 Framework Core Categories and Identifiers

FUNCTION	CATEGORY UNIQUE IDENTIFIER	CATEGORY
Identify	ID.AM	Asset management
	ID.BE	Business environment
	ID.GV	Governance
	ID.RA	Risk assessment
	ID.RM	Risk management strategy
Protect	PR.AC	Access control
	PR.AT	Awareness and training
	PR.DS	Data security
	PR.IP	Information protection processes and procedures
	PR.MA	Maintenance
	PR.PT	Protective technology
Detect	DE.AE	Anomalies and events
	DE.CM	Security continuous monitoring
	DE.DP	Detection processes
Respond	RS.RP	Response planning
	RS.CO	Communications
	RS.AN	Analysis
	RS.MI	Mitigation
	RS.IM	Improvements
Recover	RC.RP	Recovery planning
	RC.IM	Improvements
	RC.CO	Communications

Information Resources

The framework does not create anything new; it draws from other existing industry best practices that can be applied to facilitate behavioral changes in an organization. At the lowest level of abstraction in the framework core are the information resources. Each subcategory is mapped to specific sections of standards and guidelines. When a subcategory is mapped to a particular resource, defined process tasks are provided that illustrates a method to achieve the outcomes associated with that subcategory.

It is through the selection of which information resource is used by the organization that flexibility in process implementation is achieved. For example, an organization may already have business processes standardized based on Control Objectives for Information and Related Technology (COBIT 5). As such, they choose to implement the processes that achieve the framework subcategory outcomes strictly through the use of that standard. A scenario such as that would not be atypical. However, caution must be taken, in that case, regarding the coverage COBIT 5 provides for the entire scope of the framework core. Some subcategories do not map to all of the information resources referenced by the framework. The best course is to evaluate all of the resources for each subcategory, after which a decision can be made relative to the combination of resources that come closest to the existing business environment. The information resources referenced by the framework include the following:

- COBIT 5: COBIT is a framework for developing, implementing, monitoring, and improving IT governance and management practices.

    The COBIT 5 framework is published by the IT Governance Institute and the Information Systems Audit and Control Association. The goal of the framework is to provide a common language for business executives to communicate with each other about goals, objectives, and results.

    COBIT 5 is based on five key principles for governance and management of enterprise IT:
    - Principle 1: meeting stakeholder needs
    - Principle 2: covering the enterprise end to end
    - Principle 3: applying a single, integrated framework
    - Principle 4: enabling a holistic approach
    - Principle 5: separating governance from management
- Council on CyberSecurity's (CCS) Top 20 Critical Security Controls (CSC): The Top 20 Critical Security Controls (20 CSC—also known as the Consensus Audit Guidelines and formerly referred to as the SANS 20 Critical Security Controls) have emerged as a de facto yardstick from which cybersecurity programs can be measured. They are a recommended set of actions for cyberdefense that provide specific ways in which organizations can stop cybersecurity attacks. They were developed and are maintained by a consortium of hundreds of security experts from across the public and private sectors.

The 20 CSC are now governed by the CCS, an independent, expert, not-for-profit organization with a global scope.

- ANSI/ISA-62443-2-1 (99.02.01-2009), Security for Industrial Automation and Control Systems: Establishing an Industrial Automation and Control Systems Security Program:
This standard is part of a multipart ISA 62443 series that
addresses the issue of security for industrial automation and
control systems (IACSs). This part, in particular, is what
the standard refers to as "elements" related to cybersecurity
management for use in the IACS environment and provides
guidance on how to meet the requirements described for each
element.

- ANSI/ISA-62443-3-3 (99.03.03-2013), Security for Industrial
Automation and Control Systems: System Security Requirements and Security Levels: This standard is also part of a
multipart ISA 62443 series and provides detailed technical
control system requirements associated with seven foundational
requirements that are described in ISA-62443-1-1 (99.01.01),
including defining the requirements for control system capability security levels, SL-C (control system). These requirements
would be used by various members of the IACS community
along with what the standard refers to as "the defined zones
and conduits" for the system under consideration while developing the appropriate control system target SL, SL-T(control
system), for a specific asset.

- ISO/IEC 27001, Information Technology—Security Techniques—Information Security Management Systems—
Requirements: This document has quickly become the de facto
international standard for information security management.
The purpose of ISO IEC 27001 is to help organizations to
establish and maintain an information security management
system (ISMS). An ISMS is a set of interrelated elements that
organizations use to manage and control information security
risks and to protect and preserve the confidentiality, integrity,
and availability of information. These elements include all
of the policies, procedures, processes, plans, practices, roles,
responsibilities, resources, and structures that are used to
manage security risks and to protect information.

- NIST Special Publication 800-53 Revision 4, Security and Privacy Controls for Federal Information Systems and Organizations: This NIST Special Publication provides guidance for the selection of security and privacy controls for federal information systems and organizations. Revision 4 is the most comprehensive update since the initial publication. The primary goal of this update was to provide coverage of an expanding threat space and increasing sophistication of cyberattacks. This publication provides a full examination of how the NIST changes impact organizations, why privileged accounts are continually targeted by cyberattackers in advanced persistent threats, and how the proper implementation of privileged account controls can lessen the attack surface of advanced threats.

"The Informative References presented in the Framework Core are illustrative and not exhaustive. They are based upon cross-sector guidance most frequently referenced during the Framework development process" (National Institute of Standards and Technology 2014). Many industries are driven by a set or sets of defined best practices. While the resources referenced in the framework provide coverage of all subcategory outcomes, care should be taken to also refer to the standards and guidelines that define processes of the industry from which the organization belongs.

Framework Implementation Tiers

For many years, ICT managers have been examining software life cycle processes in terms of the level of quality provided through each of the process activities and the degree of process improvement is evident through management practices performed throughout the life cycle. In mid-1980s a gentleman by the name of Watts Humphrey, from the Carnegie Mellon Software Engineering Institute, developed a model called the capacity maturity model (CMM) and described it in this 1989 book *Managing the Software Process*. The CMM was originally intended as a tool for evaluating the ability of government contractors to perform a contracted software project. Though it comes from the area of software development, it can be, has been, and continues to be widely applied as a general model of the maturity of ICT life cycle processes. To that extent CMM has evolved into a new model called the capacity maturity model integration (CMMI). The model identifies five levels of process maturity for an ICT organization. Within each of these maturity levels are key process areas that characterize that level. The five maturity levels include the following:

1. Initial: Processes are usually in chaos and the organization usually does not provide a stable environment.
2. Repeatable: ICT development processes demonstrate repeatability from one project to another. There is evidence that the organization uses project management to, at a minimum, track cost and schedule.
3. Defined: The organization's set of standard processes, which is the basis for level 3, is established and improved over time. These standard processes are used to establish consistency across the organization.
4. Managed: Precise measurements and metrics are used so that management can effectively control the software development effort.
5. Optimizing: Focusing on continually improving process performance is done through both incremental and innovative technological improvements. Quantitative process improvement objectives for the organization are established, continually revised to reflect changing business objectives, and used as criteria in managing process improvement.

With the help of standards and defined software frameworks, organizations can implement process improvement mechanisms necessary to gradually progress to their desired level of process maturity. The CSF provides a similar process improvement mechanism through a tiered structure that measures an organization's ability to implement risk management activities. Tiers do not represent maturity levels, however. "Progression to higher Tiers is encouraged when such a change would reduce cybersecurity risk and be cost effective. Successful implementation of the Framework is based upon achievement of the outcomes described in the organization's Target Profile(s) and not upon Tier determination" (National Institute of Standards and Technology 2014).

The implementation tiers serve as a method to describe how well organizations have incorporated cybersecurity risk management into the environment throughout the organization. In using this technique, organizations can measure the consistency and complexity of the risk management program and how well cybersecurity information flows and influences decisions throughout the organization. However, it should not necessarily be thought of as a maturity level for a security program. Individual requirements and risk tolerance should be the driving force that guides organizations to work toward a predetermined target implementation tier. The framework describes each tier from three different perspectives: risk management process, integrated risk management program, and external participation. Table 2.3 lists each tier and a general description of the risk management characteristics evident at each tier.

Too frequently cybersecurity is erroneously thought of as an ICT problem. Realistically, however, security efforts exist only to support business operations, and when not properly aligned they can potentially be ineffective and inefficient and could even impede on organizational progress.

The need for aligning cybersecurity efforts with business processes is one of the main objectives of the CSF. It is also the reason that the framework cannot be excessively prescriptive with defining controls that should implemented by every organization. Although cohesions exist, especially in related sectors, each organization's structure, goals, risk tolerance, culture, and system design will be vary and should be assessed individually to determine adequate levels of protection.

Using business requirements as a driving factor in determining security efforts assists in understanding the possible business impacts

Table 2.3   Framework Implementation Tiers

TIER	DEGREE OF RIGOR	DESCRIPTION
Tier 1	Partial	Risk management is chaotic, with limited awareness of risks and no collaboration with others.
Tier 2	Risk informed	Risk management processes and programs are in place but are not integrated enterprise-wide; collaboration is understood but organization lacks formal capabilities.
Tier 3	Repeatable	Formal policies for risk management processes and programs are in place enterprise-wide, with partial external collaboration.
Tier 4	Adaptive	Risk management processes and programs are based on lessons learned and embedded in culture, with proactive collaboration.

for information security inadequacies and helps to prioritize defensive determinations and resource allocation toward the most important security activities. It is important to note that by communicating to cybersecurity personnel the business context will help them to precisely design controls that follow critical security principles and helps them to determine a baseline for the norms and identify the anomalies.

Therefore, to begin developing an understanding cybersecurity requirements for an organization is to have a definitive and documented understanding of the organization itself and have well-written documentation of how the organizations missions and goals, flow down to business processes supported by security programs. To that extent, cybersecurity planning and implementation efforts must extend beyond security and ICT personnel to include all stakeholders such as business process owners, executive management, and audit and accountability personnel. Just as important as other business life cycles, feedback loops must also be created to ensure that all appropriate stakeholders are informed about the performance of the security program since the program's failure could have an effect on the organization.

The framework is not meant to provide solutions for all cybersecurity-related issues or even tell an organization exactly what it must do. It does provide, however, a common body of knowledge that organizations can use to assess and streamline their own security programs. It can also be used to disseminate best practices and standards across related sectors and industries. When used in combination with critical business process reengineering efforts, best practices, security assessments, and audit from governance security program, it can help organizations to significantly reduce cybersecurity risk, better detect and respond to security breaches, and successfully recover from significant cybersecurity-related events.

Framework Profile

The framework profile is a selection or set of security activities (categories and subcategories) from the framework core. Profiles have several important purposes. Recall from a discussion earlier in this chapter that each organization performs an initial baseline activity in an effort to assess its current security capabilities and organize them into a current profile. The framework then recommends that the organization create a target profile consisting of desired security capabilities, perform a gap analysis between the current and target profiles, and develop an implementation action plan for addressing the gap.

Profiles are also a valuable tool for sharing best practices or establishing industry standards. As previously mentioned, the security activities from the framework core are not designed to be either a minimum standard or the target profile for the organization. Rather, business decisions must drive the selection of control activities. Industry partners, regulating bodies, security consultants, not-for-profit organizations, and others may use the common structure and body of knowledge of the CSF to create minimum recommended standards in the form of a profile. Establishment, dissemination, and coordination of these common profiles is required in addition to the criteria already defined in the framework to establish specific actions that should be considered minimum "cyber due care" standards for organizations.

The profile schema that organization leadership agree upon should mirror the functions, categories, and subcategories from the framework core but may also include additional security activities that are not currently found in the core but which would help to address specific security requirements.

As an example of using framework profiles to share best practices, the Council on CyberSecurity has used its list of Critical Security Controls (CSC) to develop a profile to help organizations focus on the most beneficial activities first. The CSC framework profile provides organizations with common set of prioritized, detailed, and actionable measures that should be implemented as a first step by any organization that is concerned with defending its systems and information against cyberthreats. The CSC profile can act as a road map and starting point for organizations that are looking to develop their own profiles based on their specific security requirements. Target profiles can and should be created as a baseline for industry-specific regulatory compliance requirements, which can then be easily shared.

INSIGHT   FRAMING THE FUTURE

What's Next?

This is a question on all of our minds—not just for the Framework but also cybersecurity more generally.

Executives have started to get on board, the press is paying attention, manufacturers are starting to include security in their ICS* products, grass roots organizations such as I Am The Cavalry and others are forming to help to move Automotive and Medical Device security forward, the White House has issued the Executive Order, Congressional staff discusses cybersecurity regularly, and together we have created a common practice consensus "flag" with the NIST Framework, and this very forum now exists to help us collaborate more effectively.

So, how do we use this momentum to continue to move forward coherently toward sustained risk reduction?

I've heard a lot of good ideas here, at the 6th NIST workshop, and in many other venues about what to do next, but a lot of these ideas, thrown up into the air, fall down with no structure to catch them. There is no bigger picture into which to slot next step ideas and see how they relate to past work, need, and each other.

Without such a common reference structure, making progress from here on out will be increasingly difficult and I believe we need to learn from the very recently successful past and build a framework to do so.

The new framework I'm envisioning would, far from a "2.0" of what we've already built, have a completely different goal. Instead of collecting and organizing common *solution* elements into a document, this framework would identify the types of *problems* we face doing business in a hostile, Internet and Communication Technology (ICT) enabled world and provide a context in which to organize the existing NIST Framework solutions. In other words, if we identify a common language and reference for the "cybersecurity problem space"—especially the areas outside of the CISO† organization—it should be much easier to go back, find out where the Framework excels, where it needs help, and where it simply does not apply and, from there, allow us to organize future efforts effectively and sustainably.

Maybe we should have done this earlier, but maybe it took creating a Common Practice Framework to highlight the need to go back and create a "Problem Space Framework." How many of us have looked at strategy documents that said things like "Will reduce cyber-attacks" or "Improve Cybersecurity" and thought "But wait, what does that

---

* ICS – Integrated Computer Solutions.
† CISO – Certified Information Security Officer.

mean?" Shouldn't there be goals, or non-security objectives for security to help frame, limit, and shape our efforts to some productive end?

When the executive order came out and I heard about how the NIST Framework was going to be used to support "Performance Objectives," I thought, "Great! Finally, we're going to have the electrical current that non-security-activity goals provide to security activities to drive them to defined, implementable, and effective ends."

Unfortunately, that doesn't seem to be happening and there doesn't seem to be consensus that that was even the original intent. But that doesn't mean we don't still need to create that organizing current around security activities.

The "Tier" concept in the existing framework, as incomplete as it is, definitely speaks to the need for the application of a maturity model to what we're doing, but even maturity models need to exist inside a larger context of "Why?" that is framed by all of the ways organizations—and those who work for them—introduce risk. If we don't have a framework for risk introduction in a broad business and national context, how will we ever be able to tell ourselves, each other, our customers, or anyone else that we've applied the NIST Framework in some legitimately effective or helpful way?

This shouldn't be a hard problem to solve. As with the Common Practices in the NIST Framework, we're in a situation where a lot of different people have very different but valid views into the cybersecurity problem space. The material and knowledge exists, we just need to gather it, write it down, gain consensus, and begin to apply it.

From my own point of view, I think this begins by identifying (and documenting) how the major, common roles within organizations (and **of** organizations) introduce cybersecurity risk through legitimate, authorized means in the course of doing business. If we can nail this down across the entire business value chain—from Boards and CEO's to CFO's [chief financial officers] to Operations Managers to IT to Procurement to Sales and Marketing to HR [human resources] to Industry Partners to Insurance Companies to Regulators all the way to the CISO shops that the NIST Framework already assumes solutions for—we will have a much better understanding of what we're solving for. This is because our cybersecurity risk profiles are, when it comes down to real root causes, exclusively the result of the series of decisions made by people in legitimate, authorized capacities. Whether or not the decisions are in your sphere of influence, knowing how they are influencing your cybersecurity risk profile over time is the first step in determining how to most effectively apply the controls from the existing NIST Framework. From there, that knowledge can be applied to contextualizing the maturity levels in models like the Electricity Subsector Cybersecurity Capability Maturity Model [ES-C2M2] in a way that provides "Management Metrics" to those responsible for managing organizational behavior, and those maturity levels can then guide the scope, goals, metrics, and placement of those controls that exist in the NIST Framework.

Beyond the tactical benefits of the knowledge such a framework would give us, our ability to act strategically will improve. If we know how our CEOs and those who work for them are introducing risk, if we can find commonalities across organizations, then we can describe the goals, effectiveness, and mitigating controls in terms that are much less dependent on far too rapidly changing technology and external threat actors. This would provide a much more stable platform over time from which to begin doing sustainably successful risk management, maturity modeling, and NIST Framework implementation and adoption.

That said, this is just one way we might go about creating a "Problem Space Framework"—there are others. Regardless of which one we choose, I strongly believe building one will clarify, speed up, and make our way forward much more effective at reducing risks created by the use and operation of ICT's.

Jack Whitsitt
CForum, 2014

Framework Is Descriptive and Not Prescriptive

It is noteworthy to reiterate that the CSF is not an all-in-one how to guide for organizations to use in developing their cybersecurity risk management programs. Every organization is unique in terms of its environment and business relationships with industry partners and stakeholders, as well as its culture. The framework is descriptive, not prescriptive, and should be used as a standard set of best practices used to meet the individual needs of the organization.

Section 3 of the framework, titled "How to Use the Framework," provides some high-level guidelines that organizations can use to get started. The section includes an introduction to cybersecurity and risk management, very similar to the discussion that we had in Chapter 1. Attention should be drawn to Section 3.2, however, in which the framework provides guidelines for establishing a new or improving an existing cybersecurity program.

Section 3.2, "Establishing and Improving a Cybersecurity Program," provides a set of illustrative steps that show organizations how the framework can be used to establish a security program. Further, by consistently repeating the same steps, the organization can interject continuous improvement into the program. Following are the steps that the framework recommends for establishing and improving their cybersecurity program:

- Step 1: Prioritize and scope—The organization identifies its business/mission objectives and high-level organizational priorities. With this information, the organization makes strategic decisions regarding cybersecurity implementations and determines the scope of systems and assets that support the selected business line or process. The framework can be adapted to support the different business lines or processes within an organization, which may have different business needs and associated risk tolerances.
- Step 2: Orient—Once the scope of the cybersecurity program has been determined for the business line or process, the organization identifies related systems and assets, regulatory requirements, and overall risk approach. The organization then identifies threats to, and vulnerabilities of, those systems and information assets.
- Step 3: Create a current profile—The organization develops a Current Profile by indicating which Category and Subcategory outcomes from the Framework Core are currently being achieved.
- Step 4: Conduct a risk assessment—This assessment could be guided by the organization's overall risk management process or previous risk assessment activities. The organization analyzes the operational environment in order to assess the likelihood of a cybersecurity event and the impact that the event could have on the organization. It is important that organizations seek to incorporate emerging risks and threat

and vulnerability data to facilitate a robust understanding of the likelihood and impact of cybersecurity events.

- Step 5: Create a target profile—The organization creates a target profile that focuses on the assessment of the framework categories and subcategories describing the organization's desired cybersecurity outcomes. Organizations also may develop their own additional categories and subcategories to account for unique organizational risks. Likewise, organization may also consider influences and requirements of external stakeholders such as sector entities, customers, and business partners when creating a target profile.

- Step 6: Determine, analyze, and prioritize gaps—The organization compares the current profile and the target profile to determine gaps. Next, it creates a prioritized action plan to address those gaps that draws upon mission drivers, a cost/benefit analysis, and understanding of risk to achieve the outcomes in the target profile. The organization then determines resources necessary to address the gaps. Using profiles in this manner enables the organization to make informed decisions about cybersecurity activities, supports risk management, and enables the organization to perform cost-effective, targeted improvements.

- Step 7: Implement the action plan—The organization determines which actions to take in regard to the gaps, if any, identified in the previous step. It then monitors its current cybersecurity practices against the target profile. For further guidance, the framework identifies example informative references regarding the categories and subcategories, but organizations should determine which standards, guidelines, and practices, including those that are sector specific, work best for their needs (National Institute of Standards and Technology 2014).

The rate at which these steps are repeated is determined by the organization in terms of the speed at which continuous improvement should take place. Management can also use the feedback loop created through the completion of each step to continuously update the current profile and complete that to their target profile.

Structure of the Book's Presentation of the Framework

With an understanding of the introductory material provided in this chapter, a more detailed view of the CSF can take place. Each of the five functions of the framework core will be explored in detail in its own individual chapter. The outcomes defined in each subcategory will be analyzed and matched to each of the information resources referenced by the category of the framework core. Since the underlying topic of this text is how to secure an ICT organization through governance, risk management, and audit, particular attention will be made to COBIT 5 support for each subcategory.

Some readers may find it helpful to explore COBIT 5 in detail before further exposure to the CSF. The second part of the book, beginning with Chapter 8, provides coverage of the COBIT 5 standard with emphasis on how it can be used to within the scope of cybersecurity management.

Chapter Summary

- The CSF is the result of a presidential executive order that emphasizes that the policy of the United States is improve the security and flexibility of the nation's critical infrastructure and to maintain a cyberenvironment that promotes efficiency, innovation, and economic prosperity while also promoting safety, security, business confidentiality, privacy, and civil liberties.
- The framework provides a way for organizations to assess their current cybersecurity program, set goals for maintaining cybersecurity processes already in place, and develop plans for continuous improvement of their cybersecurity efforts.
- The framework core is made up of functions, categories, and subcategories presented in different levels of abstraction in order to provide details of necessary outcomes of a cybersecurity program. The categories and subcategories are matched to industry standards that can be used to guide organizations in how to achieve the outcomes.

- The implementation tiers make up a model that the framework uses to give organizations perspective on how their cybersecurity program ranks against an accepted set of best practice criteria.
- Framework profiles are used to help the organization understand what framework outcomes currently exist within their cybersecurity program and to determine where they want their cybersecurity program to be in terms of implementation of process activities that achieve framework outcomes to a greater extent.

Case Project

Suny Corp. likes the work that you did in assessing their current governance, risk management, and audit activities. They were so impressed; they would like you to continue by developing a plan for implementing the Framework for Improving Critical Infrastructure Cybersecurity into the cyberenvironment of the entire company. Within the plan only major steps of implementation need to be organized. In other words, focus on the steps that the framework recommends for establishing and improving their cybersecurity program. The plan should take the form of a project time line that describes when each part of every step is performed. Besides providing a customized time line and plan, include the business justification for each step.

3
IDENTIFY FUNCTION

After reading this chapter and completing the case project, you will

- Understand the steps organizations take in identifying at-risk ICT assets;
- Understand the steps necessary to analyze the business environment in order to include all affected functions into the organizational cybersecurity plan;
- Understand how ICT governance is used to understand cybersecurity roles, responsibilities, and best practices for risk management decision making;
- Understand the steps taken to assess risk of ICT systems within an organization; and
- Understand the role of risk management in securing ICT systems.

The first part of this book presents a detailed examination of the functions that make up the core of the Framework for Improving Critical Infrastructure Cybersecurity (CSF). Each chapter explains how to tailor the framework's category outcomes into useful work instructions. The CSF core is composed of five function areas. Therefore, each succeeding chapter will discuss the general purposes of the function and then move on to detail the underlying activities and tasks. We will then discuss some commonly accepted ways to implement the process. The overall aim of the discussion will be to increase your knowledge about how substantive Information and Communication Technology (ICT) work can be done using the guidance of the recommendations provided in the CSF.

Before moving on, we should highlight that the CSF is not a life cycle process framework. There are several system and software life cycle frameworks, such as ISO/IEC 12207:2008 (ISO 2008), Systems and Software Engineering—Software Life Cycle Processes, which provide recommendations for each process in the order in which they are performed. While not presented as such in the CSF, Cybersecurity risk management is a life cycle process in and of itself. It provides mechanisms in the form of process activities and controls that support the information security aspects of the life cycle processes defined in the other standards, such as ISO 12207:2008, engage those activities and controls in a cyclical manner. The CSF presents those activities and controls in the form of outcomes that should be accomplished and uses the information resources as a means to allow organizations the choice of which resource to use relative to the activities that would be most beneficial to each organization's own security program. Additionally, the CSF core is not structured in exact order of priority of outcome accomplishment. For example, the CSF recommends that step 1 of establishing or improving a cybersecurity program is "Prioritize and Scope. The organization identifies its business/mission objectives and high-level organizational priorities. With this information, the organization makes strategic decisions regarding cybersecurity implementations and determines the scope of systems and assets that support the selected business line or process" (National Institute of Standards and Technology Feb. 2014). However, this step relates to cybersecurity ICT governance, which is not addressed as a category outcome of the CSF until later in the Identify Function. For those categories supported by NIST Special Publication 800-53 Revision 4, Security and Privacy Controls for Federal Information Systems and Organizations, the document provides priorities that identify when each control should be implemented. "Organizations can use the recommended priority code designation associated with each security control in the baselines to assist in making sequencing decisions for control implementation (i.e., a Priority Code 1 [P1] control has a higher priority for implementation than a Priority Code 2 [P2] control; a Priority Code 2 [P2] control has a higher priority for implementation than a Priority Code 3 [P3] control, and a Priority Code 0 [P0] indicates the security control is not selected in any baseline)" (National Institute of Standards and Technology Apr. 2014).

The first function in the CSF core describes activities that provide an understanding of how to manage cybersecurity risks to systems, assets, data, and capabilities. This function is titled Identify. The

Identify function is particularly critical to ICT and system security because it is almost impossible to ensure the secure software and system solutions without employing a well-defined and rigorous management process to guide the effort. Our national economy and defense rest on dependable ICT, so governing the processes that ensure the ICT we develop is acceptably secured is an important consideration in our everyday lives. "The necessity of secure ICT has been emphasized in every Homeland Security Presidential Directive from HSPD-1 (October 2001) to HSPD-7 (December 2003), and it is embodied in the National Strategy to Secure Cyberspace" (Shoemaker and Sigler 2015).

Identify Function Overview

The underlying objective of the Identify Function is to develop understanding at the organizational level necessary to manage cybersecurity risk to systems, assets, data, and capabilities.

The outcomes of the Identify Function serve as the foundation for effective use of the framework. Clear understanding of the organizational environment, the resources available to support critical ICT functions, and the related cybersecurity risk gives the organization the ability to plan and prioritize its efforts relative to its risk management strategy and business objectives. The outcome categories within this function include asset management, business environment, governance, risk assessment, and risk management strategy.

It is almost impossible to ensure the security of any asset if the organization lacks a clear inventory of what exactly they are protecting. It is probably not a misstatement to assert that organizations should know what they are protecting before they spend money defending it. But the fact is that almost nobody in the information security business does the common sense thing of inventorying their assets before they start building defenses. So critical things inevitably get left out of the protection scheme. No doubt, the tendency to leap and not look happens because the simple act of inventorying an asset base, which is as dynamic, complex, and virtual as information, is exceptionally time consuming as well as costly. Nevertheless, the lack of knowledge of what we are actually protecting prevents us from building watertight defenses.

This function is also focused on identifying data flows so an organization clearly understands where their data exists, both inside and outside the organization. This is not a foreign concept for management since the same approach applies to cash flow. Every organization knows exactly where their cash is, how much is on hand, and who has access to it day to day. Below are some questions management should ask internal staff regarding hardware, software, and data flow inventory:

- Have all of our systems (hardware and software) been inventoried and risk-ranked for importance?
- Have all data flows been mapped and documented?
- Do we know where our sensitive data are stored and who has access to these?
- Do we know who has the ability to connect in to our organization and access our systems/data?

The Identify Function also acknowledges that it is vital that an organization recognize its role in the economy. An organization's strategic plan and risk management program should clearly document its place in the financial sector and its role in cybersecurity. Below are some questions that management should ask related to understanding their business environment:

- Does our strategic plan include language that discusses cybersecurity and our role in the U.S. critical infrastructure?
- Does our risk management program address cybersecurity?
- Is the impact of our risk management program to cybersecurity communicated to all employees within the organization on a regular basis?

This function also ensures that the organization's existing governance structure adequately addresses cybersecurity. ICT governance can be enforced through a risk management program, a cybersecurity security program, and information security policies and procedures, as well as management and board reporting. These documents should convey how an organization manages cybersecurity and each employee's role in ensuring assets are protected from cyberthreats. Below are some questions that management should ask regarding the governance structure of their organization:

- Do we have an information security policy and does it address cybersecurity issues?
- Do we recognize our legal commitments to safeguarding data?
- Do we have a group at the executive level and at the board level that receives reports on and oversees cybersecurity?

Additionally, the Identify Function addresses the need for organizations to ensure that risk assessments are occurring and that these risk assessments take into consideration cybersecurity risks. As was the case with the asset inventory outcome, this should not be an unfamiliar concept since all organizations have been required to have comprehensive technology risk assessments and vendor risk assessments as part of federal, state, and local regulation compliance. Cybersecurity threats should be included as part of those risk assessment processes. Below are some questions that management should ask about risk assessment activities within the organization:

- Does our risk assessment process include activities associated with assessing cybersecurity threats?
- Do our vendor risk assessments include activities focused on addressing cybersecurity practices of our vendors?

Finally, organizations should ensure that risks identified through risk assessments are properly managed. The organization should document its tolerance for cybersecurity risks just as it would all other types of within any other business unit. Below are some questions that management should ask about how risk is managed within the organization:

- Have we established tolerances for cybersecurity risks?
- Does our risk mitigation process include the review and disposition of cybersecurity risks?
- Are those cyber-risk mitigation steps reviewed by executive management and communicated to the board?

Asset Management Category

The CSF describes the outcome of the asset management category as "the data, personnel, devices, systems, and facilities that enable the organization to achieve business purposes are identified and managed consistent with their relative importance to business objectives and the organization's risk strategy" (National Institute of Standards and Technology Feb. 2014). It should be noted that asset management is aligned to step 2 of the CSF recommended approach to establishing or improving an organization's cybersecurity program. As such, implementation of associated activities and controls in this category is one of the first actions organizations should take.

Generally speaking, asset management is a set of ICT processes designed to manage the life cycle and inventory of technology assets. It provides value to organizations by lowering ICT costs, reducing IT risk, and improving productivity through proper and predefined asset management. Asset management has existed only as a formal set of ICT processes for about a decade, which is immature in comparison to typical ICT life cycle processes.

It may not be completely obvious where asset management and cybersecurity security come together. After all, cybersecurity is a complex activity involving highly skilled ICT engineers, architects, and strategists charged with defending against everything from run-of-the-mill spam and phishing to multinational terrorism cells insistent on causing instability in financial markets through computer-based terrorism and everything in between.

Asset management has many goals, including maximizing the value of an organization's investment in information technology. One common approach to achieving this goal is through understanding the ICT needs of the organization and then establishing standards that serve to facilitate those needs. That in turn leads to the justification of asset types and, more often than not, the reduction of asset types. For example, organizations can see a significant reduction in the number of software applications through an application-justification process; this involves defining which types of applications meet the predefined guidelines that support the organization's ICT objectives and working to remove the applications that do not meet the guidelines. With the elimination of each application comes increased security because that is one less application to harden, patch, monitor, and audit.

Another benefit of the asset management is the increased understanding of who in the organization needs each of the ICT assets in order to perform their role within the business environment. Organizations that practice access management understand who has access to sensitive data and user permissions can be more logically restricted based on need, in some cases even serving as the basis of or logic check for privilege management systems.

CSF breaks down the asset management process into six subcategory outcomes. The outcomes are identified in Table 3.1 and described in detail in the next several sections of this chapter.

Table 3.1 Framework Core Asset Management Category

CATEGORY	SUBCATEGORY	INFORMATION RESOURCES
Asset Management (ID. AM): The data, personnel, devices, systems, and facilities that enable the organization to achieve business purposes are identified and managed consistent with their relative importance to business objectives and the organization's risk strategy.	ID.AM-1: Physical devices and systems within the organization are inventoried.	• CCS CSC 1 • COBIT 5 BAI09.01, BAI09.02 • ISA 62443-2-1:2009 4.2.3.4 • ISA 62443-3-3:2013 SR 7.8 • ISO/IEC 27001:2013 A.8.1.1, A.8.1.2 • NIST SP 800-53 Rev. 4 CM-8
	ID.AM-2: Software platforms and applications within the organization are inventoried.	• CCS CSC 2 • COBIT 5 BAI09.01, BAI09.02, BAI09.05 • ISA 62443-2-1:2009 4.2.3.4 • ISA 62443-3-3:2013 SR 7.8 • ISO/IEC 27001:2013 A.8.1.1, A.8.1.2 • NIST SP 800-53 Rev.4 CM-8
	ID.AM-3: Organizational communication and data flows are mapped.	• CCS CSC 1 • COBIT 5 DSS05.02 • ISA 62443-2-1:2009 4.2.3.4 • ISO/IEC 27001:2013 A.13.2.1 • NIST SP 800-53 Rev. 4 AC-4, CA-3, CA-9, PL-8
	ID.AM-4: External information systems are cataloged.	• COBIT 5 APO02.02 • ISO/IEC 27001:2013 A.11.2.6 • NIST SP 800-53 Rev. 4 AC-20, SA-9
	ID.AM-5: Resources (e.g., hardware and software) are prioritized based on their classification, criticality, and business value.	• COBIT 5 APO03.03, APO03.04, BAI09.02 • ISA 62443-2-1:2009 4.2.3.6 • ISO/IEC 27001:2013 A.8.2.1 • NIST SP 800-53 Rev. 4 CP-2, RA-2, SA-14
	ID.AM-6: Cybersecurity roles and responsibilities for the entire workforce and third-party stakeholders (e.g., suppliers, customers, partners) are established.	• COBIT 5 APO01.02, DSS06.03 • ISA 62443-2-1:2009 4.3.2.3.3 • ISO/IEC 27001:2013 A.6.1.1 • NIST SP 800-53 Rev. 4 CP-2, PS-7, PM-11

Source: National Institute of Standards and Technology, *Framework for Improving Critical Infrastructure Cybersecurity.* Gaithersburg, February 12, 2014.

*ID.AM-1: Physical Devices and Systems within
the Organization Are Inventoried*

The underlying objective of the CSF ID.AM-1 subcategory is to "actively manage (inventory, track, and correct) all hardware devices on the network so that only authorized devices are given access, and unauthorized and unmanaged devices are found and prevented from gaining access" (Council on Cybersecurity 2014).

In order to minimize the possibility that an organization's systems can be exploited through a cyberattack, the CSF recommends that all physical devices and systems be inventoried. Unless the physical systems and devices are identified and inventoried, they cannot be protected. This subcategory does not describe how an organization should conduct a physical inventory (e.g., manual or automated) nor does it describe who should perform the inventory and how often. Organizations can determine how to implement this outcome based on their business requirements and risk tolerance.

Cyberattackers are constantly finding ways to exploit computer systems. Organizations may have several semiprotected test and development databases or several laptops may have been bought and assigned. It is essential that all physical devices within an organizations critical infrastructure have patches applied, regardless of what purpose those devices may serve. In order to do this, however, you must first have knowledge of the devices owned by the organization.

Your inventory of devices must include all systems that have an Internet Protocol (IP) address, meaning every device that can potentially be an entry point for an attacker. You must include desktops, laptops, printers, databases, Windows and UNIX/Linux servers, backup systems, removable storage media including USB devices, voice-over-IP telephone systems, storage area networks, and lastly all network equipment such as routers, switches, and firewall software. Your inventory must be detailed, with information such as the network address, the purpose of the system, the asset owner, and the department that owns the device. It is equally important to include all virtual machines as well as wireless devices in your asset inventory.

Once an inventory of the entire system is complete, you are not done! You must frequently update the inventory to preserve accuracy on a real-time basis. System administrators must also install (freely available or commercial) software that monitors the network and immediately alerts them to the presence of new and/or unauthorized software and systems that have been installed by the organization's employees. Network scanning tools must run 24/7 at frequent intervals to catch any unauthorized devices. To prevent the installation of unauthorized devices, organizations must implement strict software installation policies that prohibit employees or contractors from installing software on their own no matter how useful it may be.

System and/or network administrators must schedule regular tests of ICT systems by installing new software and devices on the network and check whether their scanners are able to spot the unauthorized devices.

ID.AM-2: Software Platforms and Applications within the Organization Are Inventoried

The primary objective of ID.AM-2 subcategory is to "actively manage (inventory, track, and correct) all software on the network so that only authorized software is installed and can execute, and that unauthorized and unmanaged software is found and prevented from installation or execution" (Council on Cybersecurity 2014).

Most organizations do a pretty good job of keeping an inventory of their hardware such as servers, workstations, laptops, and mobile devices. However, organizations typically do not put the same type of effort into tracking software that is installed on their systems. Of course, there are many viable reasons for that, including that it is not easy to keep up to date with all the different types of software in use by organizations today. Cyberattackers are always looking for vulnerable software they can exploit. Particularly dangerous is the employee use of entrusted web sites, where they could unwittingly download malicious software that could act as Trojan software, setting up a backdoor program that can exploit the organization's entire critical infrastructure.

To keep ICT systems secure, organizations must keep an up-to-date inventory of all software, including desktop software and business software such as those that serve purposes within an enterprise resource planning environment. There must exist a list of all authorized software currently installed on each server, workstation, and laptop owned by the organization. For most medium and large companies, a software inventory tool is very useful. The tool will track and record the type of software as well as its version and patch levels. Therefore, the organization will have true picture of how up to date they are with patching and upgrading software across all business units.

Automated software tracking tools also check for and proactively monitor the installation of unauthorized software. Keep in mind that there is a wide variety of software that might be useful to the organization, and is usually installed by an employee that has earned the trust of the organization. However, if it is not an approved installation, it will be flagged by the tracking software. Moreover, the organization can also create *white lists* that let a system run only approved applications.

ID.AM-3: Organizational Communication and Data Flows Are Mapped

The main objective of ID.AM-3 is to ensure the security of information flowing within and outside the organization. To facilitate this outcome, "formal transfer policies, procedures, and controls shall be in place to protect the transfer of information through the use of all types of communication facilities" (International Organization for Standardization/International Electrotechnical Commission 2013).

This objective is adequately achieved through a well-documented mapping process. Data mapping is the process by which two different data models are created and a link between these models is defined. This mapping is most readily used in software engineering to describe the best way to access or represent some form of information. Software engineers typically use the Unified Modeling Language (UML) to develop abstract models in order to determine data relationships between two entities. The relationships could be between business units within an organization or between organization and customers, suppliers, or other external partners. This is the fundamental first step in establishing data integration and, in turn, data security of a particular part of the organizations critical infrastructure.

The main uses for data mapping include a wide variety of platforms. Data transformation is used to facilitate the relationship between an initial data source and the destination in which that data are used. It is useful in identifying the way in which data flow from one place to another. The mapping is also integral in discovering hidden information and sensitive data such as social security numbers when hidden within a different identification format. This is known as data masking.

In order to ensure the security of data flow, organizations should first look at the requirements and design specifications developed for existing an ICT system. A review of the data models existing within those specifications will help determine if all data flows have been identified. If documentation of specific data flows does not exist, the organization should act on updating that documentation. Missing data flow documentation will also lead to the conclusion that formal data transfer policies, procedures, and controls are either out of date or nonexistent.

ID.AM-4: External Information Systems Are Cataloged

The ID.AM-4 outcome recognizes that "security shall be applied to off-site assets taking into account the different risks of working outside the organizations premises" (International Organization for Standardization/International Electrotechnical Commission 2013). As a result, the organization should prepare the proper documentation that "establishes terms and conditions consistent with any trust relationships established with other organizations owning, operating, and/or maintaining external information systems allowing authorized individuals to:

1. Access the information system from external information systems; and
2. Process, store, or transmit organization-controlled information using external information systems" (National Institute of Standards and Technology April 2014).

External information systems are ICT systems or individual components of information systems that are off-site or beyond the established authorized limits of the organization, and therefore outside the scope of authority from which the organization can implement security controls and measure their effectiveness. Examples of external ICT systems include an employee's desktop or laptop that they may use to log into the network remotely, an employee's smartphone that they may use to check their e-mail, or the hotel network that may be used to do work while an employee is at a conference. This outcome also recommends the cataloging of the use of external ICT systems for the purpose of processing, storage, or transmission of organizational information. Cataloging these types of systems is becoming increasingly important given the growth and popularity of software as a service, platform as a service, and infrastructure as a service. ID.AM-4 also recommends that authorized individuals of an organization ICT system be cataloged. Those individuals likely include many of the stakeholders of the organization, such as the board of directors, management, employees, contractors, or any other individuals that have access to external ICT systems and the organization can enforce rules of authority with regard to the systems access. Restrictions that organizations impose on authorized individuals need not be uniform, as those restrictions may vary depending upon the trust relationships between organizations. The security policies of the organization will normally provide the terms and conditions for the use of external systems. The phrase *terms and conditions* has been used loosely in this section. In general, they enforce policies and procedures related to the applications that can be accessed from an organization's ICT system from external systems, and the security category of information from an organization's ICT system that can be processed, stored, or transmitted from external systems.

ID.AM-5: Resources Are Prioritized Based on Their
Classification, Criticality, and Business Value

The underlying objective of ID.AM-5 is to "develop the criteria and assign a priority rating for mitigating the risk of each logical control system" (International Society of Automation 2009).

Resource classification is a formal access control methodology used to assign a level of security to the asset and in turn restrict the number of people that can use it. Examples of classification categories are confidential, internal, and public. Any classification method must be specific enough to enable determination of priority levels, because the next step in achieving this outcome is to rank the components. It is also important that the categories be comprehensive and mutually exclusive. In other words, each asset must fit in the list somewhere and only fit into one category. It is also important to note that there is not a de facto methodology for classifying an organization's data. The organization will make that determination based on its own risk management objectives.

The U.S. government and Department of Defense (DoD) are perhaps the best-known users of classification schemes. To maintain asset security, the government and DoD have invested heavily in information security, operations security, and communication security. In fact, many developments in data communication and cybersecurity are the result of government-sponsored research and development.

One of the most difficult tasks of risk management is asset valuation. While most organizations have a general understanding of the relative worth their assets, it is much more difficult to place a business value on an individual asset. As a result, many organizations use categorical ranking to provide ranges of values for assets or they use quantitative measures. In order to assign values to assets, several questions can be posed and answers collected of a worksheet:

- Which asset or assets are most critical to the organizations success?
- Which asset or assets generate the most revenue?
- Which assets play the biggest role in generating revenue or delivering services?
- Which asset would be the most expensive to replace?
- Which asset would be the most expensive to protect?
- Which asset would expose the organization to liability or embarrassment if revealed?

When calculating, estimating, or determining the value of an asset, the organization should consider the following:

- Value retained from the cost of creating or investing in the asset
- Value retained from past maintenance of the asset
- Cost incurred for replacing the asset
- Value incurred from the cost of protecting the asset
- Value in terms of intellectual property

Other organizational criteria may add value to the asset valuation process. They should be identified, documented, and added to the process. To finalize this step of asset valuation, a weight should be assigned to each asset based on the answers to the chosen questions.

Once the classification and value assessment are complete, the organization should prioritize each asset using a process known as weighted factor analysis. In this process, each asset is assigned a score for a set of assigned critical factors. NIST SP 800-30, Risk Management for Information Technology Systems, recommends a score range of 0.1 and 1.0. In addition, each critical factor is assigned a weight ranging from one to 100 to show the criteria assigned importance to the organization.

ID.AM-6: Cybersecurity Roles and Responsibilities for the Entire Workforce and Third-Party Stakeholders Are Established

The outcome of ID.AM.6 ensures that "the organization:

1. Establishes personnel security requirements including security roles and responsibilities for third-party providers
2. Requires third-party providers to comply with personnel security policies and procedures established by the organization
3. Documents personnel security requirements
4. Requires third-party providers to notify (Assignment: organization-defined personnel or roles) of any personnel transfers or terminations of third-party personnel who possess organizational credentials and/or badges, or who have information system privileges within (Assignment: organization-defined time period) and
5. Monitors provider compliance" (National Institute for Standards and Technology April 2014).

Third-party providers include any businesses or individuals from outside the organization that provide some form of value-added service. Examples include service bureaus, contractors, and external ICT development organizations that may provide information technology services, outsourced applications, and network and security management. Organizations should include within the acquisition documents the necessary personnel security requirements. For more information about what should be included in acquisition documentation, refer to the international standard ISO/IEC 12207:2008. Third-party providers may have people working within the ICT function of the organization and have the necessary credentials, security badges, and information system privileges issued by organizations. The third-party provider should make sure that timely notification is given to organizations that they provide services of personnel changes to ensure appropriate termination of privileges and credentials. Organizations should also take care that the same procedures defined for understanding the security roles, providing privileges and credentials, and enforcing appropriate termination protocol that are applied to third party provider, be applied to internal individuals with ICT security responsibilities. This includes personnel at all levels, executives, management, and staff.

Business Environment Category

The CSF describes the outcome of the business environment category as "the organization's mission, objectives, stakeholders, and activities are understood and prioritized; this information is used to make informed cybersecurity roles, responsibilities, and risk management decisions" (National Institute of Standards and Technology Feb. 2014). As we did at the beginning of our discussion of asset management, we should make note that understanding the business environment is aligned with step 1 of the CSF recommended approach to establishing or improving an organization's cybersecurity program. As such, implementation of associated activities and controls of this category outcome is the first action organizations should take.

It is vital that an organization recognizes its role in the economy. An institution's strategic plan and risk management program should clearly document its place in the industry from which it belongs and its role in cybersecurity. Below are some questions management should ask regarding this function:

- Does our strategic plan include language that discusses cybersecurity and our role in the U.S. critical infrastructure?
- Does our risk management program address cybersecurity?
- Is this communicated to all employees on a periodic basis?

The CSF breaks down the business environment category into five subcategory outcomes. The outcomes are identified in Table 3.2 and described in detail in the next several sections of this chapter.

Table 3.2   Framework Core Business Environment Category

CATEGORY	SUBCATEGORY	INFORMATION RESOURCES
Business Environment (ID.BE): The organization's mission, objectives, stakeholders, and activities are understood and prioritized; this information is used to inform cybersecurity roles, responsibilities, and risk management decisions.	ID.BE-1: The organization's role in the supply chain is identified and communicated.	• COBIT 5 APO08.04, APO08.05, APO10.03, APO10.04, APO10.05 • ISO/IEC 27001:2013 A.15.1.3, A.15.2.1, A.15.2.2 • NIST SP 800-53 Rev. 4 CP-2, SA-12
	ID.BE-2: The organization's place in critical infrastructure and its industry sector is identified and communicated.	• COBIT 5 APO02.06, APO03.01 • NIST SP 800-53 Rev. 4 PM-8
	ID.BE-3: Priorities for organizational mission, objectives, and activities are established and communicated.	• COBIT 5 APO02.01, APO02.06, APO03.01 • ISA 62443-2-1:2009 4.2.2.1, 4.2.3.6 • NIST SP 800-53 Rev. 4 PM-11, SA-14
	ID.BE-4: Dependencies and critical functions for delivery of critical services are established.	• ISO/IEC 27001:2013 A.11.2.2, A.11.2.3, A.12.1.3 • NIST SP 800-53 Rev. 4 CP-8, PE-9, PE-11, PM-8, SA-14
	ID.BE-5: Resilience requirements to support delivery of critical services are established.	• COBIT 5 DSS04.02 • ISO/IEC 27001:2013 A.11.1.4, A.17.1.1, A.17.1.2, A.17.2.1 • NIST SP 800-53 Rev. 4 CP-2, CP-11, SA-14

Source: National Institute of Standards and Technology, *Framework for Improving Critical Infrastructure Cybersecurity.* Gaithersburg, February 12, 2014.

ID.BE-1: The Organization's Role in the Supply Chain Is Identified and Communicated

The ID.BE-1 outcome emphasizes that "agreements with suppliers should include requirements to address the information security risks associated with information and communication technology services and product supply chain" (ISO 2013).

ICT products (e.g., hardware, software, or entire information systems) are developed through a global supply chain. Supply chains are no different from any other organizational function in that they are intended to accomplish a specific purpose. The purpose of all supply chains is to provide a product or service through coordinated work that involves several organizations.

While the outcome of this subcategory focuses on identifying an organization's position and agreements within the supply chain, what the CSF is really addressing are the policies and procedures associated with the organization's supply chain risk management (SCRM) program. Proper SCRM lessens security concerns by providing a consistent and disciplined environment for developing the product, assessing what could go wrong in the process (i.e., assessing risks), determining which risks to address (i.e., setting priorities), and implementing appropriate activities that address high-priority risks. Typically, supply chains are hierarchical, with the primary supplier forming the root of a number of levels of parent–child relationships. From an assurance standpoint, what this implies is that every individual product of each individual node in that hierarchy has to be correct as well as correctly integrated with all other components up and down the production ladder. Because the product development process is distributed across a supply chain, maintaining the integrity of the products that are moving within that process is the critical concern. Responsibilities associated with maintaining integrity can be implemented with the activity and task recommendations of the agreement processes of the ISO/IEC 12207:2008.

The activities embodied in the 12207 agreement processes convey the steps that an organization should take to manage the procurement of a system, software, or service product. The agreement processes are particularly relevant to those interested in identifying the organization's roles and responsibilities corresponding to SCRM in that they provide a structured and rigorous set of activities and tasks to carry out the effort. The 12207 activities specified for acquisition convey the practices that have to be performed when an organization procures a software system or service, while the supply process (6.1.2) defines the obligations of the supplier. Using the 12207 standard, it is possible to form a detailed definition of the typical customer supplier activities involved in ICT procurement. Moreover, the addition of the risk management component to the standard procurement model represented in the 12207 agreement processes provides a complete set of practices for ICT SCRM.

ID.BE-2: The Organization's Place in Critical Infrastructure and Its Industry Sector Is Identified and Communicated

The ID.BE.2 outcome echoes and is likely the result of the Homeland Security Presidential Directive 7: Critical Infrastructure Identification, Prioritization, and Protection. Homeland Security Presidential

Directive 7 enforces a national policy for federal agencies to identify, prioritize, and communicate the placement of critical infrastructure within those agencies while protecting them from terrorist attacks. The CSF takes the outcome beyond the scope of federal agencies by including the same identification of private sector organizations position within their industry:

> Terrorists seek to destroy, incapacitate, or exploit critical infrastructure and key resources across the United States to threaten national security, cause mass casualties, weaken our economy, and damage public morale and confidence.
>
> America's open and technologically complex society includes a wide array of critical infrastructure and key resources that are potential terrorist targets. The majority of these are owned and operated by the private sector and State or local governments. These critical infrastructures and key resources are both physical and cyber-based and span all sectors of the economy.
>
> Critical infrastructure and key resources provide the essential services that underpin American society. The Nation possesses numerous key resources, whose exploitation or destruction by terrorists could cause catastrophic health effects or mass casualties comparable to those from the use of a weapon of mass destruction, or could profoundly affect our national prestige and morale. In addition, there is critical infrastructure so vital that its incapacitation, exploitation, or destruction, through terrorist attack, could have a debilitating effect on security and economic well-being.
>
> While it is not possible to protect or eliminate the vulnerability of all critical infrastructure and key resources throughout the country, strategic improvements in security can make it more difficult for attacks to succeed and can lessen the impact of attacks that may occur. In addition to strategic security enhancements, tactical security improvements can be rapidly implemented to deter, mitigate, or neutralize potential attacks (Homeland Security Presidential Directive 7 2003).

ID.BE-3: Priorities for Organizational Mission, Objectives, and Activities Are Established and Communicated

A mission statement is the core identity of an organization and the individuals who have the responsibility of performing management roles that strive toward achieving that identity. It is usually made up of three parts:

- Vision—A mental picture of what you want to accomplish or achieve.
- Mission—A statement of mission is a general statement of how you will achieve your vision. There is a very close relationship between the vision and mission. The mission is an action statement that usually begins with the word *to*. Once again, it is a very simple and direct statement that is easy to understand and remember.
- Core values—Define the business in terms of the principles and values that management will follow. They provide the bounds or limits of how the business leaders will conduct their activities while carrying out the vision and mission.

Once an organization has developed a mission statement, the next step is to create the following items:

- Goals—General statements of what the organization wants to achieve, so goals need to be integrated with the vision. They also need to be integrated with the mission of how the organization is going to achieve its vision.
- Objectives—Specific, quantifiable, time-sensitive statements of what is going to be achieved and when it will be achieved. They are milestones along the path of achieving organizational goals.
- Strategies/action plans—Specific implementation plans of how the organization will achieve your objectives and goals.

It is through the strategies and action plans that priorities should be identified and communicated. From the cybersecurity perspective, the strategies and action plans should include activities that address how the organization intends to integrate cybersecurity into its mission, vision, goals and objectives.

ID.BE-4: Dependencies and Critical Functions
for Delivery of Critical Services Are Established

The ID.BE-4 outcome recommends that "the organization identifies critical information system components and functions by performing a criticality analysis for (Assignment: organization-defined information systems, information system components, or information system services) at (Assignment: organization defined decision points in the system development life cycle)" (National Institute for Standards and Technology April 2014).

Criticality analysis is a key part of SCRM because many of the dependencies identified, such as telecommunication services, power equipment and cabling, and emergency power, are provided through the supply chain. As a result, this activity is typically performed with activities that accomplish the controls associated with the ID.BE-1 subcategory outcome. Criticality analysis consists of the prioritization of supply chain protection activities such as attack surface reduction, use of all-source intelligence, and tailored acquisition strategies. With this information, system engineers are able to see a complete functional decomposition of an ICT system to identify critical functions and components. Through that functional decomposition, the organization is able to identify core organizational operations supported by the system, decomposition into the specific functions to perform those operations, and the ability to trace those functions to the hardware, software, and firmware components that the system uses to perform those functions. This includes those functions that extend into the supply chain, external to the organization. ICT system components that allow unattended access to critical components or functions are considered critical because of the inherited vulnerabilities created by the dependencies between them. To assess the criticality of the component or function, the organization should assess them in terms of the impact failure of that component or function has on the ability for it to complete the organizational operation that it supports.

ID.BE-5: Resilience Requirements to Support Delivery
of Critical Services Are Established

The generic substitute used in business for resilience requirements is continuity management or continuity planning. The establishment of organizational continuity management or plans that support critical services is the underlying objective of subcategory ID.BE-5.

Colleges and universities, for example, are vulnerable to a variety of natural and human-made emergencies, disasters, and hazards.

Recognizing that not all events can be prevented and some risks may be considered acceptable, proper planning is essential to maintain or restore services when an unexpected or unavoidable event disrupts normal operations.

Organizational continuity planning includes the identification of vulnerabilities, priorities, dependencies, and measures for developing plans to facilitate continuity and recovery before, during, and after such a disruption. A completely comprehensive organizational continuity plan is designed and implemented to ensure continuity of operations under unanticipated conditions, such as cybersecurity attack. Plans provide the readiness of organizations for fast recovery in the event of adverse conditions, minimize the impact of such circumstances, and provide means to facilitate functioning during and after emergencies.

The development process is usually based on a single framework such as the controls defined in COBIT 5, ISO 27001:2013, or NIST SP 800-53 and involves key individuals in functional areas throughout the organization. Plans are based on a risk assessment and business impact analysis and include a process for regular maintenance, including training, testing/drills, and updates. In addition, information security and privacy should be integrated within plans:

- Scope of the plan
- Business continuity and risk management
- Developing and implementing the plan
- Framework and planning cycle
- Training, maintaining, and reassessing business continuity plans

Organizational continuity plans must recognize the need to strictly adhere to institutional security and privacy policies and regulations, even while the institution is functioning during extraordinary conditions. Good organizational continuity plans should be built in harmony with strong organizational security and privacy policies as well as state and federal regulations. This will allow important security and privacy practices to continue to be practiced, even during and after a disruptive event. Such practices should be elements of all planning, implementation, testing, and evaluation efforts.

The Homeland Security Presidential Directive 5, the Management of Domestic Incidents, states as its purpose "to enhance the ability of the United States to manage domestic incidents by establishing a single, comprehensive national incident management system to ... prevent, prepare for, respond to, and recover from terrorist attacks, major disasters, and other emergencies, the United States Government shall establish a single comprehensive approach to domestic incident management" (Homeland Security Presidential Directive 5 2003). While not all reasons for organizational continuity involve homeland security, this is an acknowledgment at the highest governmental level of the need to establish continuity plans.

Governance Category

The CSF describes the outcome of the governance category as "the policies, procedures, and processes to manage and monitor the organization's regulatory, legal, risk, environmental, and operational requirements are understood and inform the management of cybersecurity risk" (National Institute of Standards and Technology Feb. 2014).

Continuing the discussion about ICT governance was presented in Chapter 1, recall that what we call *governance* is a set of prescribed, systematic, interdependent actions that are established to get a predictable result. In the case of cybersecurity, an organization defines a set of actions to protect against the threats and vulnerabilities that impact their information assets.

The practical benefit of governance is twofold. First, it ensures that a comprehensive collection of policies, procedures, and actions are documented. Second, it ensures that those policies are operationalized in the form of tangible tasks and appropriately managed.

In practice, governance is enforced by a formal management function. The specific responsibility of that function is to ensure suitable day-to-day performance of the steps required to guarantee cybersecurity. In that respect, the activities of the management function are the actual forms of cybersecurity implementation within the organization.

This is all great in theory, but the proper question is, "How do you get your management operation to operate at the right level of capability?" That is a process question and is substantial in detail. The CSF breaks down the governance category into four subcategory outcomes. The outcomes are identified in Table 3.3 and the process mentioned above is described in the next several sections of this chapter.

Table 3.3 Framework Core Governance Category

CATEGORY	SUBCATEGORY	INFORMATION RESOURCES
Governance (ID.GV): The policies, procedures, and processes to manage and monitor the organization's regulatory, legal, risk, environmental, and operational requirements are understood and management is informed of inform the management of cybersecurity risk.	ID.GV-1: Organizational information security policy is established.	• COBIT 5 APO01.03, EDM01.01, EDM01.02 • ISA 62443-2-1:2009 4.3.2.6 • ISO/IEC 27001:2013 A.5.1.1 • NIST SP 800-53 Rev. 4 controls from all families
	ID.GV-2: Information security roles and responsibilities are coordinated and aligned with internal roles and external partners.	• COBIT 5 APO13.12 • ISA 62443-2-1:2009 4.3.2.3.3 • ISO/IEC 27001:2013 A.6.1.1, A.7.2.1 • NIST SP 800-53 Rev. 4 PM-1, PS-7
	ID.GV-3: Legal and regulatory requirements regarding cybersecurity, including privacy and civil liberties obligations, are understood and managed.	• COBIT 5 MEA03.01, MEA03.04 • ISA 62443-2-1:2009 4.4.3. • ISO/IEC 27001:2013 A. 18.1 • NIST SP 800-53 Rev. 4 controls from all families (except PM-1)
	ID.GV-4: Governance and risk management processes address cybersecurity risks.	• COBIT 5 DSS04.02 • ISA 62443-2-1:2009 4.2.3.1, 4.2.3.3, 4.2.3.8, 4.2.3.9, 4.2.3.11, 4.3.2.4.3, 4.3.2.6.3 • NIST SP 800-53 Rev. 4 PM-9, PM-11

Source: National Institute of Standards and Technology, *Framework for Improving Critical Infrastructure Cybersecurity.* Gaithersburg, February 12, 2014.

ID.GV-1: Organizational Information Security Policy Is Established

ICT governance is a not a state that can be achieved; it is a journey that organizations commit to. Done right, it passes through five progressive levels:

1. Recognition—The organization recognizes the need for security.
2. Informal realization—The organization understands informal security policies.
3. Security understanding—The security policies are planned and monitored.
4. Deliberate control—Decisions about security policies are based on data.
5. Continuous adaptation—Policies adapt to changes and are continuously improving.

The most basic level is simple recognition. The organization comes to recognize that the security of information is a valid concern. That recognition may not necessarily become evident in any organized fashion. Nevertheless, it does involve a determined level of understanding that cybersecurity is necessary. Until that ultimate state of recognition is achieved, the organization is essentially operating without any form of secure practice.

At the next level, informal realization, members of the organization are made actively aware of the elementary actions that are needed to ensure against information loss. Organizational employees follow simple assurance policies in response to that understanding.

In most organizations, those policies are implemented and enforced on an ad hoc basis. Work practices are not specifically itemized and their performance is not sufficiently overseen to ensure that security is actually part of the operation. That happens in the next step.

The third stage, security understanding, is the first level of formal organizational security policy. Although this is only the first of three levels of increasing competence, this is where most organizations normally stop. At this stage, all individuals with access to the organization's ICT system act on a commonly accepted understanding of the specific steps required to enable formal security practice. The actual steps contained in that understanding might not be extensive and are often dependent on individual willingness, but regular security policies are planned and documented for everybody in the organization to follow.

The fact that a set of formal security policies has been documented allows the organization to implement a training program. These programs are generally not oriented toward ensuring specific skills beyond general knowledge needed by everybody in the organization to perform basic work. Nevertheless, it is much better than ad hoc security practice.

Enhanced ICT governance requires the next stage. The fourth stage, deliberate control, is typical of a well-organized information assurance operation. Deliberate control is enforced by defined management accountability. Since achieving and sustaining this level of capability requires commitment and resources, there are very few organizations that actually operate at this level.

Deliberate control is built around the documentation of a tailored set of tasks for each relevant organizational function. The performance of these security tasks is monitored using quantitative measures of performance, such as number and type of incidents. These tasks are defined and overseen based on a precise knowledge of the requirements of each individual function's role.

An organization at this level of functioning can be considered to have performed proper due diligence in the protection of information and enforcement of cybersecurity. As a result of quantitative and formally monitoring, the security operation can be considered to be managed. This is a more than adequate level of assurance. However, this is not yet the highest level of governance possible.

The information assurance function is fully optimized at the continuous adaptation level. This stage not only carries out all of the policies necessary to ensure cybersecurity within the requirements of any given circumstance, but it continues to evolve those policies using the data gathered in stage four. Organizations at this level are capable of adapting to new threats as they arise. They are safe from harm because they are able to anticipate and mitigate all but the most unexpected events, and they are capable of a rapid and meaningful reaction to any unanticipated event that might occur.

ID.GV-2: Information Security Roles and Responsibilities
Are Coordinated and Aligned with Internal Roles and External Partners

The outcome of the CSF ID.GV-2 subcategory recommends that within an information security plan that has been appropriately communicated, "the organization:

1. Establishes personnel security requirements including security roles and responsibilities for third-party providers;
2. Requires third-party providers to comply with personnel security policies and procedures established by the organization;
3. Documents personnel security requirements;
4. Requires third-party providers to notify (Assignment: organization-defined personnel or roles) of any personnel transfers or terminations of third-party personnel who possess organizational credentials and/or badges, or who have information

system privileges within (Assignment: organization-defined time period); and

5. Monitors provider compliance" (National Institute for Standards and Technology April 2014).

It should be noted up front that the controls that satisfy this subcategory outcome should be implemented in an integrative manner with the controls implemented for ID.BE-1, in which the organization understands and documents its role within the supply chain.

For any type of change to take place within an organization, it is imperative that commitment of the security program begin at the senior leadership level. If top-level management fails to provide support, the implementation initiative is sure to fail. Cybersecurity of ICT systems requires a vast array of skill sets that do not necessarily manifest from one single department of an organization. As such, senior leadership must develop and document in their information security plan an approach to managing security. Senior leadership must establish a clear understanding of security accountability and responsibilities that make use of an individual's skills. The way that management proceeds in identifying and assigning roles and responsibilities is going to vary from one organization to another. In making such decisions, the culture of the organization will be a significant factor. For example, the roles and responsibilities will look very different in an organization with a collective bargaining structure from those in an organization in which management has complete control. As senior leadership makes those decisions, care must be taken to bring the internal responsibilities in line with those that had been identified through business environment activities of external partners.

ID.GV-3: Legal and Regulatory Requirements Regarding Cybersecurity, including Privacy and Civil Liberties Obligations Are Understood and Managed

The purpose of the ID.GV-3 outcome is for organizations to "avoid breaches of legal, statutory, regulatory, or contractual obligations related to information security and of any security requirements" (International Organization for Standardization/International Electrotechnical Commission 2013).

The Gramm–Leach–Bliley Act, for example, requires regulators of financial institutions to establish standards for administrative, technical, and physical safeguards in order to ensure the security and confidentiality of customer records and information. In the banking industry, the Interagency Guidelines Establishing Information Security Standards require them to implement a comprehensive written information security program, with administrative, technical, and physical safeguards appropriate to the size and complexity of the financial institution and the nature and scope of its services. When developing an information security program, the financial institution must first assess risk by identifying internal and external threats that could result in unauthorized access, misuse, alteration, or destruction of customer information or customer information systems. Beginning in the early part of the 21st century, healthcare institutions were required to ensure that appropriate information safeguards were in place to comply with Health Insurance Portability and Accountability Act, which protects the confidentiality of patient records through a standard set of security practices.

Every organization is responsible for knowing which legal and regulatory requirements they must be in compliance with; and they probably already do. That awareness must be further evident by implementation of security measures within their critical infrastructure and in appropriate documentation that supports it.

ID.GV-4: Governance and Risk Management
Processes Address Cybersecurity Risks

Recall the discussion in the last section in which we emphasized the importance of "buy-in" from senior leadership. Responsibility for the oversight of information security and cyberthreats is moving from the lower levels of the organization to boards of directors and senior executives as it becomes increasingly clear that managing these risks across an organization demands involvement at the highest levels.

Organizations in both public and private sectors are being confronted with increasing cybersecurity risks. One industry in particular is of particular significance. The banking industry is at the heart of what is considered to be critical infrastructure by the Department of

Homeland Security, and their holdings of consumer data and dollars make them especially attractive to thieves and hackers.

The outcome of ID.GV-4 recommends a governance model for information security and cybersecurity risk that does not necessarily require the board and senior executives to become technology experts but rather to implement a cross-discipline approach; and the recognition that technology, while posing a significant risk, can also be a significant competitive advantage. Organizations must update risk management skills to ensure technology risks and gaps are not only understood but also factored into decisions made by senior leadership. A well-protected organization is less likely to become a victim and stands to attract the customers of companies that do; it is also better positioned to deliver services with effective and secure technology.

Organizations that have not yet adjusted to the new cybersecurity risk paradigm typically have some common vulnerabilities:

- Boards of directors and executives that hesitate to engage on technology and cybersecurity issues;
- Risk management frameworks that do not capture the full range of technology risks, including exposure through vendors;
- Ambiguous lines of authority and a lack of accountability for protection, response, and recovery;
- Reliance upon security tools to respond to a crisis, rather than reliance upon front-end investments to prevent a crisis; and
- Inconsistent testing of their incident-response plans.

Competition for corporate time and resources is fierce, but the financial and reputational impact of security failure as well as data and privacy breaches is a huge price to pay for taking partial measures. These breakdowns are often as devastating as failures in business, public relations, customer trust, and regulatory compliance.

How organizations should best address these risks varies by their size, complexity, and lines of business. Compared with small- and medium-sized organizations, the largest have the obvious advantages that come with size: 24/7 operations that can quickly address emerging threats, more employees dedicated to protecting against cybersecurity risk, advanced information technology software and systems, and the capacity and scale to perform operations activities internally. But these resources must be deployed carefully to generate the greatest benefit. And, of course, size comes with its own disadvantages, not the least of which is the greater number of threats large organizations can expect to attract.

As the size of the organization decreases, generally so does the budget and staffing for managing cybersecurity risk. But while medium-sized organizations do not have the same flexibility that the largest ones have in deciding which activities to keep in-house, they usually have the advantage of being less technically complex. In turn, ICT systems and their protection are much less complex.

The tendency of medium- and small-sized organizations to outsource the management of cybersecurity risks is a critical distinction from the largest ones. Organizations of all sizes must be able to clearly represent their controls and capabilities regardless of who manages the implementation, which places emphasis and increased expense for competent vendor management. Managers must take an active role in evaluating the added risk or benefit of third parties and continuously monitor the overall risk posture of the organization.

The common element for all organizations in managing cybersecurity risk successfully is a governance framework that suits their risk profile. Organizations should identify where risk functions are managed and assess how much control they have over those functions. That is a key element of the rationale for outsourcing because whether to maintain a third-party relationship depends on an accurate assessment of the benefit of doing so. These decisions, which must be reconsidered on a regular basis, cannot be made unless internal teams and third parties are reporting practical information that is used to make decisions about risk.

Over time, organizations should continue to improve their cybersecurity programs through sound risk management, continuing to raise the bar by utilizing new security tools and improved processes to support it, refining security operations to be more efficient, and responding to new and emerging threats. Compliance with the rules is expected but genuine security requires steady evaluation and alignment of the cybersecurity risk framework with the organization's business objectives, governance, risk management, ICT, and regulations considered.

Risk Assessment Category

The CSF describes the outcome of the risk assessment category as that in which "the organization understands the cybersecurity risk to organizational operations (including mission, functions, image, or reputation), organizational assets, and individuals" (National Institute of Standards and Technology Feb. 2014). It should be noted that risk assessment is aligned with step 4 of the CSF recommended approach to establishing or improving an organization's cybersecurity program.

Risk assessments are important in that they help to identify threats to the organization, their likelihood, and associated consequences. Because where the risks are is a fundamental part of managing them, the term *risk assessment* is often confused with *risk management* (which will be discussed later in this chapter). Risk assessment can be seen as a tool that supports the larger scope of risk management.

Risk assessments support the strategy that is used to organize the risk management process and they give managers the information necessary to deploy specific controls that respond to those risks. Assessments also measure how effective controls are once they have been put into place. This ensures effective and the most up-to-date knowledge about existing threats. Risk assessment typically proceeds the implementation of formal risk management strategies and encompasses activities that continue throughout the risk management process. The cyclical nature of assessment can help to prioritize the implementation of controls that the organization will plan and install. As important the role of software requirements analysis of the system life cycle to identify all of the requirements of a software solution, risk assessment is also an information gathering activity that focuses on identifying and understanding all potential internal and external risks.

The best approach to assuring the most at-risk assets are secure is to implement a risk assessment framework. These frameworks establish the rules for what is assessed, who needs to be involved, the terminology used in discussing risk, the criteria for quantifying, qualifying, and comparing degrees of risk, and the documentation that must be collected and produced as a result of assessments and follow-on activities. The goal of a framework is to establish an objective measurement of risk that will allow an organization to understand business risk to critical information and assets. The result is that the risk assessment framework provides the tools necessary to make business decisions regarding investments in people, processes, and technology to bring risk to acceptable level.

There are several frameworks in use today. One of the most popular is Operationally Critical Threat, Asset, and Vulnerability Evaluation (OCTAVE), developed at Carnegie Mellon University. Another popular framework was developed by NIST and documented in NIST SP 800-30, Guide for Conducting Risk Assessments. Other frameworks in use by many organizations include ISACA's RISK IT (part of COBIT 5), and ISO/IEC 27005:2011 (part of the ISO 27000 series that includes ISO 27001 and 27002). All of the frameworks have similar approaches but differ in their high-level goals. OCTAVE, NIST, and ISO 27005 focus on security risk assessments, while RISK IT applies to the broader ICT risk management process. The choice of framework is contingent on a number of factors. However, since the CSF references COBIT 5, the ISO series, and NIST SP 800 series, we will use those resources for further discussion about risk assessment in the next several sections of this chapter. The CSF breaks down the risk assessment into six subcategory outcomes. The outcomes are identified in Table 3.4.

ID.RA-1: Asset Vulnerabilities Are Identified and Documented

The ID.RA-1 outcome recommends that organizations "continuously acquire, assess, and take action on new information in order to identify vulnerabilities, remediate, and minimize the window of opportunity for attackers" (Council on Cybersecurity 2014). In general, the associated control that achieves this outcome addresses the need to perform a vulnerability assessment.

Vulnerability assessment is a review of the level of security maintained in operational systems for the purpose of identifying potential vulnerabilities in assets. When vulnerabilities are identified, appropriate mitigation controls are implemented to protect valued assets, which is addressed in the CSF through another risk assessment subcategory outcome. Since vulnerability assessments are not exclusively conducted to identify potential vulnerabilities but also to investigate missing countermeasures, it is important to perform subsequent

Table 3.4   Framework Core Risk Assessment Category

CATEGORY	SUBCATEGORY	INFORMATION RESOURCES
Risk Assessment (ID.RA): The organization understands the cybersecurity risk to organizational operations (including mission, functions, image, or reputation), organizational assets, and individuals.	ID.RA-1: Asset vulnerabilities are identified and documented.	• CCS CSC 4 • COBIT 5 APO12.01, APO12.02, APO12.03, APO12.04 • ISA 62443-2-1:2009 4.2.3, 4.2.3.7, 4.2.3.9, 4.2.3.12 • ISO/IEC 27001:2013 A.12.6.1, A.18.2.3 • NIST SP 800-53 Rev. 4 CA-2, CA-7, CA-8, RA-3, RA-5, SA-5, SA-11, SI-2, SI-4, SI-5
	ID.RA-2: Threat and vulnerability information is received from information sharing forums and sources.	• ISA 62443-2-1:2009 4.2.3, 4.2.3.9, 4.2.3.12 • ISO/IEC 27001:2013 A.6.1.4 • NIST SP 800-53 Rev 4 PM-15, PM-16, SI-5
	ID.RA-3: Threats, both internal and external, are identified and documented.	• COBIT 5 APO12.01, APO12.02, APO12.03, APO12.04 • ISA 62443-2-1:2009 4.2.3, 4.2.3.9, 4.2.3.12 • NIST SP 800-53 Rev. 4 RA-3, SI-5, PM-12, PM-16
	ID.RA-4: Potential business impacts and likelihoods are identified.	• COBIT 5 DSS04.02 • ISA 62443-2-1:2009 4.2.3, 4.2.3.9, 4.2.3.12 • NIST SP 800-53 Rev. 4 RA-2, RA-3, PM-9, PM-11, SA-14
	ID.RA-5: Threats, vulnerabilities, likelihoods, and impacts are used to determine risk.	• COBIT 5 APO12.02 • ISO/IEC 27001:2013 A.12.6.1 • NIST SP 800-53 Rev. 4 RA-2, RA-3, PM-16
	ID.RA-6: Risk responses are identified and prioritized.	• COBIT 5 APO12.05, APO13.02 • NIST SP 800-53 Rev. 4 PM-4, PM-9

Source: National Institute of Standards and Technology, *Framework for Improving Critical Infrastructure Cybersecurity.* Gaithersburg, February 12, 2014.

vulnerability assessments to protect critical assets. The benefits of security vulnerability assessments include

- Identification of an organization's assets (information, systems, and network infrastructures, data, programs and applications);
- Classification of assets identified according to their importance to the organization, such as "critical" or "noncritical" (this classification depends on the deployed methodology);

- Identification of critical assets to an organization, for example, information such as marketing database "classified" military information and identification of which infrastructure (systems or networks) processes, stores, or transmits organization's critical information;
- Determination of the security posture of assets in order to identify potential vulnerabilities in them;
- Determination of associated security risks on asset (information, infrastructure, software and content) as follows: end-user devices (personal computers and personal digital assistants, user-support devices and the actual content or otherwise);
- Determination of security requirements and coordinate the right mix of countermeasures;
- Access to missing controls, protection measures or requirements not implemented correctly, or not implemented at all, which should have been, for the purpose of protecting critical assets; and, finally,
- Recommendation of protection controls (countermeasures) to prevent or mitigate identified vulnerabilities.

Cyberattackers stop at nothing to gain access to all of new information (e.g., software updates, patches, security advisories, and threat bulletins) and take advantage of every opportunity to exploit gaps between the appearance of new knowledge and security solutions. As research is conducted that potentially expose new vulnerabilities, attackers wait in the wings to take advantage of new opportunities. At the same time, vendors begin development and deployment of patches that act as countermeasures while organizations focus attention of assessing risk, regression-test patching, and preparing the ICT system for installation of the vendor's patches.

Generally, vulnerability assessment is performed through the use of specialized scanning tools. "Organizations that do not scan for vulnerabilities and proactively address discovered flaws face a significant likelihood of having their computer systems compromised" (Council on Cybersecurity 2014). In addition to the persistent process of scanning for vulnerabilities, organizations must consider the need for securing assets across the entire enterprise while prioritizing which assets are most valuable and managing potential side effects of not implementing countermeasures.

ID.RA-2: Threat and Vulnerability Information Is Received from Information Sharing Forums and Sources

As is the case in many business disciplines, organizations cannot rely on just the expertise of the small group of security professionals within the organization to provide the entire scope of thread and vulnerability information. The ID.RA-2 subcategory outcome suggests that "appropriate contacts with special interest groups or other specialist security forums and other professional associations shall be maintained" (International Organization for Standardization/ International Electrotechnical Commission 2013). The ICT industry is largely supported by standards and guidelines. The CSF, for example, provides a list of such documentation that can be used to implement each of the subcategory outcomes. Further research into the standard bodies and associations that develop the documents show that each provides many more resources that assist organizations in such activities as threat and vulnerability identification. Additionally, many security magazines, journals, and Internet forums exist, providing valuable resources and information sharing mechanisms that will help organizations stay up to date and in control of the latest security threats and vulnerabilities.

ID.RA-3: Threats, Both Internal and External, Are Identified and Documented

At first glance of this subcategory outcome, the mistake may be made in concluding that it was already addressed in ID.RA-1. It might be best to begin this section by describing the difference between a threat and a vulnerability. A threat is something that can compromise some aspect of your system. This includes things like a denial of service attack preventing you from accessing resources, the theft of intellectual property residing in your system, or even damaging your public image. In other words, a threat is something that you worry about happening to one of your assets. Likewise, a vulnerability is a mechanism that allows an attacker to bring your worst fears to life. That is to say, a vulnerability is a way in which a threat can be actualized. It might help to form an analogy. A threat can be likened to a plan to write some software and the vulnerability to its actual implementation.

The underlying outcome of ID.RA-3 recommends that in order to identify and document threats, both internally and externally, "the organization implements an insider threat program that includes a cross-discipline insider threat incident handling team" and at the same time "the organization implements a threat awareness program that includes a cross-organization information-sharing capability" (National Institute for Standards and Technology April 2014).

It is important to understand that cybersecurity threats do not just include possible attacks from outside the organizational boundary. In developing a cybersecurity program, attention must also be drawn to the threats that exist from within the organization. Insider threat programs include security controls to detect and prevent malicious insider activity, such as social engineering through a centralized integration and analysis process to identify potential insider threats. In addition to the integration and analysis function, insider threat programs also provide services such as preparation of insider threat policies and implementation plans, monitor individual employee activities, and provide insider threat awareness training to employees.

Anybody working within or studying about the ICT industry knows that the process associated with providing an organization information assets is evolutionary. As much as one organization evolves in how it provides and secures information, the same is true with the approaches that external attackers take in gaining access to an organization's information. Because of the constantly changing and increasing sophistication of attacker capabilities, it is becoming more likely that an organization's ICT system can be compromised. One way to minimize the possibility of external threats is by sharing information through information awareness programs. Such awareness programs can include sharing information about how threats are acted upon, tactics and techniques that organizations have found effective against certain types of threats, and knowledge about the warning signs that an attack may occur. However, organizations must be cautious. Some threat information is sensitive and should not be exposed. Other information is much less sensitive and can be freely shared.

ID.RA-4: Potential Business Impacts and Likelihoods Are Identified

"The likelihood of occurrence is a weighted risk factor based on an analysis of the probability that a given threat is capable of exploiting a given vulnerability (or set of vulnerabilities). The likelihood risk factor combines an estimate of the likelihood that the threat event will be initiated with an estimate of the likelihood of impact (i.e., the likelihood that the threat event results in adverse impacts). For adversarial threats, an assessment of likelihood of occurrence is typically based on (1) adversary intent; (2) adversary capability; and (3) adversary targeting. For other than adversarial threat events, the likelihood of occurrence is estimated using historical evidence, empirical data, or other factors" (National Institute of Standards and Technology 2012). The likelihood that a threat will occur is normally assessed based on a specific time frame. If a threat is considered to be very likely to occur, the risk assessment will consider the estimated frequency of each occurrence. While performing assessment activities consideration should be taken into the state of the organization in terms of enterprise architecture, information security program, their mission, and business processes.

Organizations normally measure likelihood of the occurrence security threats using a three-step process:

1. Assess the likelihood that threat will occur.
2. Assess the likelihood that the threat occurrence will impact (or cause considerable harm to) valuable information assets or individuals.
3. Assess the likelihood of the adverse impact of steps 1 and 2 combined

It should be noted that a single threat occurrence can exploit multiple vulnerabilities. Therefore, while determining the likelihood of a threat occurrence, the organization should examine vulnerabilities that threat occurrences could exploit as well as the mission and business functions susceptible to threats that do not have security controls in place. In some cases, ICT managers choose to implement a workaround within ICT systems where mission and business functions are most vulnerable.

ID.RA-5: Threats, Vulnerabilities, Likelihoods,
and Impacts Are Used to Determine Risk

The CSF ID.RA-5 subcategory outcome recommends that ICT managers should "determine the risk to the organization from threat events of concern considering: (i) the impact that would result from the events; and (ii) the likelihood of the events occurring" (National Institute of Standards and Technology 2012). In doing so, organizations assess the risks from threat occurrences based on what they learned from understanding the combination of likelihood and impact of each threat.

The amount of potential risk threat occurrence is a factor in determining the degree to which organizations are threatened by such events. Normally, organizations make a list of threat concerns, in the order of importance based on the risk assessment. Therefore, the greatest attention will be on threats with the highest risk. Some organizations use scoring systems to prioritize the treats with the highest risk. Normally, the level of risk is not higher than the impact level, and likelihood of the threat occurrence can help to reduce risk below that impact level. However, when managers of large organizations identify risks, many interdependencies develop. When that happens, all of the risks need to be considered together, thus possibly producing a higher risk for the entire organization. To address situations where harm occurs multiple times, organizations can define a threat as multiple occurrences of harm and an impact level associated with the cumulative degree of harm. During the activities associated with the ID.RA-1 through ID.RA-4 outcomes, an organization can gain key information related to uncertainties in risk assessments. Uncertainties can come from missing information, subjective assessments, and assumptions. The success or failure of risk assessment is partially the result of the decision making done during the assessment activities, related to determining the justifications of assumptions made during assessment.

ID.RA-6: Risk Responses Are Identified and Prioritized

Risk response is the process of developing strategic options, and determining actions, to enhance opportunities that reduce cybersecurity threats. This process ensures that each risk requiring a response has an owner monitoring the responses, although the owner may delegate implementation of a response to someone else.

Once the risks have been identified, prioritized, and the likelihood of the risk has been analyzed together with the associated impact to the organization, the ID.RA-6 subcategory outcome prescribes that "the organization

1. Implements a process for ensuring that plans of action and milestones for the security program and associated organizational information systems:
   a. Are developed and maintained;
   b. Document the remedial information security actions to adequately respond to risk to organizational operations and assets, individuals, other organizations, and the Nation;
2. Reviews plans of action and milestones for consistency with the organizational risk management strategy and organization-wide priorities for risk response actions" (National Institute for Standards and Technology April 2014).

The plan of action and milestones is a key document in the cyber-security program while emphasizing risk management across the organization, mission/business process, and ICT system. The plans should be viewed from an organizational perspective prioritizing risk response actions while at the same time keeping in mind the goals and objectives of the organization. Plan of action and milestones should be continuously updated based on results from security control assessments and continuous monitoring activities.

Risk Management Category

The CSF describes the outcome of the risk management category as "the organization's priorities, constraints, risk tolerances, and assumptions are established and used to support operational risk decisions" (National Institute of Standards and Technology Feb. 2014). At a high level of abstraction, it is easy to make the interpretation that risk management is most closely aligned with steps 1 and 4 of the CSF recommended approach to establishing or improving an organization's cybersecurity program. Likewise, you may have noticed that in each major section of this chapter, there has been some mention of risk management. In reality, risk management applies to every function of the CSF. The reason is simple. It is a process by which all of the risk-related policies, strategies, and control plans are developed and implemented which in turn affects every aspect of cybersecurity. It is one thing to identify the controls that should be implemented. Without an "umbrella" risk management structure in place, however, chances of a cybersecurity program being unsuccessful and ICT system being susceptible to cyberattacks is substantially increased. That said, risk management should be the first set of controls an organization plans for and implements before progressing through any of the steps defined by the CSF. However, knowledge of the frameworks outcomes is necessary in order to accurately establish the process the organization will implement in managing risk. As the organization continues to plan and implement the CSF recommended outcomes, the risk management process should continuously evolve based on what is learned about asset vulnerabilities, threats, and risks.

Risk management may sound overwhelming but for the most part, it is just plain common sense. For larger organizations with varied services operating over several locations, it does get a little more complicated, but for most not-for-profit groups, the task need not be overly complicated.

In order to recognize a risk, you need to know what a risk is. While some risks may apply to almost everyone, some will be specific to a single organization or one of their stakeholders. In undertaking a risk assessment the organization's specific objectives and capabilities need to be taken into account as well as external factors, such as the changing legal environment and shifting social standards.

In general, the role of risk management is to manage and mitigate risks and reduce potential impacts on information assets to an acceptable level, consider the following goals:

- Account for and protect all IT assets
- Establish and reduce the likelihood and impact of IT security risks
- Perform regular risk assessments with senior managers and key staff
- Permit access to critical and sensitive data only to authorized users

- Ensure that critical and confidential information is withheld from those who should not have access to it
- Identify, monitor, and report security vulnerabilities and incidents
- Develop cybersecurity continuity plans that can be executed, tested, and maintained

Managing cybersecurity risk is not about eliminating all risk. It is about determining and understanding the risk rating of events identified during risk assessment and putting the right processes or controls in place to manage them in accordance with the organization's tolerance to risk. It is an ongoing process, not a one-time activity. It requires an organization to understand what kind of events can have a negative impact on operations, how likely those events are to occur, and what the impact would be to the service or business if a given event does occur.

The underlying premise of all three CSF ID.RM subcategory outcomes recommend that "the organization:

1. Develops a comprehensive strategy to manage risk to organizational operations and assets, individuals, other organizations, and the Nation associated with the operation and use of information systems;
2. Implements the risk management strategy consistently across the organization; and
3. Reviews and updates the risk management strategy (Assignment: organization-defined frequency) or as required, to address organizational changes" (National Institute of Standards and Technology April 2014).

In order to better understand the risk management process, in this section, we will discuss the CSF recommendations of risk management breaking it down into understanding the plan, implementation of the process, and risk handling strategies. The CSF outcomes are identified in Table 3.5.

The Risk Management Plan

Organizations are continuously working to develop a plan that supports cybersecurity and risk management procedures. With attack

Table 3.5   Framework Core Risk Management Category

CATEGORY	SUBCATEGORY	INFORMATION RESOURCES
Risk Management Strategy (ID.RM): The organization's priorities, constraints, risk tolerances, and assumptions are established and used to support operational risk decisions.	ID.RM-1: Risk management processes are established, managed, and agreed to by organizational stakeholders.	• COBIT 5 APO12.04, APO12.05, APO13.02, BAI02.03, BAI04.02 • ISA 62443-2-1:2009 4.3.4.2 • NIST SP 800-53 Rev. 4 PM-9
	ID.RM-2: Organizational risk tolerance is determined and clearly expressed.	• COBIT 5 APO12.06 • ISA 62443-2-1:2009 4.3.2.6.5 • NIST SP 800-53 Rev. 4 PM-9
	ID.RM-3: The organization's determination of risk tolerance is informed by its role in critical infrastructure and sector specific risk analysis.	• NIST SP 800-53 Rev. 4 PM-8, PM-9, PM-11, SA-14

Source: National Institute of Standards and Technology, *Framework for Improving Critical Infrastructure Cybersecurity.* Gaithersburg, February 12, 2014.

potential continually growing, the task of securing information has become more complex, cybersecurity risk management plans need to include strategies that address all of the organizations at-risk assets extending to mobile platforms, cloud-based systems, and social ecosystems. There may be any number of strategies included in the plan. However, the plan itself is normally built around a sequence of four standard elements. You will notice that each of the elements has already been discussed in previous sections of this chapter. Hence, the connection between the risk management process acting as an umbrella over the implementation of security controls based on the recommendations of the entire CSF.

The first element is the requirement to categorize all information assets in terms of the value they represent. This is essentially an inventory and valuation process that aims to result in a prioritized list of ICT systems and their components. The goal is to identify those systems that process the most data and that are at the highest degree of risk.

The next step is to develop an integrated set of substantive risk controls. Ideally, the organization will define a set of specific activities to manage existing risks of assets identified in the first step. Such controls must be comprehensive in their application and appropriate to the situation. The controls are normally detailed in a design specification, which the organization develops through a formal process.

The third step entails the implementation of the controls. In this step, the controls for risk management are customized to fit the specific situation that they are meant to address. The risk control activities are then embedded into day-to-day operations. The purpose of this implementation step is to make the identification, analysis, and response to risk a part of the organizations day-to-day processes.

The fourth step provides support for the requirement for continuous effectiveness over time through formal assessment methods. Controlled tests and audits are conducted to ensure that the risk management process is functioning as planned. Additionally, the organization performs targeted assessments intended to evaluate the effectiveness of individual risk control functions. The goal is to confirm through observation that the actions the organization to ensure proper risk management remain effective.

If effectiveness within the risk management process can be confirmed, the organization can claim that systems falling under the risk management function are indeed secure. Given the evolution of risk to ICT assets, that assurance is always subject to restrictions of time and priorities. Nevertheless, if all of the prior steps have been completed properly and monitoring of the controls is continuous and accurate, the organization can have peace of mind that an effective risk management process is in place.

Implementing Risk Management

The steps to establish an effective risk management process involve five activities: planning, oversight, risk analysis, risk response, and continuous monitoring. The first activity entails the need for all of the operational aspects of the risk management process to be planned. As is the case in all facets of ICT life cycle management, operational planning is an essential component; therefore, every step of the organization's risk management approach must be specified including authorities, responsibilities, and timing.

An oversight process is crucial once the day-to-day risk management policies and procedures have been defined. The goal of oversight is to always stay one step ahead, in terms of the organizations risk vulnerabilities and threats. Because of the continuity of the oversight process, it should be a management function that is consistently able to provide insight and reporting of the organization's present state of identified risks.

In order to maintain understanding of risk, the organization must perform a quantitative and qualitative risk analysis in order to identify any emerging risk. The analysis must also be able to ensure that existing risks remain contained. The vital goal of this activity is continuous assurance that the risks to the ICT assets that the organization rates as high priority be properly understood and any emerging risks be identified and described in terms on their effect on the organization.

Once the analysis activity has been defined, the next step is to identify the responses the organization will apply to the existing risks. These responses should directly target all known elements of identified risks and be specifically defined in the risk management plan. It is important to have a plan for response to risk, namely, because cybersecurity risk can happen very quickly. Additionally, it is difficult for management to accurately respond to risk in the middle of an event, resulting in negative effects throughout the organization.

The final activity, and equally important as the previous, is continuous monitoring of the operational risk environment. Persistent monitoring is necessary because risks can occur at any time and in unanticipated forms. Monitoring can be done though regular testing and audits, in addition to day-to-day managerial oversight. In many cases, the best source of information on emerging risk are the end users. Those individuals can then report back to their management the suspicion of risk. Middle managers can, in turn, evoke actions defined in the risk management plan. Those actions will likely call for further testing based on established test plans and may also require further action in the form of audit when appropriate.

Risk Handling Strategies

Organizations are faced with four options in dealing with risk. One, they can accept the risk and consequences of losses. Two, they can take necessary actions to avoid loses. Three, they can choose to mitigate the losses. Lastly, they can choose to transfer the risk to third parties through contracts, insurance, or various other mechanisms. Regardless which approach is chosen, the organization must adopt a strategy that addresses reach of its priority risks.

Accepting the risk and consequences of loss is typically the most common strategy. The reason for this is that many risks are not identified or acknowledged within the risk management process. Most organizations are willing to accept risks that are rare or have little impact on their ICT assets. The opinion of management in those cases is that the cost of addressing the risk outweighs the cost of harm. When an organization chooses to accept risk, this is referred to as residual risk. These types of risks, however, are still tracked through the risk analysis process.

Alternatively, the organization can choose a risk avoidance strategy. Cybersecurity has three essential components: prevention, detection, and response. The activities associated with prevention are examples of risk avoidance. Cybersecurity awareness programs are another example of this strategy. Because the least amount of harm will occur by having measures in place to address risks when they occur, the cybersecurity program is heavily focused on avoidance.

The last two components of cybersecurity, detection and response, are contained within risk mitigation and risk transfer strategies. Risk mitigation strategies address the activities that should be taken to minimize loss in the presence of risk. For example, an intrusion detection system will not prevent an attack on the network. However, it provides the information needed for the organization to act quickly to minimize the losses as a result of the attack.

In risk transfer, a third party such as an insurance agency absorbs the consequences of the risk. Obtaining insurance against predetermined risks does not prevent the risk from occurring. However, the financial burden of losses will be transferred from the organization to the agency that underwrites the policy. As you can see, risk transfer works well to address risks that incur financial losses. However, they are less effective in alleviating the consequences associated with such things as customer loyalty, organizational reputation, or regulation compliance.

INSIGHT   ADDING CYBER SECURITY
TO CORPORATE RISK MANAGEMENT

Corporate boards and senior management like to focus on business. They love the numbers, the strategy and the success of a business operation. They have a passion for it and that is why they are sitting on board or managing a global company.

They do not like to talk as much about risks, much less plan for them. When it comes to information governance and protecting the company from hackers and cyber-intruders who can harm the company, corporate leaders inevitably turn to their information technology specialists.

This dynamic has to change. Information governance is now part of the corporate risk management fabric. If you look at all the data breach incidents, one significant omission is the failure of the company to have in place an incident response plan to escalate and minimize any damage.

Even more than an incident plan is needed these days—companies have to devote resources and attention to assessing data vulnerabilities and protecting against hackers and other intruders. At the same time, companies face serious internal risks created by BYOD* policies and practices, as well as simple employee mistakes.

Cyber risks have become a fundamental focus for investors, and the SEC requires disclosures of material events relating to cyber intrusions. So far, few companies have made such disclosures.

Corporate boards have to become proactive in this area—they need to ask the tough questions.

- Does the company have an incident response plan in place to reduce the impact of a security breach?
- Are the key stakeholders assigned specific roles in this process?
- Does the board have a reporting mechanism in place to monitor these occurrences and ensure that the company responds appropriately to such an incident?

It is easy to focus on the crisis management scenario without adequately investing in the up-front measures to protect a cyber intrusion. Companies have to spend more on the proactive approach to minimize risks. This is a familiar refrain when addressing a number of risks but when you consider the financial and reputational damage from a cyber attack, a company has to prioritize cyber risks.

Cyber security is not just an issue that should be relegated to the information technology specialists. Board members and senior

---

* Bring your own device (BYOD) is a business trend toward employee-owned devices within a business. Smartphones are the most common, but employees bringing their own tablets, laptops and USB drives into the workplace to use on the job.

managers have to become more familiar with technology issues in order to manage these risks. Reporting lines and authorities have to be made clear well in advance of cyber-attack so that the risks can be managed.

Finally, once a governance structure is put in place to address these issues, the company has to devote time and energy to test its incident responses. Companies will quickly learn some strategies that work and some that do not. Call it a cyber-fire drill but such exercises are well worth the time and attention in order to avoid disastrous events.

In addressing cyber risks, companies often ignore the risks created by their vendors. Companies have to assess the risks that vendors create for their companies. It is too easy to ignore vendor risks and focus on internal risks. A vendor-created cyber security risk complicates risk management and a response and usually spills into lengthy and complex litigation (Volkov 2014).

Linking COBIT to the Identify Function

COBIT 5 defines IT risk as "business risk, specifically, the business risk associated with the use, ownership, operation, involvement, influence and adoption of IT within an enterprise" (Information Systems Audit and Control Association 2012). Further, the framework suggests that IT risk consist of IT events that have an impact on the organization. COBIT is consistent with the other information resources in that it emphasizes the uncertainty, frequency, and impact risk events have on the organization, and recognizes the challenges that risk events cause in meeting organizational goals and objectives.

The COBIT framework recognizes that managed risk is an enabler to all of the resources, processes, and conditions vital for continued success and growth of an organization, and provides opportunities such as business process alignment that might not have otherwise been identified. Additionally, COBIT emphasizes that managed risk provides management an understanding of the security strengths and weaknesses within the organization.

COBIT addresses the underlying risk management process through what it labels as "the risk management Perspective." That perspective combines the CSF governance and management outcomes into a common process. That process includes how to identify, analyze, and respond to risk, and how to use the COBIT 5 framework for that purpose. As such, this perspective requires COBIT 5 core risk processes EDM03 Ensure risk optimization and APO12 Manage risk to be implemented.

Chapter Summary

- The outcomes of the Identify Function of the CSF develop a detailed understanding of systems, assets, data, and capabilities at the organizational level necessary to manage cybersecurity risk.
- Asset management is a set of ICT processes designed to manage the life cycle and inventory of technology assets. Its purpose is to lower ICT costs by reducing IT risk and improving productivity through proper and predefined asset management techniques.
- The business environment category of the CSF is intended to understand and prioritize the organization's mission, objectives, stakeholders, and activities in order to use that information to make informed cybersecurity roles, responsibilities, and risk management decisions.
- Through a properly defined governance process the organization is able to create and implement risk management policies and procedures, in addition to understanding processes to manage and monitor regulatory, legal, risk, environmental, and operational requirements that have an effect on managing cyber security risk.
- Through risk assessment, the organization is able to understand cybersecurity's tangible and intangible risks to organizational operations and make informed decision on how to address those risks through a risk management process.
- The risk management process aims to define and plan the organization's priorities, constraints, risk tolerances, and assumptions in order to insight into operational risk decision making.

Case Project

Suny Corporation would like you to continue the work you have been doing on the plan for implementing the Framework for Improving Critical Infrastructure Cybersecurity. Now that you are familiar with the outcome of the Identify function, they would like you to update your plan with more specific criteria related to have asset management, business environment analysis, and risk assessment. They would also like detail related to how you plan to implement an ICT governance structure within the company. Within the plan, only major steps of implementation need to be organized. In other words, focus on steps that the framework recommends for establishing and improving their cybersecurity program. The plan should continue to take the form of a project timeline that describes when each part of every step is performed. Besides providing a customized timeline and plan, include the business justification for each step.

4

PROTECT FUNCTION

After reading this chapter and completing the case project, you will

- Understand the steps organizations take in controlling access to ICT assets;
- Understand the steps necessary to ensure that personnel are provided appropriate professional development to foster awareness of cybersecurity;
- Understand the importance of security policy within a cyber-security program;
- Understand the importance of implementing security controls associated with maintaining ICT systems; and
- Understand the steps necessary to protect communication systems and removable media.

The second function in the CSF core describes controls that get into the meat and potatoes of developing and implementing safeguards to minimize cybersecurity risks to an organization's systems, assets, data, and capabilities. This function is titled Protect. The controls that support outcomes of this function are normally addressed after the development and implementation of controls in the Identify Function discussed in Chapter 3. Once all the critical data, system software, and processes are identified, relevant threats and risks against those resources need to be evaluated and proper mitigating solutions must be put in place to assure the availability of these systems. Examples of mitigating solutions include access control, patch management, anti-virus, firewalls, backups, security awareness, and training. Effective implementation of security controls in the system components is a critical activity that can affect the security state and risk endured by an organization.

Protect Function Overview

Protective security control implementation should be consistent with the organization's enterprise architecture and information security architecture. The information security architecture serves as a basis for assigning security controls (including, for example, security mechanisms and services) to an ICT system and any business functions that it supports. Security controls targeted for deployment within the ICT system (including subsystems) should be assigned to specific system components that carry the responsibility of supporting a predefined security capability. It should be noted that not all subsystems need to have security controls allocated to them. Organizations should strive to achieve an acceptable balance based on the categorization of subsystems, information security architecture, and which controls are assigned. Industry best practices are typically used when implementing the controls within the ICT system including system and software engineering processes, security engineering principles, and secure coding techniques. Moreover, organizations must ensure that mandatory configuration settings are identified and implemented on ICT products consistent with government regulations and organizational policies.

For all practical purposes, security engineers with the assistance of the Chief Information Security Officer develop a complete security engineering process that identifies and improves information security requirements and provides mechanisms for developing of those requirements into ICT products and systems through a focused approach to security design or configuration. When organizations utilize security products and services from outside vendors, those products and service must have been tested, evaluated, or validated through approved assessment procedures. Additionally, organizations must satisfy minimum assurance requirements when implementing security controls. Assurance requirements are those activities and tasks that security control development teams define and implement to increase the level of confidence that the controls have been implemented correctly, operate as required, and produce the required outcome from the perspective of meeting the security requirements for the ICT system. Assurance requirements are meant to define the desired quality of design, development, and implementation of the security controls in the ICT system. For ICT systems that the organization has ranked at a higher priority, where the threat of more advanced cyberattacks are thought to be more likely, additional assurance measures are considered.

One important point that deserves mention is that organizations may implement controls that are the same across or inherited from different systems or subsystems. That is referred to as the implementation of common controls. In cases such as these, organizations must take into consideration any implementation issues related to the integration or interfaces with common controls and system-specific controls.

When common controls are inherited, security engineers and chief information security officers work with the common control provider to determine the best way to apply the common controls to the organization's ICT systems. There are times when formal integration into ICT products, systems, and services may not be necessary. This tends to be the case for certain operational and management controls. However, some types of operational or technical controls require implementation of additional components, products, or services to allow the ICT system the ability to take full advantage of the previously selected common controls.

There are cases when common controls that have been inherited from other systems do not align with protection priorities and have undesirable weaknesses or deficiencies. In those situations, the owner of the system should identify alternative controls to be implemented. To the extent allowable by the organization's risk management plan, organizations and their suppliers must conduct developmental testing and evaluation during development and implementation processes. By conducting testing and evaluation during development and implementation of the system life cycle, there is greater chance for early detection of weaknesses and deficiencies in addition to providing a cost-effective approach to correcting the problem. Issues found during these tests can be addressed by management in a timely manner and be resolved as needed.

The preceding discussion, although a bit detailed, was important in understanding the overarching principles of implementing security controls. As mentioned above, the Protect Function of the CSF provides the outcomes achieved through the development and implementation of security controls specifically designed to safeguard critical infrastructure. By doing so, this function "supports the ability to limit or contain the impact of a potential cybersecurity event. Examples of outcome Categories within this Function include: Access Control; Awareness and Training; Data Security; Information Protection Processes and Procedures; Maintenance; and Protective Technology" (National Institute of Standards and Technology Feb. 2014).

Access Control Category

The CSF describes the outcome of the access control category as the development and implementation of controls in which "access to assets and associated facilities is limited to authorized users, processes, or devices, and to authorized activities and transactions" (National Institute of Standards and Technology Feb. 2014). This category, as will be the case with the remaining functions and categories discussed in the next four chapters, is aligned with step 7 of the CSF recommended approach to establishing or improving an organization's cybersecurity program. With that in mind, all initial security and risk management plans should have been developed. Additionally, the organization should have completed initial risk assessment as a basis for creating a target profile containing cybersecurity outcomes that require development and implementation of appropriate protective, detection, and recovery controls.

Cybersecurity access control is an important aspect of any system. It is the process in which organizations ensure that an authenticated user accesses only what they are authorized to and nothing else. Unfortunately, security is rarely at the top of an organization's priorities, although mention terms such as *data confidentiality, sensitivity,* and *ownership* and they quickly become interested. The good news is that there is a wide range of techniques that can be applied to help secure access to system. The bad news is that the human factor is the weakest link. Cybersecurity is too often merely an illusion that is sometimes made worse when gullibility, naïveté, or ignorance come into play. Cybersecurity is not a technology problem; it is a people and management problem. Having said that, it is an understatement to say that the technology factor and the people factor go hand in hand; organizations need to address both issues to succeed.

Before moving on to the access control outcomes defined by the CSF, it would be beneficial to understand the difference between authentication and authorization. Authentication is the act of determining the identity of a user and of the system that he or she is using. The goal of authentication is to first verify that the user, either a person or a system that is attempting to interact with your system, is allowed to do so. The second goal is to gather information regarding the way that the user is accessing your system. For example, a banker cannot attempt to make financial transactions during off-hours from an Internet café although they should be able to do so from their secured workstation at their branch. Therefore, gathering basic system information, such as its location and security aspects of its connection (Is it encrypted? Is it via a physical line? Is the connection private?), is critical. Alternatively, authorization is the act of determining the level of access that an authorized user has to system functions and data. Fundamentally, to set an effective approach to authorization, the first question that you need to address is "what will we control access to?" Organizations can secure access to both data and functionality, such as access to sales figures and the ability to see another employee's payroll data. Stakeholder requirements will drive the answer to that question. However, the granularity of access, and the ability to implement it effectively, is a definite constraint. For example, although the requirements specifications may dictate controls to access specific columns of specific rows within a database based on complex business rules, security engineers may not be able to implement this in a cost-effective manner that also conforms to performance constraints. The second question that needs to be answered is "what rules are applicable?" The answer to this question is also driven by stakeholder requirements, although you may need to explore various security factors that the stakeholders may not be aware of. These factors include connection type, update access, time of day, existence, cascading authorization, global permissions, and combination of privileges.

The CSF breaks down the access control category into six subcategory lower-level outcomes. Those outcomes are identified in Table 4.1 and described in detail in the next several sections of this chapter.

PR.AC-1: Identities and Credentials Are Managed for Authorized Devices and Users

The underlying objective of the CSF PR. AC-1 subcategory is to "actively manage the life-cycle of system and application accounts—their creation,

Table 4.1   Framework Core Access Control Category

CATEGORY	SUBCATEGORY	INFORMATION RESOURCES
Access Control (PR.AC): Access to assets and associated facilities is limited to authorized users, processes, or devices, and to authorized activities and transactions.	PR.AC-1: Identities and credentials are managed for authorized devices and users.	• CCS CSC 16 • COBIT 5 DSS05.04, DSS06.03 • ISA 62443-2-1:2009 4.3.3.5.1 • ISA 62443-3-3:2013 SR 1.1, SR 1.2, SR 1.3, SR 1.4, SR 1.5, SR 1.7, SR 1.8, SR 1.9 • ISO/IEC 27001:2013 A.9.2.1, A.9.2.2, A.9.2.4, A.9.3.1, A.9.4.2, A.9.4.3 • NIST SP 800-53 Rev. 4 AC-2, IA Family
	PR.AC-2: Physical access to assets is managed and protected.	• COBIT 5 DSS01.04, DSS05.05 • ISA 62443-2-1:2009 4.3.3.3.2, 4.3.3.3.8 • ISO/IEC 27001:2013 A.11.1.1, A.11.1.2, A.11.1.4, A.11.1.6, A.11.2.3 • NIST SP 800-53 Rev. 4 PE-2, PE-3, PE-4, PE5, PE-6, PE-9
	PR.AC-3: Remote access is managed.	• COBIT 5 APO13.01, DSS01.04, DSS05.03 • ISA 62443-2-1:2009 4.3.3.6.6 • ISA 62443-3-3:2013 SR 1.13, SR 2.6 • ISO/IEC 27001:2013 A.6.2.2, A.13.1.1, A.13.2.1 • NIST SP 800-53 Rev. 4 AC-17, AC-19, AC-20
	PR.AC-4: Access permissions are managed, incorporating the principles of least privilege and separation of duties.	• CCS CSC 12, 15 • ISA 62443-2-1:2009 4.3.3.7.3 • ISA 62443-3-3:2013 SR 2.1 • ISO/IEC 27001:2013 A.6.1.2, A.9.1.2, A.9.2.3, A.9.4.1, A.9.4.4 • NIST SP 800-53 Rev. 4 AC-2, AC-3, AC-5, AC-6, AC-16
	PR.AC-5: Network integrity is protected, incorporating network segregation where appropriate.	• ISA 62443-2-1:2009 4.3.3.4 • ISA 62443-3-3:2013 SR 3.1, SR 3.8 • ISO/IEC 27001:2013 A.13.1.1, A.13.1.3, A.13.2.1 • NIST SP 800-53 Rev. 4 AC-4, SC-7

Source: National Institute of Standards and Technology, *Framework for Improving Critical Infrastructure Cybersecurity.* Gaithersburg, February 12, 2014.

use, dormancy, deletion—in order to minimize opportunities for attackers to leverage them" (Council on Cybersecurity 2014).

There are numerous ICT system account types that must be managed; some examples are individual, shared, group, guest or anonymous, developer, and temporary. It is important that there is consistency between the definition of authorization and the access privileges of users and requirements defined for other security controls in the security plan. Normally, an organization will define access privileges by account, by account type, or by a combination of the two. However, there are additional attributes that require consideration, including restrictions on time of day, day of week, and location of access. When defining those and other attributes, organizations must give some thought to system-related requirements, such as system downtime for upgrades or maintenance. Consideration must also be given to organizational requirements including time zone differences, customer requirements, or remote access. Without these attributes defined, the availability of the ICT system could be affected.

Temporary accounts are those intended for short-term use. Organizations create temporary accounts when there is a need for a group of accounts to be used on a short-term basis. Moreover, these accounts are often used in emergencies where there is immediate need for account activation. In most cases, temporary account activation bypasses the normal account authorization processes. However, procedures must be in place to log their availability and usage. In addition to account activation processes, the organization must also define procedures account disabling or deactivation. Circumstances forcing disabling or deactivation of accounts include when temporary accounts are no longer required and when an employee is transferred or terminated.

PR.AC-2: Physical Access to Assets Is Managed and Protected

The primary objective of PR.AC-2 subcategory is "to prevent unauthorized physical access, damage and interference to the organization's information and information processing facilities" (International Organization for Standardization/International Electrotechnical Commission 2013). This outcome not only addresses the need to lock the door behind you but also includes implications such as physical access authorization and control, access control for transmission medium along with associated power equipment and cabling, access control for output devices, and monitoring physical access once it is established.

Access control is a way of limiting access to a system or to physical or virtual resources. For ICT systems, access control is a process by which users are granted access and certain privileges to systems, resources, or information.

To use access controlled systems, users must present credentials before they can be granted access. For physical systems, these credentials may come in many forms but credentials that cannot be transferred provide the most security. For example, a key card may act as an access control and grant the bearer access to a classified area. Because this credential can be transferred or even stolen, it is not a secure way of handling access control. A more secure method for access control involves two-factor authentication. The person who desires access must show credentials and a second factor to corroborate identity. The second factor could be an access code, a personal identification number (PIN), or even a biometric reading.

There are three factors that can be used for authentication:

- Something known only to the user, such as a password or a PIN
- Something that is part of the user, such as a fingerprint, a retina scan, or another biometric measurement
- Something that belongs to the user, such as a card or a key

For purposes of cybersecurity, access control includes the authorization, authentication, and audit of the individual trying to gain access. Access control can be represented as a model having a subject and an object. The subject is the human user or the one trying to gain access to the object, usually the software. Organizations should also maintain an access control list containing all of the authorization credentials and the individuals to whom these credentials apply. Such list should be viewable based on predefined privileges and managed through access controls. This allows an administrator to secure information and set privileges as to what assets can be accessed, who has access, and at what time that access can occur.

PR.AC-3: Remote Access Is Managed

The main objective of PR.AC-3 is to ensure the security of information flowing from outside the organization. To facilitate this outcome, formal remote access policies, procedures, and controls should be in place to protect the transfer of information by the use of all types remote of communication facilities. This includes access via virtual private networks (VPNs), mobile devices, and use of external information systems. It should be noted that external information systems are also addressed in the asset management subcategory of the Identify Function. However, in that subcategory, focus was on systems of third-party vendors and contractors that are integrated into the functionality of an organization's ICT system. This access control aims to protect an ICT system that provides access via personally owned information systems or devices or privately owned devices located in commercial or public facilities, for example.

Simply put, *remote access* is the act of accessing organizational ICT systems by individuals or computer processes acting on behalf of individuals communicating through external networks such as the Internet. Normally, an organization uses encrypted VPNs to enforce confidentiality and integrity over remote connections. Considering connection to ICT systems via external system, it is important to note that remote access controls apply to information systems other than public web servers or entities designed for public access. With that in mind, organizations should address authorization prior to allowing remote access without specifying the formats for such authorization.

PR.AC-4: Access Permissions Are Managed, Incorporating the Principles of Least Privilege and Separation of Duties

The PR.AC-4 outcome recognizes that account privileges and passwords need to be effectively managed and the policies established by management be properly enforced in order to minimize cybersecurity attacks. It might be a good idea to first understand what is meant by *principles of least privilege* and *separation of duties.*

The *principle of least privilege* (POLP) is a term used in cybersecurity that states that a user should be able to access only the information and resources required for legitimate reasons. POLP states that every component of a system, such as a process, user, or program, should have the least authority possible to perform its job. Separation of duties (SoD) is a type of security control designed to prevent error and fraud by ensuring that at least two individuals are responsible for the separate parts of any task. SoD involves breaking down tasks that might otherwise be completed by a single individual into multiple tasks so that no one person is in control. Payroll management, for example, is an administrative area where both fraud and error are risks. A common separation of duties for business function is to have one employee responsible for the accounting portion of the job and another responsible for signing checks.

The mismanagement of privileges is a primary method for attackers to spread inside an organization. Two very common attacker techniques take advantage of uncontrolled privileges. In the first, a workstation user running as a privileged user is victim of a security attack such as phishing, pharming, spoofing, or downloading malware. If the victim user's account has privileges to valuable information assets, the attacker can completely take over the victim's machine and install keystroke loggers, sniffers, and remote control software to find passwords and other sensitive data.

The second common technique used by attackers is to simply use process of elimination to guess or crack a password of a user to gain access to a system. If access privileges are haphazardly and widely distributed or identical to passwords used on systems said to pose less risk, the attacker has a much easier time gaining full control of systems because there are many more accounts that can act as avenues for the attacker to compromise access privileges.

To alleviate the password exploitation issue, organizations should have built-in operating system functions that contain lists of accounts (especially those with superuser privileges). Such functionality should verify that users with high-privileged accounts do not use those accounts for their day-to-day web surfing and e-mail reading.

Enforcement of strong password requirements is also a good way to avoid attacks. Those same built-in operating system functions can be configured to enforce a minimum password length to prevent users from choosing short passwords. Many organizations enforce even more complex password policies in order to minimize the chance of any user passwords being stolen.

PR.AC-5: Network Integrity Is Protected, Incorporating
Network Segregation Where Appropriate

The underlying objective of PR.AC-5 is "to ensure the protection of information in networks and its supporting information processing" and "to maintain the security of information transferred within an organization and with any external entity" (International Organization for Standardization/International Electrotechnical Commission 2013). What this outcome is really defining is the requirement for network security management.

Network security management entails monitoring and implementing necessary security controls related to all communications that take place on internal networks in addition to communications between internal networks and external interfaces. One of the most widely implemented techniques of securing information flows within an organization, to networks within an organization, and external interfaces is through network segregation. This process can be complex but the basics are straightforward. Simply put, it is the process of logically grouping network assets, resources, and applications together into compartmentalized areas that have no trust of each other. The topic of network segregation is beyond the scope of this book. However, there are some key requirements to take into consideration when segregating networks:

- Gain visibility of traffic, users, and assets
- Protect communications and resources on both inbound and outbound requests
- Implement granular controls on traffic, users, and assets
- Set a default deny policy on all intersegment connections

Regardless of the network segmentation approach, each of those four requirements should be considered while focusing on only a single segment at a time. Begin with areas that are simpler to segment away from the wider network, such as development or test areas. Pick the lowest hanging fruit first and learn lessons on the way to the more complex areas.

Awareness and Training Category

The CSF describes the outcome of the awareness and training category as "the organization's personnel and partners are provided cybersecurity awareness education and are adequately trained to perform their information security-related duties and responsibilities consistent with related policies, procedures, and agreements" (National Institute of Standards and Technology Feb. 2014). Securing and protecting digital information, ICT systems, and critical infrastructure requires building and retaining a responsive and skilled workforce that can adapt to a variety of cybersecurity situations. This is one of the foundational goals of the National Initiative for Cybersecurity Education (NICE), a federal project that began in 2010. The justification for starting the project was that building our nation's cybersecurity workforce requires two complementary components: workforce planning and professional development. While the initiative was originally aimed at providing workforce planning and development within the federal agencies, it is quickly becoming recognized by all industries. Generally speaking, workforce planning consists of analyzing the capabilities needed to achieve the current mission of the organization and forecasting the capabilities needed in the future. Based on this analysis, gaps in talent can be identified and addressed through hiring a skilled workforce and professional development programs. In response to these needs, more than 20 federal departments and agencies contributed to a process that resulted in the development of the National Cybersecurity Workforce Framework.

The NICE Framework uses categories and specialty areas as a structural basis to group similar types of cybersecurity work. Seven categories serve as a primary structure for the NICE Framework, grouping related specialty areas together within each category. Within each specialty area, typical tasks and knowledge, skills, and abilities are provided. The point that needs to be made is that the NICE Framework provides organizations the mechanisms it needs to identify cybersecurity skills necessary, hire individuals with the correct skill sets, and provide appropriate professional development programs. To learn more about the NICE Framework, the book *Cybersecurity: A Guide to the National Initiative for Cybersecurity Education (NICE) Framework (2.0)* by Dan Shoemaker, Anne Kohnke, and Ken Sigler can be useful.

The CSF breaks down the awareness and training category into five subcategory outcomes. The outcomes are identified in Table 4.2. Unique to this category is that the controls that satisfy each of the five subcategory outcomes are generally the same (with the exception of PR.AT-3). Therefore, in a removal from the standard structure used

Table 4.2 Framework Core Awareness and Training Category

CATEGORY	SUBCATEGORY	INFORMATION RESOURCES
Awareness and Training (PR.AT): The organization's personnel and partners are provided cybersecurity awareness education and are adequately trained to perform their information security-related duties and responsibilities consistent with related policies, procedures, and agreements.	PR.AT-1: All users are informed and trained.	• CCS CSC 9 • COBIT 5 APO07.03, BAI05.07 • ISA 62443-2-1:2009 4.3.2.4.2 • ISO/IEC 27001:2013 A.7.2.2 • NIST SP 800-53 Rev. 4 AT-2, PM-13
	PR.AT-2: Privileged users understand roles and responsibilities.	• CCS CSC 9 • COBIT 5 APO07.02, DSS06.03 • ISA 62443-2-1:2009 4.3.2.4.2, 4.3.2.4.3 • ISO/IEC 27001:2013 A.6.1.1, A.7.2.2 • NIST SP 800-53 Rev. 4 AT-3, PM-13
	PR.AT-3: Third-party stakeholders (e.g., suppliers, customers, partners) understand roles and responsibilities.	• CCS CSC 9 • COBIT 5 APO07.03, APO10.04, APO10.05 • ISA 62443-2-1:2009 4.3.2.4.2 • ISO/IEC 27001:2013 A.6.1.1, A.7.2.2 • NIST SP 800-53 Rev. 4 PS-7, SA-9
	PR.AT-4: Senior executives understand roles and responsibilities.	• CCS CSC 9 • COBIT 5 APO07 • ISA 62443-2-1:2009 4.3.2.4.2 • ISO/IEC 27001:2013 A.6.1.1, A.7.2.2 • NIST SP 800-53 Rev. 4 AT-3, PM-13
	PR.AT-5: Physical and information security personnel understand roles and responsibilities.	• CCS CSC 9 • COBIT 5 APO07.03 • ISA 62443-2-1:2009 4.3.2.4.2 • ISO/IEC 27001:2013 A.6.1.1, A.7.2.2 • NIST SP 800-53 Rev. 4 AT-3, PM-13

Source: National Institute of Standards and Technology, *Framework for Improving Critical Infrastructure Cybersecurity.* Gaithersburg, February 12, 2014.

to describe each subcategory, the subcategory outcomes of Table 4.2 will be described cumulatively in the section.

PR.AT-1 through PR.AT-5: Awareness and Training Subcategories

The outcomes of subcategories PR.AT-1, 2, 3, 4, and 5 recommend that, in order to promote awareness and training of all users of the ICT system while ensuring that roles and responsibilities are understood, "the organization establishes an information security workforce development and improvement program" (National Institute for Standards and Technology Apr. 2014).

As we mentioned in the overview of this category, cybersecurity workforce development and improvement programs include

- The ability to gain the knowledge and skill levels needed to perform roles and responsibilities related to information security;
- Role-based training programs for individuals assigned to information security roles and responsibilities;
- Standards for measuring and building individual qualifications for individuals currently working in and applicants of information security-related positions—by early 2016, certifications are expected for each of the seven categories of the NICE Framework; and
- The ability for information security professionals to advance in the field and enter positions that carry a higher level of responsibility.

Information security workforce development and improvement programs are intended to complement organizational security awareness and training programs already in place. The intention is for the information security workforce development and improvement programs to focus on developing fundamental information security skills of selected individuals that are needed to protect an organization's operations and information assets.

The challenge faced by many organizations is the degree to which third-party partners, as described in PR.AT-3, provide their information security professionals the necessary workforce development in order to ensure security of information assets crossing organizational boundaries. This, in part, is what makes the NICE Framework such a useful document. As NICE continues to grow in popularity, more organizations will adopt its recommendations. In turn, a common approach to cybersecurity awareness and training will be adopted by all organizations, thus reducing the possibility of dealing with untrained third-party information security professionals.

Data Security Category

Without data, an organization has no record of transactions, ability to serve its customer, and ability to make managerial decisions. In modern times, every organization within every private or public sector relies on ICT systems, and those systems rely on data to produce the information necessary to operate effectively. Therefore, data security is a critical aspect of cybersecurity. Put simply, data security can be defined as the policies and procedures associated with protecting data in transmission, in processing, and at rest (storage). The CSF defines it as "information and records (data) are managed consistent with the organization's risk strategy to protect the confidentiality, integrity, and availability of information" (National Institute of Standards and Technology Feb. 2014). The value that organizations have on data is what motivates attackers to steal or corrupt it. An effective security program will protect the integrity and value of an organization's data.

Much of the critical data that organizations store is accessible through database management systems (DBMSs). The process of maintaining the confidentiality, integrity, and availability of the data managed by a DBMS is known as database security. Database security is accomplished by applying a wide range of managerial, physical, and technical controls consistent with the priorities defined in the risk management plan. Managerial controls include policies, procedures, and governance. Technical controls include access control and authentication (as we described earlier in the chapter), auditing, application security, backup and recovery, encryption, and integrity processes. The CSF breaks down the data security category into seven subcategory outcomes. The outcomes are identified in Table 4.3 and described in the next several sections of this chapter.

PR.DS-1: Data-at-Rest Are Protected

Recall from the discussion above that *data-at-rest* is simply a term used to refer to data in storage. As the title of this subcategory outcome implies, organizations must put mechanisms in place to address the confidentiality and integrity of information in active and archived databases; this includes user information as well as vital system information. There are numerous ways in which organizations can achieve confidentiality and integrity protection. One common technique for maintaining confidentiality is the use of cryptography and file share scanning. *Data integrity* is a term used to refer to the accuracy and reliability of data. Data must be complete, with no

Table 4.3 Framework Core Data Security Category

CATEGORY	SUBCATEGORY	INFORMATION RESOURCES
Data Security (PR. DS): Information and records (data) are managed consistent with the organization's risk strategy to protect the confidentiality, integrity, and availability of information.	PR.DS-1: Data-at-rest are protected.	• CCS CSC 17 • COBIT 5 APO01.06, BAI02.01, BAI06.01, DSS06.06 • ISA 62443-3-3:2013 SR 3.4, SR 4.1 • ISO/IEC 27001:2013 A.8.2.3 • NIST SP 800-53 Rev. 4 SC-28
	PR.DS-2: Data-in-transit are protected.	• CCS CSC 17 • COBIT 5 APO01.06, DSS06.06 • ISA 62443-3-3:2013 SR 3.1, SR 3.8, SR 4.1, SR 4.2 • ISO/IEC 27001:2013 A.8.2.3, A.13.1.1, A.13.2.1, A.13.2.3, A.14.1.2, A.14.1.3 • NIST SP 800-53 Rev. 4 SC-8
	PR.DS-3: Assets are formally managed throughout removal, transfers, and disposition.	• COBIT 5 BAI09.03 • ISA 62443-2-1:2009 4. 4.3.3.3.9, 4.3.4.4.1 • ISA 62443-3-3:2013 SR 4.2 • ISO/IEC 27001:2013 A.8.2.3, A.8.3.1, A.8.3.2, A.8.3.3, A.11.2.7 • NIST SP 800-53 Rev. 4 CM-8, MP-6, PE-16
	PR.DS-4: Adequate capacity to ensure availability is maintained.	• COBIT 5 APO13.01 • ISA 62443-3-3:2013 SR 7.1, SR 7.2 • ISO/IEC 27001:2013 A.12.3.1 • NIST SP 800-53 Rev. 4 AU-4, CP-2, SC-5
	PR.DS-5: Protections against data leaks are implemented.	• CCS CSC 17 • COBIT 5 APO01.06 • ISA 62443-3-3:2013 SR 5.2 • ISO/IEC 27001:2013 A.6.1.2, A.7.1.1, A.7.1.2, A.7.3.1, A.8.2.2, A.8.2.3, A.9.1.1, A.9.1.2, A.9.2.3, A.9.4.1, A.9.4.4, A.9.4.5, A.13.1.3, A.13.2.1, A.13.2.3, A.13.2.4, A.14.1.2, A.14.1.3 • NIST SP 800-53 Rev. 4 AC-4, AC-5, AC-6, PE-19, PS-3, PS-6, SC-7, SC-8, SC-13, SC-31, SI-4
	PR.DS-6: Integrity checking mechanisms are used to verify software, firmware, and information integrity.	• ISA 62443-3-3:2013 SR 3.1, SR 3.3, SR 3.4, SR 3.8 • ISO/IEC 27001:2013 A.12.2.1, A.12.5.1, A.14.1.2, A.14.1.3 • NIST SP 800-53 Rev. 4 SI-7
	PR.DS-7: The development and testing environment(s) are separate from the production environment.	• COBIT 5 BAI07.04 • ISO/IEC 27001:2013 A.12.1.4 • NIST SP 800-53 Rev. 4 CM-2

Source: National Institute of Standards and Technology, *Framework for Improving Critical Infrastructure Cybersecurity.* Gaithersburg, February 12, 2014.

variations or compromises from the original, to be considered reliable and accurate. Compromises to data integrity can happen in a number of ways. In industries where data are handled, identifying and addressing potential sources of damage to data is an important aspect of data security. Integrity can be preserved by implementing mechanisms such as write-once, read-many (WORM) technologies. WORM technology is a data storage technology that stores inerasable and/or nonmodifiable information after it has been written on a drive. The data are stored on WORM devices. These device disks prevent users from accidentally erasing or altering sensitive information. Organizations can also implement other security controls including the use of off-line storage instead of online alternatives. It is important to note that no single control is going to adequately protect an organization's data storage. Decisions must be made of the best combination that meet the specific priority needs as identified in the risk management plan.

PR.DS-2: Data-in-Transit Are Protected

It is important to remember that data transmission takes place internally as well as between internal and external networks. Therefore, while implementing the controls that support this outcome, organizations must consider components of internal and external systems, such as servers, mobile devices, tablets, printers, network enabled copiers, scanners, and fax machines. Communications that take place between internal networks and outside the protection of the organization are the most difficult to protect due to their exposure to the possibility of interception and modification. Nevertheless, protecting the confidentiality and integrity of organizational information once it leaves internal networks can be accomplished by physical means such as using protected distribution systems or logical means by using various encryption techniques. Organizations that use commercial providers for transmission services rather than fully dedicated services have additional constraints to consider. In those cases, it may be more difficult to achieve the needed security controls for transmission confidentiality and integrity because the organization must rely on the security mechanisms put into place by that provider. When commercial providers are used, the organization must evaluate the service packages or their provider to determine what confidentiality and integrity controls are available. If the required level of security is not available through the provider's service packages, organizations must implement their own compensating security controls or accept the additional risk.

PR.DS-3: Assets Are Formally Managed
throughout Removal, Transfers, and Disposition

The main objective of the PR.DS-3 outcome is "to prevent unauthorized disclosure, modification, removal or destruction of information stored on media" (National Institute of Standards and Technology Feb. 2014). In doing so, organizations must establish formal, documented media disposal procedures. Documented procedures are critical since they help ensure that effective processes are consistently applied, regardless of staffing changes or turnover.

While security standards provide some flexibility on how the requirements of handling media and disposal can be met, there are many best practices that organizations can adopt to ensure that they are protected from unauthorized access to sensitive data. In addition, organizations should be mindful of the data retention requirements for any data contained on storage media to be disposed. Below is a list and summary of commonly accepted best practices:

- Practice 1: Maintain secure control and custody of media to be disposed.
  - Media to be disposed must stay within the control of the organization from the time it is collected to the time it is erased.
  - Pick-up/transit—Storage media to be disposed should be collected by and in the constant possession of dedicated and trusted personnel.
  - Media should be maintained in a secure, locked area until it can be sanitized.
- Practice 2: Render all data on the media unusable.
  - Do not delete the data—destroy it.

- All data should be rendered unusable using special software designed for this purpose.
- Meet the requirements of adopted security standards.
- Practice 3: Physical destruction is an option.
  - Organizations have the choice of physically destroying the media itself rather than erasing it. This typically takes the form of shredding or pulverization, ensuring the media can never be used again.
  - Any media that cannot be erased through the use of software tools must be physically destroyed.
- Practice 4: Keep detailed records.
  - Organizations should maintain records that document all media disposal activities, since this can provide them with the means of confirming that specific media was disposed of properly if it is later called into question.
- Practice 5: Provide evidence of disposal.
  - In addition to keeping records, it is a good idea to identify media that has been sanitized. This can include affixing a sticker or a document to the device indicating that the data erasure process was completed. This helps organizations easily identify and segregate devices internally and lets others know that the media has been wiped and can be made available for use by others.

PR.DS-4: Adequate Capacity to Ensure Availability Is Maintained

The PR.DS-4 outcome is one of the few instances within the framework that is not clear in its intentions. Each of the controls listed as information resources varies significantly from the others. As such, the reader is left to interpret the intended outcome based on its title. Consequently, we will not provide elaboration.

PR.DS-5: Protections against Data Leaks Are Implemented

Simply put, data leakage occurs when classified information is accessed by an undesirable party. This can be accidental or malicious and is commonly associated with e-mail trails that are not adequately secured. Often, organizations do not comprehend the severity of the issue until they experience the consequences. Once the leakage has occurred, repercussions include the following:

- Fines—When public privacy has been breached, organizations can face enormous fines from federal, state, and local governments.
- Reputation compromising—When data leakage goes public, it can spell disaster for an organization's reputation. Not only will they lose current clients but will also significantly hinder their chances at sourcing new ones.
- Legal action—As well as hefty fines, organizations breaching confidential data guidelines can face serious legal action which may lead to court cases, account crippling settlements, bankruptcy files, and even jail time.
- Loss of invaluable information—The leaking of highly confidential information such as product ideas, marketing tactics, and business growth plans can be devastating for companies that want to set themselves apart from their competitors.

For the reasons listed above, it is absolutely crucial for the organization's risk management plan to include protective measures that minimize damaging consequences that go hand in hand with data leakage.

In order to completely eliminate the risk of data leakage while maintaining productivity, organizations must implement an effective and seamless security strategy. Cloud-based services are designed to safeguard information against accidental and malicious leaks, while single web-based consoles offer users complete control over all policies. Below is a list of key areas needed to warrant a successful data leak prevention strategy:

- Real-time changes—These are important as they ensure that regardless of site or server numbers, changes are applied simultaneously to all traffic.
- Flexibility—Offering managers flexibility over policy controls is essential to ensuring a data leak prevention solution that is able to cater for different users and groups.
- Transport Layer Security (TLS) encryption—TLS encryption feature safeguards on data in transit and are a fundamental part of meeting corporate governance and compliance needs.

If you want to safeguard an organization against data leaks, understanding the risks and addressing them with an effective security solution is absolutely critical.

PR.DS-6: Integrity Checking Mechanisms Are Used to Verify Software, Firmware, and Information Integrity

Integrity, from the perspective of data and network security, is the assurance that information can be accessed or modified only by those authorized to do so. Organizations should implement measures to ensure integrity by controlling the physical environment of networked devices and servers, restricting access to data, and maintaining strict authentication procedures. Data integrity can also be threatened by environmental conditions, such as heat, dust, and electrical surges.

Organizations should implement controls to protect data integrity in software and firmware by making administrative functions of servers accessible only to network administrators, keeping transmission media (such as cables and connectors) covered and protected to ensure that they cannot be tapped, and protecting hardware and storage media from power surges, electrostatic discharges, and magnetism.

Network administration controls to ensure data integrity include maintaining current authorization levels for all users; documenting system administration procedures, parameters, and maintenance activities; and creating disaster recovery plans for occurrences such as power outages, server failure, and virus attacks.

PR.DS-7: Development and Testing Environment(s) Are Separate from the Production Environment

It would not be an exaggeration that every ICT system within an organization could rightly be considered business critical. Whether it provides decision support for one business function, a custom application, or an entire ERP system, business units would be hard-pressed to efficiently complete their day's activities if the system was down or not operating as it should. There are a number of items that should be considered when making a change to ICT systems including ensuring proper documentation, training, system design, and testing. One of the most overlooked best practices to ensure success is having a development area where applications can be rigorously developed, tested, and deployed.

Why are separate environments needed? The most basic is answer is this—you should never make changes to a working production environment without first ensuring that the changes are correct and well tested. Of course, if you do not have a separate development environment, it is impossible to follow this simple rule. Even seemingly small changes can lead to a bug, a security flaw, or a regression. Ask yourself, "If I made this proposed change and the system became totally unusable for all my users during normal business hours, would that be OK?" If you hesitate in your answer at all, then do not even think about making the change without first putting it through its phases outside the production environment.

A development environment is where system developers live. This environment will typically have development tools like Visual Studio .NET installed. Other development tools for logging, performance monitoring, and debugging may also be present. This environment can typically be refreshed very easily (i.e., via a virtual machine snapshot or a disk partition image) and may be loosely controlled when it comes to system access to allow the developers to make registry, database, and network changes easily.

A test environment is very different from the development environment. Instead of containing special tools and software or being configured with special permissions or access, the test environment is identical to the production environment. This environment is closely controlled so that software versions, permissions, and configuration options match the production environment. All testing takes place in this environment. A test environment will serve multiple audiences. Programmers will use it to test changes and enhancements to custom applications. Systems administrators will use it to test new versions of software or software patches. Security engineers use it to test security controls, and users will use it do to unit testing and verify if an application meets their specific business needs.

Some may wonder if it is overkill to have multiple environments and multiple physical or virtual servers. The answer depends on whether the organization can afford for all of the users to be down during business hours because a change did not work as planned. If there is no problem with that scenario, then it may be overkill. However, for the type of systems that we talked about at the outset of this section, most people would probably agree that downtime for business critical systems has a significant cost to the business.

INSIGHT   WANTED: MORE VIGILANCE ON DATA SECURITY SNAPCHAT, TARGET INCIDENTS COULD PROVIDE IMPETUS FOR NEW SAFEGUARDS

Your data is out there, and people are coming for it. If you're lucky, the villains will only get the most harmless stuff. Perhaps they'll filch just your phone number from Snapchat, a number you thought would be kept confidential because the messaging company makes a show of its commitment to your privacy. You believed it would actually take steps to keep its promise (so did I). In fact, Snapchat was lax, and now your selfie-stained number is out there, dangling in the wind.

If you aren't so lucky, the bad guys could get much more damaging data. You used a credit card to shop at Target. Naturally, you assumed such a big company took adequate measures to keep the data safe. Well, it didn't. So now your credit cards are being traded on murky online bulletin boards, and you're scrambling to make sure that your credit isn't compromised.

I'm not breaking any news in declaring that we live in an age ruled by hackers, by people who, for reasons both noble and savage, are systematically breaking into every valuable cache of information stored in any digital format anywhere. According to the research firm Risk Based Security, 2012 was a record year for security breaches, with the number of intrusions more than doubling from a year earlier. If recent events are an indication, 2013 will soon be declared another banner year for world-wide data insecurity.

Is this just how life is going to be from now on? With reports that the National Security Agency is now building its own quantum computer that could potentially snoop into even encrypted data, should we just get used to the idea of permanent insecurity?

No. We shouldn't.

I'm hoping that the rash of high-profile security incidents we've seen over the past few months will spark renewed interest in the security sector, prompting new money and entrepreneurial energy to pour into the business of protecting our data. We'll never get perfect security; data, like money, will always be vulnerable to theft. At the moment, though, there is an innovation gap in security, with our ability to collect data far outstripping our ability to protect it. That balance needs to be restored.

Considering the expense of some of these hacks—the significant downturn in business at Target after the credit-card breach, for instance—there is ample incentive for companies that hold our data to start thinking about new ways to safeguard it. This could create a threat-protection gold mine. If you've got a new idea for securing data, you might well clean up.

We're already seeing these incentives affect the security market. Look at FireEye, a 10-year-old company that makes an innovative threat-detection system that sits around an organization's entire network. FireEye's system tests network traffic in a "virtual execution engine," which you can think of as a bomb shelter in which suspicious code (say an email attachment) can be "detonated" in order to determine if it poses any threat to the organization.

FireEye, which began trading its stock on the Nasdaq Stock Market last fall, has been one of the most successful tech initial public offerings in recent years. Last week it said it had spent nearly $1 billion to purchase Mandiant, a company that acts as a post-detection threat-response team—a kind of security force that will swoop in to stop an attack after FireEye's systems have detected one.

But it isn't just that we need new techniques to prevent security breaches. We—customers, companies and the media—need a new attitude about security. Tech companies, especially startups, often seem to consider security an afterthought or expensive add-on rather than something they bake in to their technology from the ground up. That's because there is often a trade-off between convenience and security, and we usually side with convenience.

The Snapchat breach is telling. The hack involved a feature that allows people to upload their address books in order to find friends who are using Snapchat. Last August, researchers at Gibson Security published a warning that Snapchat's system could be easily exploited. All an attacker had to do was quickly send every phone number in the U.S. to the app; he would get back a user name for each hit, allowing him to create a database matching Snapchat user names to phone numbers.

On Christmas Eve, seeing that Snapchat hadn't taken adequate steps to improve its system, Gibson published detailed guidelines of a possible attack on Snapchat. The company responded with a cocky blog post arguing that such an attack was only "theoretically" possible. Turns out the theory was correct—just before the year was out, attackers had exploited the flaw to collect 4.6 million Snapchat user names and phone numbers. (They published partially redacted phone numbers.)

Some in the tech industry have called for lenience toward Snapchat, saying that the attack wasn't really so damaging—your phone number, after all, might well have been public in a phone book anyway and users' actual messages weren't made public.

But I'd rather not give Snapchat the benefit of the doubt. The company's public response to the hack has been entirely too cavalier, and its response to the security researchers' vulnerability seemed to lack any sense of urgency. It is precisely that attitude that allows such large hacks to take place—and it makes you wonder how well the company protects the rest of its data.

All tech companies need to be forced into taking security more seriously. That's why, in Snapchat's case, I propose a temporary boycott: If you use the app regularly and you consider your privacy important, you should take a break for a short while. Only if the company sees that its users are serious about security will it adopt a new attitude toward your data. If you don't do this—if you keep using Snapchat despite the company's obvious shortcomings—you're part of the problem. (Manjoo 2014)

Information Protection Processes and Procedures Category

Information security policies are required for every organization and form the basis for an information security program. To be effective, policies must be issued at the highest level of the organization and apply to all subordinate business functions. Security policies must be promulgated, stakeholders must follow the policies, the policies must be monitored, and must be enforced. A selective set of information security policies should apply to all members of the workforce, including staff, volunteers, student interns, independent contractors, and vendors. Moreover, in order to provide adequate support for proper implementation, policies must clearly document the procedures and expectations of all staff within an organization. However, they should not be confused with IT security procedures that provide greater detail and may change frequently.

Organizations must issue security policies to

- Create their information security program and assign responsibility for it;
- Outline their approach to information security;
- Address specific issues of concern to the organization;
- Outline decisions for managing a particular system;
- Define sanctions; and
- Set expectations for all staff.

This discussion may be familiar to you because we have touched on security policy, processes, and procedures in each chapter thus far and will continue to do so in our discussions going forward. The point is that for every aspect of cybersecurity, and in turn every function of the CSF core, development, implementation, and maintenance of security policy supporting that function is critical to ensuring that the organization is in position to understand their cybersecurity threats and vulnerabilities in addition to minimizing the impact to business functions resulting from exploitation. In particular, the PR.IP Function of the CSF core recommends that an organization's "security policies (that address purpose, scope, roles, responsibilities, management commitment, and coordination among organizational entities), processes, and procedures are maintained and used to manage protection of information systems and assets" (National Institute of Standards and Technology Feb. 2014). The CSF breaks down the information protection processes and procedures category into 12 subcategory outcomes. The outcomes are identified in Table 4.4 and described in the next several sections of this chapter.

PR.IP-1 and PR.IP-3: Configuration Management Baselines
Are Established and Change Control Is Put into Place

Since the mid-1980s, the control of any form of ICT activity has fallen under the generic heading of configuration management (CM). This important system live cycle supporting process defines and enforces control over an organization's assets. CM is an essential technique for monitoring and controlling all forms of development activity. It specifies the methods for controlling changes to assets throughout their useful life cycle.

Table 4.4   Framework Core Information Protection Processes and Procedures Category

CATEGORY	SUBCATEGORY	INFORMATION RESOURCES
Information Protection Processes and Procedures (PR. IP): Security policies (that address purpose, scope, roles, responsibilities, management commitment, and coordination among organizational entities), processes, and procedures are maintained and used to manage protection of information systems and assets	PR.IP-1: A baseline configuration of information technology/ industrial control systems is created and maintained.	• CCS CSC 3, 10 • COBIT 5 BAI10.01, BAI10.02, BAI10.03, BAI10.05 • ISA 62443-2-1:2009 4.3.4.3.2, 4.3.4.3.3 • ISA 62443-3-3:2013 SR 7.6 • ISO/IEC 27001:2013 A.12.1.2, A.12.5.1, A.12.6.2, A.14.2.2, A.14.2.3, A.14.2.4 • NIST SP 800-53 Rev. 4 CM-2, CM-3, CM-4, CM-5, CM-6, CM-7, CM-9, SA-10
	PR.IP-2: A system development life cycle to manage systems is implemented.	• COBIT 5 APO13.01 • ISA 62443-2-1:2009 4.3.4.3.3 • ISO/IEC 27001:2013 A.6.1.5, A.14.1.1, A.14.2.1, A.14.2.5 • NIST SP 800-53 Rev. 4 SA-3, SA-4, SA-8, SA10, SA-11, SA-12, SA-15, SA-17, PL-8
	PR.IP-3: Configuration change control processes are in place.	• COBIT 5 BAI06.01, BAI01.06 • ISA 62443-2-1:2009 4.3.4.3.2, 4.3.4.3.3 • ISA 62443-3-3:2013 SR 7.6 • ISO/IEC 27001:2013 A.12.1.2, A.12.5.1, A.12.6.2, A.14.2.2, A.14.2.3, A.14.2.4 • NIST SP 800-53 Rev. 4 CM-3, CM-4, SA-10
	PR.IP-4: Backups of information are conducted, maintained, and tested periodically.	• COBIT 5 APO13.01 • ISA 62443-2-1:2009 4.3.4.3.9 • ISA 62443-3-3:2013 SR 7.3, SR 7.4 • ISO/IEC 27001:2013 A.12.3.1, A.17.1.2, A.17.1.3, A.18.1.3 • NIST SP 800-53 Rev. 4 CP-4, CP-6, CP-9
	PR.IP-5: Policy and regulations regarding the physical operating environment for organizational assets are met	• COBIT 5 DSS01.04, DSS05.05 • ISA 62443-2-1:2009 4.3.3.3.1 4.3.3.3.2, 4.3.3.3.3, 4.3.3.3.5, 4.3.3.3.6 • ISO/IEC 27001:2013 A.11.1.4, A.11.2.1, A.11.2.2, A.11.2.3 • NIST SP 800-53 Rev. 4 PE-10, PE-12, PE-13, PE-14, PE-15, PE-18
	PR.IP-6: Data are destroyed according to policy.	• COBIT 5 BAI09.03 • ISA 62443-2-1:2009 4.3.4.4.4 • ISA 62443-3-3:2013 SR 4.2 • ISO/IEC 27001:2013 A.8.2.3, A.8.3.1, A.8.3.2, A.11.2.7 • NIST SP 800-53 Rev. 4 MP-6

(Continued)

Table 4.4 (Continued)   Framework Core Information Protection Processes and Procedures Category

CATEGORY	SUBCATEGORY	INFORMATION RESOURCES
	PR.IP-7: Protection processes are continuously improved.	• COBIT 5 APO11.06, DSS04.05 • ISA 62443-2-1:2009 4.4.3.1, 4.4.3.2, 4.4.3.3, 4.4.3.4, 4.4.3.5, 4.4.3.6, 4.4.3.7, 4.4.3.8 • NIST SP 800-53 Rev. 4 CA-2, CA-7, CP-2, IR-8, PL-2, PM-6
	PR.IP-8: Effectiveness of protection technologies is shared with appropriate parties.	• ISO/IEC 27001:2013 A.16.1.6 • NIST SP 800-53 Rev. 4 AC-21, CA-7, SI-4
	PR.IP-9: Response plans (incident response and business continuity) and recovery plans (incident recovery and disaster recovery) are in place and managed.	• COBIT 5 DSS04.03 • ISA 62443-2-1:2009 4.3.2.5.3, 4.3.4.5.1 • ISO/IEC 27001:2013 A.16.1.1, A.17.1.1, A.17.1.2 • NIST SP 800-53 Rev. 4 CP-2, IR-8
	PR.IP-10: Response and recovery plans are tested.	• ISA 62443-2-1:2009 4.3.2.5.7, 4.3.4.5.11 • ISA 62443-3-3:2013 SR 3.3 • ISO/IEC 27001:2013 A.17.1.3 • NIST SP 800-53 Rev.4 CP-4, IR-3, PM-14
	PR.IP-11: Cybersecurity is included in human resources practices (e.g., deprovisioning, personnel screening).	• COBIT 5 APO07.01, APO07.02, APO07.03, APO07.04, APO07.05 • ISA 62443-2-1:2009 4.3.3.2.1, 4.3.3.2.2, 4.3.3.2.3 • ISO/IEC 27001:2013 A.7.1.1, A.7.3.1, A.8.1.4 • NIST SP 800-53 Rev. 4 PS Family
	PR.IP-12: A vulnerability management plan is developed and implemented.	• ISO/IEC 27001:2013 A.12.6.1, A.18.2.2 • NIST SP 800-53 Rev. 4 RA-3, RA-5, SI-2

Source: National Institute of Standards and Technology, *Framework for Improving Critical Infrastructure Cybersecurity.* Gaithersburg, February 12, 2014.

The main objective of configuration management is to control changes to changed items in a way that preserves their integrity CM provides two primary advantages: It maintains the integrity of configurations and it allows changes to be evaluated and made rationally. It also gives the top managers and policy makers direct input into the evolution of a organization's ICT asset base. It does this by ensuring that managers are involved in decisions about the form of the controlled asset. CM provides the basis to measure quality, improve the system development and maintenance cycle, make testing and quality assurance easier, remove error-prone steps from product releases, provide traceability of related components, and dramatically ease problems with change management and problem tracking.

Configuration management involves three major elements in the system life cycle: development, which supports the identification process; maintenance, which supports authorization and configuration control; and assurance, which supports verification. The latter two functions are cornerstones of the process because they ensure correct configuration of all of the products under configuration control.

Configuration management incorporates the two processes of configuration control and verification control, which are implemented through three interdependent management activities, which must be fitted to the needs of each project. The three activities are change process management, which is made up of change authorization, verification control, and release processing; baseline control, which is composed of change accounting and library management; and configuration verification, which includes status accounting to verify compliance with specifications.

Each role in the process is assigned to an appropriate manager or management team. The configuration manager ensures that the requirements of change management are carried out. The configuration manager's general role is to process all change requests, manage all change authorizations, and verify that the changes are complete. The organization also appoints a baseline manager who ensures that all configuration items (CIs) in the project configuration management plan are identified, accounted for, and maintained consistently with a specified identification scheme. The baseline manager establishes a change management ledger (CML) for each controlled product, records all changes and promotions, and maintains all libraries associated with a given product.

The baseline manager accounts for product configuration by working with appropriate development personnel to set up and maintain the CML. This ledger represents a complete list of CIs for each controlled software product, including a CI description label, promotion/version level, and change activity. Because items not in the ledger are not CIs by definition, the baseline manager is responsible for keeping the ledger up to date. The baseline manager maintains accounts that reflect the current state of all configurations and is responsible for authorizing entries in the CML.

The verification manager has the responsibility for ensuring that product integrity is maintained during the change process. The general role of the verification manager is to confirm that items in the CML conform to the identification scheme, verify that changes have been carried out, and conduct milestone reviews. The verification manager also maintains documentation of all reviews. The verification manager must guarantee that items maintained in the CML reflect the status of the product at any point in time.

Because it establishes the "day one" baseline, the cornerstone of configuration management is the configuration identification scheme. That scheme is usually established during the requirement analysis phase of the specification process. All components are given a unique identifying label and then arrayed based on their interrelationships and dependencies. The result of this activity is a baseline, which represents the basic configuration of the product. Baseline configurations are usually defined in development.

Once established, the identification scheme is maintained throughout the life cycle. The unique labels for items defined at any level are typically referred to as product identification numbers (PINs). Generally, PINs are associated with the structure itself; they designate the position of items in the overall "family tree" of the product. Change occurs when new baselines are created during a promotion or release. If items in the evolving structure represent a new baseline, the identifying labels are modified to reflect it.

The organization must explicitly define the management level authorized to approve changes to each baseline. Authorization is always given at the highest practical level. As an ICT product evolves, increasing levels of authority will probably be required to authorize a change. Changes at any level in the basic structure must be maintained at all levels. The configuration control board (CCB) operates at defined levels of authorization. CCBs are hierarchical and composed of managers with sufficient authority to direct the change process. At a minimum, an ICT organization has three control boards: one composed of top-level policy makers and one for each of the major system components (a software CCB and a hardware CCB). The members of these boards have the proper level of authority to oversee decisions. Generally, it is not a good idea for policy makers to sit on technical boards or for programmers to serve on top-level CCBs. The scope of the board's oversight must be defined formally and explicitly, usually in the general configuration management plan.

Configuration management is a major process within an organization, so a strategic plan is required to guide it. The plan describes configuration management activities, the procedures and schedule for performing those activities, the organization(s) responsible for performing each activity, and the relationships of those organizations with other entities.

The plan lists and specifies typical activities for configuration management within the organization, such as development or maintenance, and it includes activities that might involve external organizations, such as subcontractors. Because of its importance, this plan is generally part of the overall scheme for system management. At the end of this step, the organization has a correct and fully documented life cycle plan for ensuring configuration integrity.

The next step in the process is the identification scheme. In this step, the organization develops a formal plan to accurately identify hardware and software items and their versions. These items will be controlled for the project. Then, the organization identifies the documentation, which establishes baselines, version references, and other identification details for each CI and its versions. This documentation must embody all identified CIs into a coherent baseline configuration for every official version of the system, software item, or service. These baselined versions are controlled for the duration of the project.

To end users, configuration control is the most visible part of the process. Moreover, it is the part that has the biggest payoff for the organization. Configuration control is important to configuration management because it ensures that all changes are made rationally and correctly. Configuration control receives change requests, analyzes and evaluates the impacts of a change, and passes that analysis along to decision makers who either approve or disapprove of the request.

After confirmation that the change request is appropriate, a timely review is conducted by the proper authorities, as designated in the configuration management plan. During the authorization review, the configuration management team provides a map of all interfaces between items proposed for change, an analysis of anticipated impacts, and a resource analysis. The appropriate entity (usually the CCB) either authorizes the change or denies it. After receiving authorization to make the change, the configuration management team modifies, verifies, and incorporates the software item into the new controlled baseline. The change control team performs the modifications and then releases the modified item.

Configuration control establishes an audit trail to track each modification. Configuration management uses this audit function, which is normally captured in the baseline management ledger, to record and track the explanation and authorizing agent for each change. The purpose of this step is to ensure that the modification can be traced. In particular, configuration control ensures that audits regulate all access to the baseline items responsible for safety or security functions. Configuration management also controls and audits access to controlled libraries that contain authenticated development or release baselines.

The configuration management team must also account for all baseline configurations, as well as maintain a related reporting function. The reporting captures the status and history of each baseline item. This accounting process helps the organization to prepare reports that describe the status and history of controlled software items, including baselines. Status reports normally include the number of changes for a project, the latest software item versions, release identifiers, the number of releases, and comparisons of releases.

Evaluation is an important function of configuration management. Evaluation normally comes at the conclusion of a change, which was actually executed by maintenance or development. Evaluation helps ensure the functional completeness of a changed item against requirements and the physical completeness of any hardware elements. Criteria for evaluation typically include whether the design and code reflect updated technical descriptions. These requirements are normally communicated to the evaluation team through a statement of work that is authorized by a suitable body (usually the CCB) and prepared by the configuration manager.

In practice, the release and delivery of a product and its documentation must be formally controlled. As a result, master copies of code and documentation are maintained for the life of the product. Configuration management controls the release and delivery of modifications through the library function. In particular, the code and documentation for safety or security functions are handled, stored, packaged, and delivered in accordance with policies of the relevant organizations.

PR.IP-2: A System Development Life Cycle to Manage Systems Is Implemented

Because many products can be built from a single correct process, the creation of an enterprise-wide architecture from an ideal model of overall best practice is likely to solve many problems associated with improper management of the ICT process, and in turn reduce the likelihood of cybersecurity attack. In that respect, the ISO 12207-2008 standard (which was originally mentioned in Chapter 3) provides the generic model that defines the ideal structure of the ICT process as a whole. It serves as a stable basis for defining a life cycle management framework that it is applicable to any form of ICT operation. In addition, ISO 12207 provides a commonly recognized worldwide basis for standardizing terminology and processes to effectively manage any software or ICT development, sustainment, or acquisition process.

ICT manufacture requires precise command of both the logical and physical details of the production process; however, the construction of systems is ultimately creative. Practically speaking, detailed control is necessary in order to assure proper execution of the process, yet ICT managers face the daily dilemma that they know less about what is actually going on in their processes than the technical people they supervise. The real threat that this represents is that the manager is ultimately responsible for the success or failure of the product.

Therefore, the quintessential first step in establishing adequate control over the ICT development and sustainment process is to create a tangible, well-defined, and standardized ICT life cycle management function for the organization. Logically, if a reliable basis for coordinated management control is not available, it is hard to establish and maintain the correctness of any action as dynamic and abstract as ICT work. Management is not science. However, the people who work in ICT often have backgrounds in science and mathematics. As a result, business and process considerations sometimes do not fit into their repertoire of inclinations or interests. Instead, the tendency in many ICT organizations is to favor technology solutions over process, which has been generally described as the silver bullet mind-set. As a result, the industry has tried to solve complex organizational problems with the latest flavor of the month in ICT toolsets.

The alternative to the silver bullet approach is a fully defined and standardized process that must be set at a level sufficient to encompass any set of activities, methods, and practices used in the production and evolution of ICT. However, because decisions about the activities and tasks to include in such a model are more of an art than a science, a commonly accepted and properly focused best practice framework of activities and tasks is needed to guide the definition of the life cycle process for a given organization.

A body of knowledge in best practice has always existed within the ICT industry, and it is documented in a wide range of professional standards. When properly applied, these standards give ICT managers direct visibility into the functioning of their processes. Specifically, because standards serve as benchmarks for best practice, they can be used as a measuring stick to leverage management control. In practice, a set of independently audited standards creates and maintains the consistent policy and procedure framework necessary for managers to judge performance.

For many years, there was no single comprehensive framework that itemized and described all potential forms of activity in the ICT process. However, in 1995, the ISO 12207 standard was released. ISO 12207 is formally designated as the ISO/IEC International Standard for Software Life Cycle Processes, and it documents the common elements in the ICT life cycle. Because of the definitions in ISO 12207, any size or type of organization can define and interrelate all components of ICT activity into a single practical understanding. The ensuing set of processes allows for rational control of all aspects of the life cycle.

ISO 12207 is the comprehensive framework that allows enterprise architects to decompose a standard life cycle process from a generic set of management activities down to their instantiation in the form of concrete everyday tasks. The standard covers the life cycle of ICT from conceptualization through retirement and consists of processes for acquiring and supplying ICT products and services; establishing, enabling, and supporting development and sustainment projects; and fostering reuse. By definition, the processes itemized in ISO 12207 represent a complete set. The template of activities and tasks provided by the standard is intended to be applicable at all levels of ICT operation, from the organizational level down through projects and all the way to the application development and maintenance stage.

ISO 12207 activities encompass "all facets of system definition necessary to establish the full context for the development, maintenance and use of ICT products and services" (International Standards Organization 2008). The specific process, activities, and tasks itemized in the standard are meant to describe all ICT projects. The activities that may be performed during the life cycle are grouped into categories: agreement processes, organizational project enabling processes, project processes, technical processes, ICT-specific processes, ICT support processes, and ICT reuse processes. Each category contains three to eleven life cycle processes that are further divided into a set of activities, and each activity is subdivided into tasks.

A concrete understanding of the specific life cycle needs of an organization can be arrived at through a process of hierarchical decomposition. Nevertheless, practitioners still need specific best practice advice to help them detail the work required to achieve real-world goals. As you saw earlier, this work is done in three steps. First, the organization must adopt a unified process model as a foundation for tailoring a specific application to the business; the only currently recognized model of this type is the ISO 12207 standard. Then, the organization must establish activity specifications for each process element.

The tangible definition of this process is usually carried out using standards, such as those promulgated by the Institute of Electrical and Electronics Engineers, Military, or proprietary business standards. The only rule is that the standard used must define the process specified by the higher-order framework in terms of the level of abstraction. Finally, specific policies and procedures are defined within the detailed structure that fit the culture and goals of the business exactly.

Within this top–down framework for decomposition, specific operational elements are tailored out by identifying the unique problems and criteria of the project environment, and then documenting the adjustments needed to modify the overall activity and task specifications for the specific project. If this decomposition procedure is followed correctly, the outcome is a unique representation of best practice within the organization for each element of the higher-order standard (for example, ISO 12207:2008). When applied correctly, this standards-based decomposition approach allows an organization to ensure commonly recognized best practice while retaining its own distinctive characteristics and culture.

PR.IP-4: Backups of Information Are Conducted,
Maintained, and Tested Periodically

Information that is worth acquiring and maintaining on a system is generally worth retaining. ICT systems are prone to failure, whether by security attack or other means, resulting in irretrievable loss of information. It is for that reason that the PR.IP-4 subcategory outcome recommends that the organization perform frequent backups. Backup is the process of copying information from a portion of the ICT system to another device for the purpose of recovery or archival. Causes for information loss can include a security attack, equipment malfunction, software bugs, human error, and some other natural or human-made disaster.

Backup copies of valuable information should be available in the event that any of these events occur. When data are lost or damaged, vital information can be copied back from the backup media into the production system. This is called data restoration.

The caveat is how do we know that the backed up data are able to be restored? Periodically, the operations staff should perform tests on the backup media to ensure that the correct data are being backed up in the first place and that it can be restored without issue.

Backup media that contains copies of valuable business information needs to be given the same level of physical and logical protection as the original data. This includes secure storage, surveillance, and visitor logs. Accurate records need to be kept on the backup media so that the correct business information can be restored. If a particular file or database needs to be recovered, operators need to know what volume contains the information needing restoration. Records will indicate the location of each volume.

Generally, backup media should be kept in locked storage close to the system from which the information originated so that restoration can take place quickly and seamlessly. The locked storage should be accessible only to authorized individuals as defined in the organization's security plans. The problem with having the backup media located close to the system from which the information originated is that the backup media and original system component is at risk of destruction in the event of disaster. For this reason, it is necessary to have a copy of the archived data located far away from its original location.

This practice is known as off-site storage. Because of the critical nature of the backed up business information, it needs to be protected during transit as well as during storage. Factors to consider when searching for a suitable off-site storage facility include the following:

- Distance from business location—The off-site storage facility should not be so close to the originating business location that both are vulnerable to regional disasters such as a flood. However, it should not be so far that critical data cannot be restored in a timely manner.
- Security of transportation—The mode and security of the transportation between the originating location and storage facility should be proportional to the value of the data in transit.
- Security of storage facility—The facility itself should have good record management controls in place that handle the storage of media properly.
- Resilience against disasters—The storage facility should have robust physical controls to ensure the safety of the facility and stored records from events such as earthquakes, fires, and floods.

PR.IP-5: Policy and Regulations Regarding the Physical Operating Environment for Organizational Assets Are Met

As we have discussed at many points in the first four chapters, and likely several more, cybersecurity requires the protection of both data and physical assets. Some of the controls mentioned to protect data have included implementation of firewalls, monitoring systems, and intrusion detection. However, those controls can easily be overcome if the attacker is able to gain physical access to the devices being controlled. In other words, a hard drive may be secure when it is attached to the system. However, if stolen, that same hard drive is no longer secure. Therefore, the CSF recommends that organizations review policies and regulations associated with the physical security and the physical operating environment in particular to ensure that compliance is evident. The National Institute of Standards and Technology (NIST) SP 800-53 lists six primary aspects of the physical operating environment that require control policy and regulation review and compliance:

1. The ability to shut off power to ICT systems or individual components in emergencies
2. The need for emergency lighting to illuminate emergency exits and evacuation routes from the facility in the event of power outage
3. Evidence of proper fire suppression and detection devices particularly within areas containing ICT systems and resources
4. Proper temperature and humidity controls
5. The ability to protect the ICT system and resources from water damage
6. The need to position ICT system components in locations within the facility where damage is minimized and unauthorized access is eliminated

As with all areas of security, the implementation of these controls requires sound organizational policy. Physical environment policies and regulations guide users in the appropriate use and protection of information resources and assets, as well as protecting their own safety in day-to-day operations.

PR.IP-6: Data Are Destroyed According to Policy

It may appear that the CSF repeats itself in the outcome required in PR.IP-6 from the discussion we already had on PR.DS-3. However, it is important to note that PR.DS-3 addresses the management of all asset disposal, while PR.IP-6 emphasizes the importance of implementing a data destruction policy.

Having a consistent data destruction policy followed by everyone within an organization at all times is vital, especially when faced with litigation. Legally and properly destroying data prevents extensive fishing expeditions by your opponents in litigation (which is a legalized and ritualized form of warfare). A regular business process addressing data destruction should also get you some safe harbor protections under the Federal Rules of Evidence relating to electronic evidence should litigation arise. Be aware that the safe harbor protections exist. Organizations should work with their attorney to take advantage of them.

Whether an organization is obligated to take certain steps in destroying data really depends on the laws, rules, or regulations that an organization is obliged to demonstrate adherence. Regulated industries have requirements in place through a variety of sources. For example, depending on the industry there may be Sarbanes–Oxley, Graham–Leach–Bliley, and the Fair and Accurate Credit Transactions Act or HIPAA implications.

If an organization is not heavily regulated, they can look to some of the other destruction standards. The U.S. Department of Defense standards and methods might be good places to start. Other resources include international, national, state, and local laws, rules, and regulations. One excellent resource is NIST SP 800-88 *Guidelines for Media Sanitization.*

After review of the applicable laws, rules, and regulations, the organization needs to add steps to their data destruction policy. The data destruction policy needs to address how to classify and handle each type of data residing on all forms of media. It needs a process for the review and categorization of the types of data the organization has and what kinds can be removed. Classifications and contents of data will also play a role. Data and media containing confidential information, trade secrets, and the private information of customers require the strictest controls and destruction methods. Data and media containing little to no risk to the organization may have relaxed levels of control and destruction.

PR.IP-7: Protection Processes Are Continuously Improved

The CSF PR.IP-7 subcategory outcome clearly emphasizes that once protection processes are developed and implemented, they do not remain static. Just as organizational goals and objectives change, so too should the processes that protect the organization's assets that allow them to achieve those goals and objectives. One vital requirement of process improvement is the use of measurements.

Measurement can provide understanding into many aspects of software and system development, such as project management, compliance, assurance, return on investment (ROI), and process management. A measurement infrastructure must be in place to enable and facilitate measurement. A well-established measurement infrastructure requires the following: processes and procedures be defined, documented, and institutionalized; data that are available and easily collected; and a measurement process that is an integrated into day-to-day operations. Process implementation evidence that results from integration of the security life cycle into the system development life cycle creates data that can be used to support implementation, efficiency and effectiveness, assurance, and ROI measurements. Applying capability maturity models enhances the ability of an organization to reliably collect and use security measurement in a consistent and repeatable manner. Process appraisals according to capability maturity models such as Capacity Maturity Model Integration (CMMI) and ISO/IEC 21827 Systems Security Engineering Capability Maturity Model (SSE-CMM) can provide insight into the process maturity of processes and practices. An integrated appraisal of the CMMI and SSE-CMM with a result of level two or higher, for example, indicates that processes and practices are in place to support the integration of information assurance into the life cycle. Additionally at level two, basic infrastructure exists to facilitate measurement of security.

PR.IP-8: Effectiveness of Protection Technologies
Is Shared with Appropriate Parties

The CSF PR.IP-8 subcategory outcome suggests that effectiveness is achieved when "knowledge gained from analyzing and resolving information security incidents shall be used to reduce the likelihood or impact of future incidents" (International Organization for Standardization/International Electrotechnical Commission 2013). Perhaps the most effective way of accomplishing this task is by the use of knowledge management systems.

Knowledge management (KM) is a concept and a term that arose approximately two decades ago, roughly in 1990. Quite simply, it means organizing an organization's information and knowledge holistically but that sounds a bit wooly and, surprisingly enough, even though it sounds overbroad, it is not the whole picture. It is a discipline that promotes an integrated approach to identifying, capturing, evaluating, retrieving, and sharing all of an enterprise's information assets. These assets may include databases, documents, policies, procedures, and previously uncaptured expertise and experience in individual workers. Perhaps the most central thrust in KM is to capture and make available the information and knowledge that is in people's heads as it were and that has never been explicitly set down, so that it can be used by others in the organization. Putting it into the context of our discussion here, the information and knowledge relates to the effectiveness of protection technologies. In essence, it is a documentation trail of lessons learned contained in databases in order to make security processes more repeatable.

Lessons learned databases are databases that attempt to capture and to make accessible knowledge that has been operationally obtained and typically would not have been captured in a fixed medium (to use copyright terminology). In the KM context, the emphasis is typically upon capturing knowledge and making it explicit. Early in the KM movement, the phrase typically used was *best practices*, but that phrase was soon replaced with *lessons learned*. The reasons were that *lessons learned* was a broader and more inclusive term and because *best practice* seemed too restrictive and could be interpreted as meaning there was only one best practice in a situation. What might be a best practice in North American culture might well not be a best practice in another culture.

PR.IP-9: Response Plans and Recovery Plans Are in Place and Managed

The need to plan for crisis management, business continuity, and disaster recovery has never been greater. Organizational survival is in more jeopardy within the past decade as two global trends have increased operational risk in all industries and made it more difficult for organizations to maintain resiliency. The first is an increase in external forces that can threaten a society. Terrorism is one of these forces. The objective of terrorist threats is to disrupt society through attacks on high-profile or strategic sites, or on the products and services that sustain the population. These strategic sites are not just limited to governments, but are now defined as 18 critical infrastructure categories that encompass all sectors of society from banking, manufacturing, to the food and water supply. Distance from an at-risk site also impacts the risk to organizational survival. In addition to the terrorist threats is a landscape of national political instability in which crisis can be triggered with little warning and upset stability within a nation or region.

The second trend is increasing reliance on resources imported through global business. In the interest of competitive forces, many businesses have increased their supply chains until they are truly without boundaries. Not only natural resources but also parts, supplies, finished goods, labor, services, information, and knowledge are obtained in an international environment sustained by ICT systems that navigate across the globe. While businesses have become more competitive and efficient through international sourcing, they also have become more vulnerable to disruptions in distant parts of the world. Some of these new supply regions do not have the long history of strict security controls that we have been discussing so far. They may also lack telecommunications and electrical grid redundancy and other components that strengthen the infrastructure and provide confidence to international customers and consumers of goods.

Adding these two trends to the traditional risks of natural disasters or weather-related incidents, such as earthquakes and hurricanes, means that risk or potentials for loss have increased largely unnoticed over the past decade.

Response plans (more often referred to as business continuity plans) and disaster recovery plans are at the foundation of preparedness. For individual organizations, they are components of sound risk management and the means of preserving organizational resiliency during extreme duress. Moreover, they are part of a national security infrastructure designed to ensure unrestricted delivery of goods and services.

Simply put, business continuity plans are the creation of a strategy through the recognition of threats and risks as described above, with a focus on ensuring that personnel and assets are protected and able to function in the event of a disaster. Business continuity planning involves defining potential risks, determining how those risks will affect operations, implementing safeguards and procedures designed to mitigate those risks, testing those procedures to ensure that they work, and periodically reviewing the process to make sure that it is up to date.

Disaster recovery is the process in which an organization resumes business after a disruptive event. The event might be something large like an earthquake or a terrorist attack, or something small like malfunctioning software caused by a computer virus.

Given the human tendency to not play devil's advocate, many managers are prone to ignoring disaster recovery because disasters seem unlikely. While business continuity planning suggests a more comprehensive approach to making sure that organizations can keep their cash flow, not only after a natural disaster but also in the event of smaller disruptions including illness or departure of key staffers, supply chain partner problems, or other challenges that businesses face from time to time. Despite these distinctions, the two terms are often married under the acronym BC/DR (business continuity and disaster recovery) because of their many common considerations.

All BC/DR plans need to include how employees will communicate, where they will go, and how they will keep doing their jobs. The details can vary depending on the size and scope of an organization and its business objectives. For some organizations, issues such as supply chain logistics are most crucial and are the focus on the plan. For others, information technology may play a more pivotal role, and the BC/DR plan may have more of a focus on systems recovery.

PR.IP-10: Response and Recovery Plans Are Tested

Once the organization has developed their BC/DR plan, it is just as important to test it. Testing verifies the effectiveness of the organization's plan, trains plan participants on what to do in a real scenario, and identifies areas where the plan needs to be strengthened. Testing methods will vary depending upon the organizational priorities. However, the testing process generally consists of the following five steps:

1. Conduct a plan review at least quarterly. Gather a group of key business continuity plan participants (typically division leaders or department heads). Discuss the elements of the

plan with a focus on the discovery of any areas where the plan can be strengthened. Train new managers regarding the plan and incorporate any new feedback.

2. Conduct disaster role-playing sessions that allow plan participants to walk through the parts of the BC/DR plan, gaining familiarity with their responsibilities given a specific emergency scenario. Conduct the dry-run training to document errors and identify inconsistencies for correction and improvements. Schedule at least two to three of these sessions each year.

3. Perform a simulation of a possible disaster scenario. Include business leaders, partners, vendors, management, and staff in the BC/DR test simulation. Test data recovery, staff safety, asset management, leadership response, relocation protocols, and loss recovery procedures. Plan a full simulation at least once each year with different, realistic scenarios that test the effectiveness of the BC/DR plan.

4. Accommodate any work stoppages due to the testing of the BC/DR plan by scheduling simulations and other testing exercises between Friday and Saturday. Conduct sessions that include management and higher-level staff exclusively on the weekends, and plan review sessions usually lasting 2 to 4 hours that can be scheduled during the business week.

5. Communicate the importance and benefit of the BC/DR plan to all levels of the organization. Promote the review and active participation in the BC/DR simulation. Use the simulation to identify competencies within the workforce that may signify additional resources during a disaster situation.

PR.IP-11: Cybersecurity Is Included in Human Resources Practices

Human resources (HR) directors can play a key role in keeping organizations safe in cyberspace by

- Taking ownership of the security risk posed by employees: Most employees assume that cybersecurity is a technical issue and it is not until after a successful attack that they start taking personal responsibility for security. Attitudes like this make an organization vulnerable. To improve their chances of success, hackers are now searching out the organizations that are likely to be less aware of the cyberthreat: those that have not been attacked yet, such as smaller companies or those with a lower public profile. HR has a vital role to play in educating employees about the impact their attitudes and behavior have on the organization's security.

- Ensuring that security measures are practical and ethical: Controls can stop people acting in a way that places the organization at risk, but they must be consistent with the way people behave and think. For example, randomly generated passwords are hard to crack but most people have to write them down, which defeats their purpose. Monitoring can allow organizations to examine what employees are doing but often raises questions of trust and crosses the boundary between private life and business. The HR team is best placed to advise on whether policies are likely to work and whether they are appropriate.

- Identifying employees who may present a particular risk: Breaking into a network takes minutes. However, finding and safely extracting what they want may take criminals months or even years of research and planning. To shorten this process, cyberattackers are getting help from insiders in more than half of all advanced attacks.

  Attackers use social media to identify a useful target and to create a relationship with them. They target people with a predisposition to break security controls such as those with strong views, who do not react well to authority. They look for a trigger event that will break the employee's psychological contract with their employer such as demotion, change in role, redundancy, or dismissal. Employees who take action against their employer are most likely to do so within 30 days of such an event. This gives the HR team a chance to intervene, including taking steps to increase monitoring and deter them. Managing an employee's exit with a view to security is also one of the most critical of all the contributions the HR team can make.

PR.IP-12: A Vulnerability Management Plan Is Developed and Implemented

Vulnerability management planning is the initial step in developing a comprehensive system of practices and processes designed to identify, analyze, and address flaws in hardware or software that could serve as attack potentials.

As we discussed earlier in the book, a vulnerability is a weak point that an intruder could exploit to gain access to system resources for data theft or malicious purposes. The essential elements of vulnerability management include detection, assessment, and remediation. Methods of detection, such as vulnerability scanning, penetration testing, and Google hacking, help find potential attack potentials.

A vulnerability scanner uses a database containing all the information required to check a system for security holes in services and ports, anomalies in packet construction, and potential paths to exploitable programs or scripts.

Pen tests, which may be automated or performed manually, involve gathering information about the target before the test, identifying possible entry points, attempting to breach the system, and reporting back.

Google hacking is the practice of using advanced search techniques in search engine queries to locate hard-to-find information. Security researchers and intruders can both use targeted queries to locate information that was not intended to be public. Manipulation and further engagement can turn up vulnerabilities that can be exploited.

During vulnerability analysis, any security holes found are identified, defined, and classified. Analysis may also involve evaluating the potential effectiveness of proposed controls and subsequently evaluating how well they performed in practice.

Remediation is the step of the vulnerability management in which security holes that are determined pose an unacceptable risk to the organization are patched.

Because the nature of threats is constantly evolving, vulnerability management planning comprises a continuous and repetitive body of practices that must be frequently improved to ensure it is effective given the threats currently in existence.

Maintenance

This outcome assumes that a formal, documented information system maintenance policy that addresses purpose, scope, roles, responsibilities, and management commitment and formal, documented procedures to implement the policy and associated system maintenance controls already exist. For organizations in the public sector, such a policy and procedures should be made consistent with applicable federal laws, executive orders, directives, policies, regulations, standards, and guidance. Private sector organizations must also be cognizant of industry standards and regulations. Oftentimes, the information system maintenance policy is included as part of the information security policy for the organization. Including it within the general security policy will normally prevent overlap of policies related to the same security controls. There is a great deal of flexibility in the implementation of system maintenance procedures. Some organizations choose to include maintenance as part of their overall security program, while others prefer to include security procedures directly within the maintenance plan for each individual ICT system when required. Regardless of how an organization chooses to address the documentation of security procedures, the organizational risk management strategy is a key factor in the development of the system maintenance policy; and management should perform frequent reviews of the two in order to ensure consistency. The CSF breaks down the maintenance category into two subcategory outcomes. The outcomes are identified in Table 4.5 and described in the next couple of sections of this chapter.

PR.MA-1: Maintenance and Repair of Organizational Assets Is Performed and Logged in a Timely Manner, with Approved and Controlled Tools

The underlying objective of PR.MA-1 is that the organization schedules, performs, documents, and reviews records of maintenance and repairs on ICT components based on what has been defined in manufacturer or vendor specifications and organizational requirements. In the section above, you learned that security maintenance policies and procedures are normally aligned within the general scope of the organizational security program, or at least within the maintenance plans for individual ICT systems. It is through that supporting

Table 4.5   Framework Core Maintenance Category

CATEGORY	SUBCATEGORY	INFORMATION RESOURCES
Maintenance (PR. MA): Maintenance and repair of industrial control and information system components is performed consistent with policies and procedures.	PR.MA-1: Maintenance and repair of organizational assets is performed and logged in a timely manner, with approved and controlled tools.	• COBIT 5 BAI09.03 • ISA 62443-2-1:2009 4.3.3.3.7 • ISO/IEC 27001:2013 A.11.1.2, A.11.2.4, A.11.2.5 • NIST SP 800-53 Rev. 4 MA-2, MA-3, MA-5
	PR.MA-2: Remote maintenance of organizational assets is approved, logged, and performed in a manner that prevents unauthorized access.	• COBIT 5 DSS05.04 • ISA 62443-2-1:2009 4.3.3.6.5, 4.3.3.6.6, 4.3.3.6.7, 4.4.4.6.8 • ISO/IEC 27001:2013 A.11.2.4, A.15.1.1, A.15.2.1 • NIST SP 800-53 Rev. 4 MA-4

Source: National Institute of Standards and Technology, *Framework for Improving Critical Infrastructure Cybersecurity.* Gaithersburg, February 12, 2014.

documentation that vendor-specific or organizational requirements are identified and justified as necessary consistent with the organization's established risk strategy.

This outcome also mandates that the following criteria be included within the maintenance policy:

- The organization remains in control of all maintenance activities, regardless if service is performed on site or remotely
- The organization designates an official that explicitly approves the removal of the ICT system or system components from organizational facilities for off-site maintenance or repairs
- Procedures are in place to sanitize equipment to remove all information from media that is being removed from organizational facilities for off-site maintenance or repairs
- Procedures are in place to check all potentially impacted security controls, following maintenance or repair, to make sure that the controls are still functioning properly

The CSF also stipulates that the organization establish a process for maintenance personnel authorization and maintain an updated list of third-party maintenance organizations or personnel. Doing so will ensure that individuals performing maintenance on the

ICT system have required access authorizations and identifies personnel with technical competence required to supervise the maintenance process.

Individuals that have not previously been identified in the ICT system, such as third-party personnel and consultants, may legitimately require privileged access to the system, for example, when required to conduct ad hoc maintenance or diagnostic tasks. Based on a prior assessment of risk, the organization may decide to issue temporary authorization to these individuals. Temporary authorization may be for one-time use or for a predetermined time frame.

PR.MA-2: Remote Maintenance of Organizational Assets Is Approved, Logged, and Performed in a Manner That Prevents Unauthorized Access

As mentioned above, it is not uncommon for the organization to utilize a third party for their maintenance and repair needs; in those cases, it is important that the maintenance policy specifies criteria for authorization, monitoring, and control of all maintenance and diagnostic activities. Moreover, the organization should allow the use of related third-party maintenance and diagnostic tools only as consistent with organizational policy and documented in the security plan for the ICT system.

Third-party maintenance and diagnostic activities are those conducted by individuals communicating through a network, either an external network (e.g., the Internet) or an internal network. Local maintenance and diagnostic activities are those carried out by individuals physically present at the information system or information system component and not communicating across a network connection. The key point of this category outcome is that identification and authentication techniques used in the establishment of third-party maintenance and diagnostic sessions are consistent with the network access requirements defined for organizational users.

Protective Technology

The sixth and final category of the Protect Function deals with the controls associated with protection of technology. Technical security architecture, as it is often referred to, focuses on the mapping between the control architecture and the protection processes, life cycle issues, and contextual drivers. It typically defines controls for protection settings that can be implemented by technical mechanisms and identifies what is commonly called technical security policy, as opposed to enterprise policy. The interaction between other elements is the prime focus of technical security architecture but it commonly encompasses the elements of context more than any other area. These are the *who, what, where, why, when*, and *how* of the Protect Function. The CSF describes this category as the controls in which "technical security solutions are managed to ensure the security and resilience of systems and assets, consistent with related policies, procedures, and agreements" (National Institute of Standards and Technology Feb. 2014). The category is broken down into the four subcategories identified in Table 4.6 and described in the next several sections of this chapter.

PR.PT-1: Audit/Log Records Are Determined, Documented, Implemented, and Reviewed in Accordance with Policy

The purpose of audit is to assess the execution of a specific set of activities, which take place within a given setting. The goal, therefore, is to verify the correctness of how those activities are performed. Audits typically confirm three things. The first is the continuous applicability and relevance of policies that guide the process. The second is whether the procedures that have been created to execute the process remain correct and complete. The third is whether management of the process is capable of overseeing the process execution.

The audit process maintains accountability by accumulating evidence (logs) to support conclusions about the audit target. For that reason, the audit process has to be able to objectively describe every relevant aspect of the operation (or in the case of technology, entity) being audited. Audit gathers sufficient objective evidence by observing and documenting specific aspects of the operation or entity under examination. The aim is to gather sufficient evidence to be able to characterize performance over time with some degree of assurance.

Since the audit process has to guarantee consistent interpretation, substantive steps must be taken to ensure that, when faced with the same evidence, all auditors will make the same observations and in

Table 4.6 Framework Core Protective Technology Category

CATEGORY	SUBCATEGORY	INFORMATION RESOURCES
Protective Technology (PR. PT): Technical security solutions are managed to ensure the security and resilience of systems and assets, consistent with related policies, procedures, and agreements.	PR.PT-1: Audit/log records are determined, documented, implemented, and reviewed in accordance with policy.	• CCS CSC 14 • COBIT 5 APO11.04 • ISA 62443-2-1:2009 4.3.3.3.9, 4.3.3.5.8, 4.3.4.4.7, 4.4.2.1, 4.4.2.2, 4.4.2.4 • ISA 62443-3-3:2013 SR 2.8, SR 2.9, SR 2.10, SR 2.11, SR 2.12 • ISO/IEC 27001:2013 A.12.4.1, A.12.4.2, A.12.4.3, A.12.4.4, A.12.7.1 • NIST SP 800-53 Rev. 4 AU Family
	PR.PT-2: Removable media is protected and its use restricted according to policy.	• COBIT 5 DSS05.02, APO13.01 • ISA 62443-3-3:2013 SR 2.3 • ISO/IEC 27001:2013 A.8.2.2, A.8.2.3, A.8.3.1, A.8.3.3, A.11.2.9 • NIST SP 800-53 Rev. 4 MP-2, MP-4, MP-5, MP-7
	PR.PT-3: Access to systems and assets is controlled, incorporating the principle of least functionality.	• COBIT 5 DSS05.02 • ISA 62443-2-1:2009 4.3.3.5.1, 4.3.3.5.2, 4.3.3.5.3, 4.3.3.5.4, 4.3.3.5.5, 4.3.3.5.6, 4.3.3.5.7, 4.3.3.5.8, 4.3.3.6.1, 4.3.3.6.2, 4.3.3.6.3, 4.3.3.6.4, 4.3.3.6.5, 4.3.3.6.6, 4.3.3.6.7, 4.3.3.6.8, 4.3.3.6.9, 4.3.3.7.1, 4.3.3.7.2, 4.3.3.7.3, 4.3.3.7.4 • ISA 62443-3-3:2013 SR 1.1, SR 1.2, SR 1.3, SR 1.4, SR 1.5, SR 1.6, SR 1.7, SR 1.8, SR 1.9, SR 1.10, SR 1.11, SR 1.12, SR 1.13, SR 2.1, SR 2.2, SR 2.3, SR 2.4, SR 2.5, SR 2.6, SR 2.7 • ISO/IEC 27001:2013 A.9.1.2 • NIST SP 800-53 Rev. 4 AC-3, CM-7
	PR.PT-4: Communications and control networks are protected.	• CCS CSC 7 • COBIT 5 DSS05.02, APO13.01 • ISA 62443-3-3:2013 SR 3.1, SR 3.5, SR 3.8, SR 4.1, SR 4.3, SR 5.1, SR 5.2, SR 5.3, SR 7.1, SR 7.6 • ISO/IEC 27001:2013 A.13.1.1, A.13.2.1 • NIST SP 800-53 Rev. 4 AC-4, AC-17, AC-18, CP-8, SC-7

Source: National Institute of Standards and Technology, *Framework for Improving Critical Infrastructure Cybersecurity.* Gaithersburg, February 12, 2014.

turn draw the same conclusions. Those requirements imply the need for very specific audit criteria.

Audits are scheduled by plan. The auditing personnel must be given the freedom to perform the audit in the plan. Moreover, the resources necessary to conduct the audits should be specified and cross-referenced to the audit objectives. An audit manager is typically assigned to oversee the audit process. The role of this manager is to supervise, monitor, and evaluate the activities of the audit team. He or she selects the auditors, assigns roles and responsibilities, plans, schedules audit activities, and oversees audit reporting. The auditors themselves must have the technical know-how to perform a proper audit.

When it comes to technology, it is important when planning the audit to keep two rules in mind. One, electronic records need to be audited using the same methodology and level of rigor that is applied to the more traditional body of audit evidence. Two, the outcomes and conclusions of the review of electronic records have to be recorded in the same fashion as the traditional audit evidence. Checklists are particularly important in ensuring proper coverage in both respects, because they direct the auditor's attention to items that may not have otherwise been considered. In applied terms, if a technical item is not on the checklist it is not likely to be reviewed. Typically, the checklist ensures that meaningful aspects of technical items, like the operating system and network utilities, are always examined.

PR.PT-2: Removable Media Is Protected
and Its Use Restricted According to Policy

ICT system removable media includes both computerized and non-computerized media. Computerized media includes diskettes, magnetic tapes, external/removable hard disk drives, flash drives, and compact disks, for example. Noncomputerized media includes paper and microfilm. This outcome also applies to mobile devices with information storage capability, such as smartphones, tablets, and laptops.

Earlier in the chapter, we discussed the need for organizations to restrict user access to media. This outcome restricts the use of certain types of media on ICT systems. An organization may prohibit the use of flash drive or external hard drive usage with part or all of their ICT components. Technical and nontechnical safeguards such as policies, procedures, and rules of behavior should be communicated throughout the organization in order to restrict the use of information system media found potentially harmful.

PR.PT-3: Access to Systems and Assets Is Controlled,
Incorporating the Principle of Least Functionality

An initial interpretation of this subcategory outcome would lead to the notion that the CSF is repeating an outcome that had already been addressed in the access control category of this same function. Recall that earlier in the chapter, access control was described as all standardized controls utilized to ensure only authorized individuals have access to ICT assets. However, this outcome approaches that definition from the principle of least functionality, which is achieved through the activities defined by the CM-7 control of NIST SP 800-53.

CM-7 is part of the configuration management family of controls, but the activities defined can be applied to technology access control as well. The control states that "the organization:

1. Configures the information system to provide only essential capabilities; and
2. Prohibits or restricts the use of the following functions, ports, protocols, and/or services" (National Institute for Standards and Technology Apr. 2014).

The idea behind least functionality is that ICT systems afford organizations a wide variety of functions and services. Some of those functions and services are provided by default and do not directly support the overall objectives of the organization. In some cases, it is necessary to offer multiple services from single ICT components, but that in turn increases risk over limiting the services provided by any one component. That is where least functionality comes in. Whenever possible, organizations should limit component functionality to a single function per device (e.g., e-mail servers or web servers, but not both). By doing so, access to each device can be better managed relative to the authorized privileges to the functions that device provides. On a regular basis, organizations should review functions and services offered by ICT systems or individual components to determine which functions and services are candidates for elimination. In addition to functions and services, organizations should consider disabling physical and logical ports/protocols that are no longer in use to prevent unauthorized connection of devices.

PR.PT-4: Communications and Control Networks Are Protected

Communication and control network protection practices have not changed significantly in the last decade. Most perimeters rely for protection on stateful inspection firewalls with "holes" liberally poked through them, backed up by noisy and largely ignored intrusion prevention or detection systems. Although communication protections have not changed, business and collaboration requirements have driven the use of Internet applications and interorganization connectivity skyward. These services, located in the demilitarized zone at the perimeter of the control network, often traverse the perimeter with little to no oversight or control. Regulatory compliance has mandated many ICT teams to "bolt on" certain controls such as data loss prevention and encryption. From *encrypt everything* strategies to *check box* implementations of these solutions, many organizations are still left blind to what gets through the network perimeter.

The external border of the network is the face of an organization. The traffic permitted to flow through, both good and bad, can determine the success or potential collapse of an organization. The challenge is to maximize the network's utility and accountability while minimizing its vulnerability. Most communication and control network security needs a facelift. Providing the appropriate level of security today means modernizing defenses to handle the following:

- Management of aging firewall policies: Firewall policies contain rules of uncertain origin, business requirement, and active use. Important rules may not be active, while unimportant rules may be cluttering up and slowing down perimeter defenses. Most organizations have poor visibility into how well rules implement the policies that regulations and governance committees define.
- Automated attacks: Public-facing services are at risk from distributed denial of service campaigns that threaten business continuity.
- Targeted attacks: Communication system vulnerabilities (such as an unpatched web server) must be identified and mitigated to prevent their exploitation.
- Identification of who is doing what and where: To decrease undesirable and risky traffic, the network should help identify and

control outbound communications by internal users, protecting against interactions with known villains and risky geographies.

- Noisy intrusion prevention systems (IPSs): Being on the network perimeter, IPSs see every packet of traffic the firewall allows through or users send out. Many times, the overwhelming volume of alerts means they are only referred to for post-event forensics. During forensics, the volume also makes it difficult to normalize data when correlating events against disparate data sources.

- Management of tunneling applications: Tunneled communications can provide unfiltered command and control communication for malware and botnets. Plus, tunneling applications such as Skype can allow invisible data leakage.

- Blind spots created with encryption: Many organizations either do not have technology in place to allow scanning of encrypted traffic or have not enabled this facility where appropriate on their perimeters. A high percentage of malicious traffic is encrypted to take advantage of this limitation. Also, determined insiders may encrypt sensitive information to send it outside the company.

An effective communication and control network architecture enhances the organization's security posture, as well as its visibility. Instead of a hodgepodge of point products that keep critical threat intelligence in silos, the effective security measures will build an accountable and complete picture of communications that permits the organization to easily, effectively, and securely manage traffic flow:

- Reputation-aware perimeter devices: Communication devices should have the ability to review an external host's history of behavior before accepting a connection. This function is most prevalent in e-mail gateways for spam and malware detection, but is also a feature of some other perimeter protection devices.

- Vulnerability management and exploit prevention: Communication devices (such as e-mail and web servers) should be scanned on a regular basis for known and new vulnerabilities. Since patch management schedules revolve around maintenance windows, business uptime requirements, and threat severity, the network security systems must mitigate vulnerabilities until patches can be installed. Finally, a full data correlation and reporting system should aggregate the current status of these systems.

- Application discovery and control: Many applications seek outbound connectivity over the communications paths and ports that are commonly open. This traffic includes both critical business applications and malicious traffic. The solution should reliably identify and exert policies over applications including those within hypertext transfer protocol and hypertext transfer protocol secure traffic.
- Detection of tunneling applications: Complete solutions should include traffic flow analysis to perform additional validation of protocols and applications regardless of the channel of communication. Additionally, systems that present external services should be aware of and force compliance to the protocols on which their services are offered. This should also include command and control communication.
- Appropriate and pervasive encryption management: The solution must be able to decrypt, inspect, and reencrypt both inbound and outbound traffic to ensure it complies with policies and does not contain malware. However, the system must be flexible enough to recognize and allow certain traffic to pass without decryption as appropriate. This traffic might include sensitive or protected traffic, such as personal health information.
- Systems, policy, and event management: The solution must provide practical visibility into events and the systems that are affected, as well as report on the applicability and effectiveness of policy as enforced by active rules. By leveraging an in-depth reporting function, the solution should provide real-time as well as historical situational awareness.

Linking COBIT to the Protect Function

It is important to remember that while many of the outcomes defined in the CSF Protect Function are technical in nature, COBIT is focused on the management practices associated with how each of the controls is implemented within the ICT system. As such, each of the COBIT 5 controls listed as an information resource for each of the subcategory outcome addresses the management controls necessary to ensure safeguarding ICT assets.

The COBIT framework categorizes the controls that align to this function, as well as the functions discussed in the next three chapters, to step 7, implement action plan, of the CSF's suggested approach to establishing or improving a cybersecurity program. More formally, COBIT aligns the controls to the principle of enabling a holistic approach. COBIT defines this principle as "efficient and effective governance and management of enterprise IT require a holistic approach, taking into account several interacting components. COBIT 5 defines a set of enablers to support the implementation of a comprehensive governance and management system for enterprise IT. Enablers are broadly defined as anything that can help to achieve the objectives of the enterprise. The COBIT 5 framework defines seven categories of enablers:

1. Principles, Policies and Frameworks
2. Processes
3. Organizational Structures
4. Culture, Ethics and Behavior
5. Information
6. Services, Infrastructure and Applications
7. People, Skills and Competencies" (Information Systems Audit and Control Association 2014)

The COBIT controls aligned to the CSF action plan implementation provide an opportunity for stakeholder communications, which should be written using a level of understanding and terminology appropriate for each audience. For instance, management may be interested in specific facilities and processes, while board and executives may be more interested in competitive forces or market opportunities.

According to the COBIT framework, action plan execution is gradually implemented, building on project success and process improvement. The actual execution of the plan provides a mechanism for effective risk management throughout the organization. Additionally, performance measures and incremental metrics should be used to document success and support any required adjustments. Many of those measures are described in the COBIT 5 processes, especially those in the Build, Acquire and Implement (BAI) and Deliver, Service and Support (DSS) families of COBIT controls.

Chapter Summary

- The Protect Function supports the ability to limit or contain the impact of a cybersecurity event. Examples of outcomes include access control; awareness and training; data security; information protection processes and procedures; maintenance; and protective technology.
- Access control approaches determine how users interact with data and other network resources. Furthermore, access control measures ensure that data are protected from unauthorized disclosure or modification.
- A good cybersecurity awareness and training program should educate employees about corporate policies and procedures for working with ICT systems. The NICE Framework is an excellent resource for establishing an awareness and training program. While the CSF describes the outcomes necessary of a well-defined cybersecurity program, the NICE framework identifies the tasks that will achieve those outcomes and the knowledge necessary to perform those tasks.
- Data security is achieved through protective digital privacy measures that are applied to prevent unauthorized access to computers, databases, and websites. It also protects data from corruption. It is not uncommon for data security to be the main priority for organizations of every size.
- The backbone to any established cybersecurity program are security policies that define purpose, scope, roles, responsibilities, management commitment, and coordination among organizational entities.
- Cybersecurity provisions should be included in the maintenance plans of entire ICT systems and the plans for individual ICT projects.
- Technical and nontechnical audits are necessary within an established security program in order to assess the execution of a specific set of activities according to security policy and procedures. The goal is to verify the correctness of how those activities are performed.

Case Project

Suny Corporation would like you to continue the work you have been doing on the plan for implementing the Framework for Improving Critical Infrastructure Cybersecurity. Now that you are familiar with the outcomes of the Protect Function, they would like you to update your plan with more specific criteria related to access control, data security, and configuration management. They would also like details related to how you plan to implement cybersecurity workforce development within the company. Within the plan, only major steps of implementation need to be organized. In other words, focus on steps that the framework recommends for establishing and improving their cybersecurity program. The plan should continue to take the form of a project timeline that describes when each part of every step is performed. Besides providing a customized timeline and plan, include the business justification for each step.

5
DETECT FUNCTION

After reading this chapter and completing the case project, you will

- Understand the challenges organizations face in detecting cybersecurity attacks;
- Understand the steps organizations should take in detecting anomalies and events;
- Understand the meaning of security continuous monitoring, and the proactive measures organizations take in ensuring its effectiveness; and
- Understand the importance of requirement compliance, testing, and communicating of detection processes as an underlying practice of continuous process improvement.

From a national perspective, one of the main objectives of homeland security is to secure the nation from the many threats through its critical infrastructures. In addition to the countless physical implications, homeland security includes cyber specialized areas such as: video surveillance, image detection, and cyberattack detection (more commonly referred to as intrusion detection or threat intelligence). This chapter focuses on the intrusion detection within national and private sector critical infrastructures. In the past decade, cybercrime and cyberterrorism have increased exponentially. To quickly detect exploitation of ICT assets, a set of ethical rules and security controls is necessary. In this chapter, we will also explore cybersecurity intelligence controls by way of their support for achieving the outcomes of the CSF Detect Function subcategories. Recall from our discussions in previous chapters that cyberattacks are actions that attempt to bypass security mechanisms of ICT systems. Cybersecurity intrusion detection can then be simply defined as the policies and procedures associated with identifying individuals who are using ICT systems without authorization and those who have legitimate access to the system but are abusing their privileges. We can add to this definition the more global identification of attempts to use an ICT system without authorization or to abuse existing privileges. In other words, cybersecurity intelligence controls should not be limited to detecting human access. Organizations must have mechanisms in place to detect *any* attempts to access unauthorized ICT assets.

Detect Function Overview

Cybersecurity has been front-page news for the past decade and we should expect that trend to continue well into the future because the behavior of cybercriminals has fundamentally changed. During the 1990s, the majority of cyberattacks were based on viruses and malware designed to be deployed across a large number of potential victims. Today, cybercriminals are targeting specific organizations. They look for weaknesses and identify the easiest ways to gain access to targeted corporate networks. Once they are inside, they expend significant resources on evading detection so they can maximize access to confidential data. This shift in tactics was a key factor in many recent mega–data breaches including Target, JP Morgan, Michaels, and Sony.

The technical sophistication behind these attacks, and the criminals' ability to evade detection by traditional security tools, has left many organizations concluding that there is very little that can be done to protect their confidential data. In reality, that is an incorrect assessment and we learned in Chapter 4 of numerous outcomes that the CSF defines in order to protect ICT assets. Nevertheless, larger organizations on the cutting edge of cybersecurity are building solutions that use machine learning and automation to radically reduce the time needed to detect and respond to a cyberattack in progress.

One of the biggest challenges faced with detecting an advanced cyberattack is that large organization network infrastructures are naturally in a constant state of change. Every cyberattack leaves behind detectable changes but cybercriminals are able to hide in plain sight by disguising these changes as normal network activity.

Detecting anomalous and destructive changes among hundreds of thousands of routine changes made by the organization is a key to quickly identifying those changes that indicate a cyberattack is in progress. This problem is rapidly becoming more difficult by orders of magnitude. The indicators of malicious change are constantly shifting, and the volume of normal change on organizational networks is routinely very high, especially for large organizations that have hundreds of thousands of mission critical systems and associated network devices. This makes detecting malicious changes laborious and time consuming. This detection problem can be particularly daunting if the problem-solving approach relies on applied human intelligence.

One of the trends in cybersecurity defense is the development of a wide range of community and commercial intrusion detection feeds that make it possible to dynamically search for specific malicious changes, also called indicators of compromise, such as IP addresses associated with malicious attacks, malware file names and hashes, and specific attack vectors. These services allow organizations to share information about current cyberattacks.

These feeds are a critical source of valuable information, but many organizations find them difficult to apply across the entire enterprise infrastructure. It can be difficult to translate a list of data into actionable intelligence. To use this information effectively, organizations need to quickly determine if any of the devices on their networks show signs of infection for a constantly changing array of malware.

The good news is that there are many organizations that have found a way to apply intrusion detection in near real time. This allows them to correlate known external threat agents and their tactics with the specific malicious changes on critical systems resulting in the automated detection of specific cyberattacks. When this information is paired with the business context and detailed system state data, organizations can pinpoint remediation efforts focusing scarce resources on those systems that are most vulnerable to specific active threats, effectively automating the process of detecting and thwarting cybercriminals in near real time.

Applying intrusion detection in this way makes it possible for organizations to adapt to rapid changes in the cyberthreat landscape and scale their response up or down, depending on the unique requirements of their specific business. It also makes it possible to dynamically shift resources and defenses in response to attack patterns. This transformation of cybersecurity business process stands in sharp contrast to traditional approaches that attempt to apply equal security measures across the entire corporate network. The most common example of more traditional security approaches is the application of software patches. Most organizations wait for a vendor to release patches and then deploy them evenly across all functional areas. The emerging agile cybersecurity model, by constantly adapting to the rapid changes in cyber threats, would prioritize the deployment of these patches to specific systems that are uniquely vulnerable to specific threats.

It is not an exaggerated statement that cybercrime will continue to evolve and become more sophisticated. However, no matter how sophisticated the attack, it will continue to leave at least one simple clue on critical systems either file or configuration changes. Cybercrime defenses simply need to use automation and dynamic intelligence to detect these changes and we can stop cybercriminals in their tracks.

INSIGHT APTs: Minimizing Losses with Early Detection

Let's travel back to 2006, the year the blockbuster, "The Departed," came out. Matt Damon plays a young criminal who has infiltrated the state police as an informer for South Boston's Irish Mob. Working his way up the ranks, he gathers sensitive information about the plans and counter-plans of the operations he has penetrated and leaks them to his organized crime cohorts. Eventually, police suspect that there's a mole in their midst. Now, we all know how this ends—Damon is exposed and killed by Mark Wahlberg for his stint—but not before wreaking havoc throughout the department.

There are some solid parallels between Damon in the Departed and the recent spate of high profile data breaches in which access is gained via authorized credentials and the perpetrator remains undetected for an extended period of time. This situation, unfortunately, is so common for organizations with high-value information that many experts advise them to operate on the assumption that they've already been breached.

With a seemingly infinite number of security products on the market, one might ask how we find ourselves in this situation. One explanation is that human nature makes us susceptible to a whole host of social exploits and phishing schemes, and once hackers gain legitimate access, signature based perimeter defenses are largely ineffective. Once inside the network, it appears that cyber criminals have carte blanche to move laterally, secure their objectives and steal whatever they want.

And given that the average breach goes undetected for months, they seem to be able to take their sweet time doing it.

Attackers try hard to mask their activities—but try as they might, in order to accomplish their goals, their behaviors are likely to be anomalous at some point in time. Quickly detecting these anomalies as they develop could make the difference between losing tens of millions of customer records and losing a few hundred—or none at all.

While it seems somewhat obvious that looking for "unusual" activity would be beneficial to early detection, it turns out that in practice, it's not as easy as it might sound. In fact, in a late 2014 Analytics and Intelligence survey performed by the SANS Institute, respondents said that the Inability to understand and baseline "normal behavior" (in order to detect abnormal behavior) is one of the top impediments to effective attack detection and response.

This is where machine learning anomaly detection technology comes in. It can process millions of data points each minute, establishing, or learning a "normal" baseline, comparing data points to past behavior, and identifying anomalous differences in values over time, differences in rates over time, and population outliers. Using this technology, user transactions, server processes, internet traffic, IPS alerts and proxy logs can all be analyzed for unusual activities.

An anomaly in a single dimension, say access to a never before seen external uniform resource locator (URL), may be uninteresting, so we certainly wouldn't want to generate more useless alerts for the incident response team to investigate. Instead, anomaly detection software analyzes multiple data relationships, increasing the anomaly level or "score" when an activity is anomalous in multiple dimensions. For example, a large hypertext transfer protocol (HTTP) POST access to a new URL, from an internal system that typically doesn't use the POST method might be an indicator of some sort of data exfiltration. Or an unusual number of domain name system (DNS) requests with a very large number of unique subdomains might be an indicator of malware command and control communication (C2).

While these are simple examples, and you might argue that a skilled IT team could perform these analyses manually or with scripts, albeit much more slowly, the real power of machine learning anomaly detection comes from the automated learning of baselines across multiple sources of system log and event data, relationships that security pros thought were virtually impossible to analyze using existing technology that relies on manual searching or script-based analysis.

As practical implementations of this type of big data security analytics become available to security teams, you might be tempted to think that we'll no longer read about major data breaches going undetected. Unfortunately, this will take some time. A survey from Lieberman Software suggests that despite the continued occurrence of massive data breaches, an alarming 65 percent of security professionals believe that perimeter security technologies, such as firewalls and anti-malware solutions, are sufficient in defending against advanced persistent threats (APTs*). Hopefully, given the news of late, they have awakened to the fact that there is no defense sufficient to prevent APTs and that the emphasis must be shifted to early detection.

In the battle between IT teams and cyber criminals, the only way of spotting the metaphorical Matt Damon in your network may be machine learning anomaly detection. (Paquette 2015)

Anomalies and Events Category

The CSF describes the outcome of the anomalies and events category as the development and implementation of controls in which "anomalous activity is detected in a timely manner and the potential impact of events is understood" (National Institute of Standards and Technology Feb. 2014). This category, addresses the outcomes organizations should realize through controls implemented to support anomaly detection.

It might be the best way to understand anomaly detection by beginning with a hypothetical. George Wilson had just returned from traveling abroad. He was at a car rental company when a polite agent informed him that his bank credit card did not work. Flustered and embarrassed, he tried a different credit card, one that worked. Already late for work, he put aside trying to figure out what happened.

---

* APT – Advanced Persistent Threat: Normally target organizations in sectors with high-value information, such as the federal government, manufacturing and the financial industry and is characterized as an unauthorized person gaining access to a network while staying undetected for a long period of time. The purpose of such a threat is to steal data rather than to cause malicious damage to the network.

That evening, he called his bank. A cheerful customer service representative reminded him it was his responsibility to inform the bank when he traveled outside the United States. He did not know it then, but that was his first encounter with an anomaly-detection system.

Why did the bank freeze his account? His credit card being used in a foreign country was considered a high-risk anomaly. With all the data breaches and stolen credit/debit card information traversing the internet, banks and organizations, of both the private and public sectors, are being careful.

First, let us define *anomaly*. *The American Heritage Dictionary* describes anomaly as a deviation or departure from the normal or common order, form, or rule. Anomalies have also been called outliers, exceptions, or peculiarities. When it comes to ICT, an anomaly detector is a software tool that seeks out abnormal digital entities in computing devices or network infrastructure.

Detecting anomalies is not hard once a baseline of what is considered normal has been created. However, there is a complication: how to decide if the detected anomaly is good, bad, or indifferent. For example, a detector will flag a new computer as an anomaly. Moreover, it will do so every scan as the new computer is a departure from the normal baseline, so there must be a way to differentiate good unknowns from bad unknowns from indifferent unknowns. That something would be a classifier. A classifier is a machine learning program that is used to categorize anomalies, keep track of them, and update the anomaly detector to avoid unwarranted alerts.

Referring back to the travel example, as soon as George explained his predicament to customer service, the representative reactivated his credit card, shifted his using a credit card in Paris from an unknown anomaly to an acceptable classifier, which in turn configured the bank's anomaly detector to allow any additional charges he made while in France.

What is significant about anomaly detection is that it takes away the bad guys' element of surprise. The system is still reactive but moves way up the curve, giving ICT departments more of a fighting chance.

The CSF breaks down the anomalies and events categories into five subcategory lower-level outcomes. Those outcomes are identified in Table 5.1 and described in detail in the next several sections of this chapter.

Table 5.1   Framework Core Anomalies and Events Category

CATEGORY	SUBCATEGORY	INFORMATION RESOURCES
Anomalies and Events (DE.AE): Anomalous activity is detected in a timely manner and the potential impact of events is understood.	DE.AE-1: A baseline of network operations and expected data flows for users and systems is established and managed.	• COBIT 5 DSS03.01 • ISA 62443-2-1:2009 4.4.3.3 • NIST SP 800-53 Rev. 4 AC-4, CA-3, CM-2, SI-4
	DE.AE-2: Detected events are analyzed to understand attack targets and methods.	• ISA 62443-2-1:2009 4.3.4.5.6, 4.3.4.5.7, 4.3.4.5.8 • ISA 62443-3-3:2013 SR 2.8, SR 2.9, SR 2.10, SR 2.11, SR 2.12, SR 3.9, SR 6.1, SR 6.2 • ISO/IEC 27001:2013 A.16.1.1, A.16.1.4 • NIST SP 800-53 Rev. 4 AU-6, CA-7, IR-4, SI4
	DE.AE-3: Event data are aggregated and correlated from multiple sources and sensors.	• ISA 62443-3-3:2013 SR 6.1 • NIST SP 800-53 Rev. 4 AU-6, CA-7, IR-4, IR5, IR-8, SI-4
	DE.AE-4: Impact of events is determined.	• COBIT 5 APO12.06 • NIST SP 800-53 Rev. 4 CP-2, IR-4, RA-3, SI 4
	DE.AE-5: Incident alert thresholds are established.	• COBIT 5 APO12.06 • ISA 62443-2-1:2009 4.2.3.10 • NIST SP 800-53 Rev. 4 IR-4, IR-5, IR-8

Source: National Institute of Standards and Technology, *Framework for Improving Critical Infrastructure Cybersecurity.* Gaithersburg, February 12, 2014.

DE.AE-1: A Baseline of Network Operations and Expected Data Flows for Users and Systems Is Established and Managed

Generally, a lot of time in network security is spent discussing the discovery of anomalies that can indicate attack; one thing that sometimes gets forgotten, however, is how fundamental it is to first understand what normal looks like. Establishing baseline data for normal traffic activity and standard configuration for network devices can go a long way toward helping security analysts spot potential problems. There are so many different activities in ICT networks with a high amount of variance that it is extremely difficult to discover security issues without understanding what normal looks like. When ICT organizations establish baseline data, it makes it easier to track deviations from that baseline.

Using DNS traffic as an example, if it is known that the use of dynamic DNS services is at a low 0.25% of normal DNS traffic, an increase to 5% is an anomaly that should be investigated and might well lead to the detection of a cyberattack.

However, simply understanding normal can be a challenging task. Baselining activities can mean tracking many different attributes across multiple dimensions, which means understanding normal host behavior, network behavior, user behavior, and application behavior, along with other internal information, such as the function and vulnerability state of the host. Additionally, external context, such as reputation of IP, plays a factor.

For example, on any given host, understanding normal means knowledge of which processes and services are currently running, which users have access privileges to the host, how often, and what files, databases, and/or applications do those users access. On the network, it means, which hosts communicate with other hosts, what application traffic is generated, and how much traffic is generated.

This is not an easy task and, unfortunately, the open nature of Internet traffic and differing user behavior make it hard to come up with specific baseline recommendations for any organization.

Put simply, networks serve the needs of their users. Users are unique individuals and express their different tastes, preferences, and work styles in the way they interact with the network. The collected metadata about those preferences can act like an impression for that network. And each network impression is going to be as unique as its users who generate the traffic.

Another added dimension to developing baseline is time. The time interval for sampling data for establishment of a benchmark often depends on what kind of abnormality the organization hopes to eventually discover.

For instance, if there is interest in detecting abnormal file access, the organization would want a longer benchmark period building a history of file access per user over a predefined period (such as a month) to compare to a period of the identical length. Moreover, if they want to monitor the number of authentication successes and failures to production systems, they may need to benchmark only the previous day compared to the current day.

While baselines can be useful for detecting deviations, it may actually be useful to think in terms of pattern contrasts rather than normal and abnormal. The term *anomaly* is used a lot because people think of pattern *A* as normal and patterns not *A* as the anomaly, but it might be best to just think about it as a contrast between patterns. Especially as we develop advanced analytics for big data, the general characteristics of data contrasts provide some very useful information.

This type of analysis also makes it less likely to fall victim to attackers who understand how baselines can be used to track deviations. Instead of a single, static baseline, advanced organizations will constantly track patterns and look for contrasts across time. The attacker will always try to understand the target norms because that allows them to elude detection. Think about how hard it would be on an attacker when the organization establishes its own norms and changes them on a regular basis. Regardless of the priorities for establishing the patterns, when a contrast of patterns does identify anomalies, immediate analytical response should be initiated.

When the organization has identified the appropriate parameters needed to classify traffic from the *unknown* to the *known bad* column, it is important to share that information, first internally to control the security of the network, and then more widely, so others might learn how they can detect anything similar on their own networks.

DE.AE-2: Detected Events Are Analyzed
to Understand Attack Targets and Methods

During the process of detecting an anomaly in an organization's ICT systems, two tasks are normally performed: monitoring ICT systems with a variety of tools, normally referred to as intrusion detection systems (IDSs), and followed by sending and receiving notifications of detected events. In order to effectively detect an anomaly, there needs to be an implied knowledge about the organizations' ICT systems and services. For example, it might be useful to know how many e-mails are generated and passed through the system in a day, so a higher number of e-mails signals a potential anomaly. Monitoring tools such as antivirus software can be used to detect viruses and to generate reports about virus activity in the infrastructure. IDSs can be used to "sniff" network traffic to find matches with the signatures of known attacks. A number of challenges hinder monitoring tools' effective usage, however. First, to install an IDS and interpret its output, security personnel must have extensive knowledge of the type of network traffic that is allowed within their organization. Unfortunately, this information is rarely explicitly documented and difficult to obtain. A second challenge relates to the fact that it is sometimes necessary to involve external stakeholders, complicating communication. For example, in the case of IDS installation, a vendor's input is normally required to verify that its server is not blocking IDS traffic, and they generally do not know anything about the target organizational networks. Third, IDSs are embedded into actual production networks that must continue to be operational, complicating the troubleshooting process when issues arise during installation. A fourth challenge is a lack of usability; for example, during the IDS installation, diagnosis of issues can be complicated by misleading and uninformative error messages.

During active monitoring with an IDS, some organizations find it very challenging to generate meaningful reports on monitoring outcomes, largely due to the overwhelming amount of false positives generated. To reduce false positives, an IDS needs to be customized to fit a given organization's characteristics, a time-consuming and difficult process that some organizations prefer to avoid. Another way to target specific networks is by risk assessment (as described in previous chapters). As the above examples demonstrate, tools for monitoring typically have pros and cons. In some instances, security practitioners combined tools in unique ways to maximize their utility, a practice known as bricolage. Due to usability issues and budget constraints, many organizations choose to create their own tools to detect anomalies in the ICT infrastructure. Such tools are typically scripts customized to the organization's specific needs. To create effective scripts, however, organizations need individuals with both technical expertise and knowledge about the IT infrastructure within their organization.

Organizations must also consider how the appropriate administrators are notified of anomalies. The complexity of ICT systems and the lack of resources to actively monitor all systems mean that organizations have to rely on notifications as a passive method of detecting security incidents. Most organizations receive notifications from various stakeholders, including ICT professionals and end users. Often, these notifications require communication among stakeholders. For example, an external organization may detect malicious traffic generated from one of the systems they administer. They may have received this notification from another third party who was notified by another. Organizations also receive notifications about incidents from end users in the form of complaints that the Internet access was blocked.

Once a potential anomaly is detected, security professionals investigate it further by doing at least three tasks: verification, assessment, and tracking the source of the anomaly. During anomaly verification, organizations try to confirm, often with alternate data sources, that a compromise actually occurred. Verification may also require collaboration with external organizations. When organizations have access to machines that stakeholders have reported infected by malicious software, they do not necessarily need tools to confirm the infection. Some techniques use experience to identify patterns that indicate the machine has had malicious software. Likewise, experience can be used during verification to know what type of connection pattern is normal from one server to another.

If an incident is confirmed during its assessment, security professionals estimate the incident's magnitude and consequences. In some organizations, the policy is for the potential cost of the incident to the organization to be communicated to managers who will make a determination of whether to proceed. However, some incidents that do not meet the organization's criteria for high risk may still be investigated by the security team in order to protect their systems.

In tracking the anomaly source, organizations aim to determine the source of the incident. Many organizations use their knowledge about hacking patterns to diagnose the source of an anomaly related to malicious software. They also rely on their technical knowledge to perform forensic tasks on compromised servers. If the source of an incident was due to the actions of an internal employee, stakeholders within human resources may be contacted, for example. When the source of an incident is difficult to diagnose, organizations find it helpful to interact with other specialists, particularly ones who could offer a novel perspective, as they are new to the investigation or have a different background.

In addition to collaboration, another strategy organizations use to identify the cause of an incident involves simulation of the incident. This can be accomplished by collecting information from actual situations and then repeating the conditions of failure. Another approach, perhaps to get more information about malicious traffic causing anomalies, the security team may decide to download the same suspected malicious software to provide such information.

Some security incidents can be solved during the analysis process. In other instances, incident containment is necessary. This is accomplished in various ways, including turning off ports or services in external organizations and cleaning up ICT systems by reinstalling software.

DE.AE-3: Event Data Are Aggregated and Correlated from Multiple Sources and Sensors

As each event occurs, data are collected about that event in log files. The implemented intrusion detection system reviews each log file, looking for patterns or signatures that may indicate an attack or intrusion is in progress or has already occurred. While an individual host intrusion detection and prevention system (IDPS) can examine the activity in only one system, a log file monitor can look at multiple log files from different systems.

The NIST Guide to Computer Security Log Management states that information regarding an incident may be recorded in several places, such as firewalls, routers, network IDPS, host IDPS, and application logs. Organizations should deploy one or more centralized log file monitors and configure logging devices throughout the organization to send duplicates of their log entries to the centralized log monitor. In general, this outcome recommends the creation of a log management infrastructure, which consists of the hardware, software, networks, and media used to generate, transmit, store, analyze, and dispose of log data.

DE.AE-4: Impact of Events Is Determined

There are two perspectives to the interpretation of the DE.AE-4 CSF outcome. The first would be the case in which the organization takes a reactive approach to determining the impact of events. Such an approach puts the organization in a position of suffering the consequences of damages caused by the event; after which an analysis of the data generated by the event results in new or improved cybersecurity policies, procedures, and countermeasures. The second, and probably preferred, approach would be to be proactive in determining the impact of events before they happen. Such considerations are made during the risk assessment process.

Recall from discussions in previous chapters that before an organization commits resources to cybersecurity and ICT controls, it must know which assets require protection and the extent to which those assets are vulnerable. Risk assessment determines the level of risk to the organization if a given event occurs. The caveat to that, however, is that not all risks can be anticipated or measured in terms of their impact, but most organizations will be able to acquire some understanding of the risks they face. Managers working with ICT security specialists should try to determine the value of assets, points of vulnerability, likelihood of the event, and potential for damage.

DE.AE-5: Incident Alert Thresholds Are Established

Let us revisit the hypothetical situation that was introduced at the beginning of the section "Anomalies and Events Category" of this chapter. In order to adequately detect an event, George Wilson's bank likely established an incident alert threshold. The threshold is normally a number or percentage of instances of the event, but that does not always have to be the case. George was in Paris when he attempted to use his credit card. His financial institution may have chosen to flag all incidents taking place outside the boundary of North America. More commonly, financial institutions will establish a threshold of three to five declined transactions, or three to five transactions on a given day in amounts greater than 25% of the average amount for that credit card. Another common use of thresholds is for authentication into privileged areas of an organization's network. For example, three unsuccessful attempts could trigger locking of access privileges until verification of the event can take place.

Many organizations use thresholds as a metric to determine the frequency certain ICT components and assets are reassessed. A particular event exceeding the defined threshold may evoke action in the form of updated security countermeasures, policies, and procedures. In some cases, the threshold may be found to be inadequate, in which case the organization may choose to make an adjustment. However, such changes should be implemented consistent with the organization's risk management strategy.

Security Continuous Monitoring Category

Since it is impossible to prevent all attacks, organizations need to ensure that they detect attacks as quickly as possible. The concept of continuous monitoring has been gaining momentum, driven by both compliance mandates and the U.S. government's guidance on Continuous Diagnostics and Mitigation, as a means to move beyond periodic assessment. This makes sense given the speed that attacks can increase within an ICT environment.

Given the different definitions of security monitoring, we suggest a risk-based approach to monitoring and assessing critical devices. That means ensuring that the most critical assets are truly monitored continuously, and by *continuous*, we mean uninterrupted. The vast majority of devices in an ICT environment probably do not need continuous monitoring. Yet for those devices that are very critical, intermittent assessment leaves a window of exposure for the attackers, a window that you cannot afford.

Despite our interpretation of the word *continuous*, the CSF describes this category outcome as "the information system and assets are monitored at discrete intervals to identify cybersecurity events and verify the effectiveness of protective measures" (National Institute of Standards and Technology Feb. 2014). That description aligns with the NIST definition of information security continuous monitoring:

> Information security continuous monitoring (ISCM) is maintaining ongoing awareness of information security, vulnerabilities, and threats to support organizational risk management decisions.
>
> The terms "continuous" and "ongoing" in this context mean that security controls and organizational risks are assessed, analyzed and reported at a frequency sufficient to support risk-based security decisions as needed to adequately protect organization information. Data collection, no matter how frequent, is performed at discrete intervals. (Dempsey et al. 2011)

The CSF breaks down the security continuous monitoring category into eight subcategory outcomes. The outcomes are identified in Table 5.2.

DE.CM-1: Network Is Monitored to Detect Potential Cybersecurity Events

As data breaches become a more frequent and damaging occurrence, organizations are being forced to focus on analyzing every possible way that a malicious attacker is able to exploit their ICT systems.

Table 5.2   Framework Core Security Continuous Monitoring Category

CATEGORY	SUBCATEGORY	INFORMATION RESOURCES
Security Continuous Monitoring (DE.CM): The information system and assets are monitored at discrete intervals to identify cybersecurity events and verify the effectiveness of protective measures.	DE.CM-1: The network is monitored to detect potential cybersecurity events.	• CCS CSC 14, 16 • COBIT 5 DSS05.07 • ISA 62443-3-3:2013 SR 6.2 • NIST SP 800-53 Rev. 4 AC-2, AU-12, CA-7 • CM-3, SC-5, SC-7, SI-4
	DE.CM-2: The physical environment is monitored to detect potential cybersecurity events.	• ISA 62443-2-1:2009 4.3.3.3.8 • NIST SP 800-53 Rev. 4 CA-7, PE-3, PE-6, PE20
	DE.CM-3: Personnel activity is monitored to detect potential cybersecurity events.	• ISA 62443-3-3:2013 SR 6.2 • ISO/IEC 27001:2013 A.12.4.1 • NIST SP 800-53 Rev. 4 AC-2, AU-12, AU-13 • CA-7, CM-10, CM-11
	DE.CM-4: Malicious code is detected.	• CCS CSC 5 • COBIT 5 DSS05.01 • ISA 62443-2-1:2009 4.3.4.3.8 ISA 62443-3-3:2013 SR 3.2 • ISO/IEC 27001:2013 A.12.2.1 • NIST SP 800-53 Rev. 4 SI-3
	DE.CM-5: Unauthorized mobile code is detected.	• ISA 62443-3-3:2013 SR 2.4 • ISO/IEC 27001:2013 A.12.5.1 • NIST SP 800-53 Rev. 4 SC-18, SI-4. SC-44
	DE.CM-6: External service provider activity is monitored to detect potential cybersecurity events.	• COBIT 5 APO07.06 • ISO/IEC 27001:2013 A.14.2.7, A.15.2.1 • NIST SP 800-53 Rev. 4 CA-7, PS-7, SA-4, SA9, SI-4
	DE.CM-7: Monitoring for unauthorized personnel, connections, devices, and software is performed.	• NIST SP 800-53 Rev. 4 AU-12, CA-7, CM-3, CM-8, PE-3, PE-6, PE-20, SI-4
	DE.CM-8: Vulnerability scans are performed.	• COBIT 5 BAI03.10 • ISA 62443-2-1:2009 4.2.3.1, 4.2.3.7 ISO/IEC 27001:2013 A.12.6.1 • NIST SP 800-53 Rev. 4 RA-5

Source: National Institute of Standards and Technology, *Framework for Improving Critical Infrastructure Cybersecurity.* Gaithersburg, February 12, 2014.

While it is important to know where vulnerabilities lie, large organizations including the U.S. government are still experiencing devastating cyberattacks after analyzing their systems' weaknesses.

The intrusions suffered by these groups exploited not only the complexity of modern ICT systems but also human nature. Some organizations become vulnerable by their use of interconnected systems, while others are victims of sophisticated spear phishing schemes. With so many places to gain entry and a wide variety of methods to attack, data breaches are all but guaranteed to happen to an organization. With this in mind, organizations need to move away from just trying to prevent cyberattacks and instead provide additional focus on mitigating the associated risks.

ICT professionals need to understand how to proceed after different types of assets have been compromised. If financial data are exploited or intellectual property is stolen, what are the backup plans in place to make the fallout as minimal as possible? Once those processes are put in place, risk management teams should develop strategies to detect breaches as soon as possible, since mitigation efforts will not mean anything if the company does not know it has been infiltrated.

With a network monitoring solution, organizations receive continuous surveillance of systems in order to identify malicious activity as soon as possible. Network monitoring refers to the practice of overseeing the operation of a computer network using specialized management software tools. Network monitoring systems are used to ensure availability and overall performance of host computers and network services. These systems are typically employed on larger scale corporate and university IT networks.

A network monitoring system is capable of detecting and reporting failures of devices or connections. It normally measures the processor (central processing unit) utilization of hosts, the network bandwidth utilization of links, and other aspects of operation. It will often send messages (sometimes called watchdog messages) over the network to each host to verify if it is responsive to requests. When failures, unacceptably slow response, or other unexpected behavior is detected, these systems send additional messages called alerts to designated locations (such as a management server, an e-mail address, or a phone number) to notify system.

The ping program is one very simple example of a network monitoring program. Ping is a software tool available on most computers that sends IP test messages between two hosts. Anyone on the network can run these basic ping tests to verify that the connection between two computers is working and also measure the current connection performance.

While ping is useful in some situations, more sophisticated network monitoring systems exist. These software programs are designed for use by professional administrators of larger computer networks.

DE.CM-2: Physical Environment Is Monitored to
Detect Potential Cybersecurity Events

Recall from Chapter 4 that access control is a large part of how organizations protect ICT assets (including data, external media, and physical equipment). The CSF emphasizes the need for access control, again, by defining an outcome requiring organizations monitor their physical environment as a facet of cybersecurity detection. Ensuring appropriate access to the physical environment can be accomplished in many ways depending upon the individual risk priorities of the organization. Nevertheless, most organizations choose electronic monitoring and alarm systems to detect unauthorized access.

Monitoring equipment record events that a human being might miss and are useful in areas where other types of physical controls are not practical. Electronic monitoring is not used exclusively to safeguard ICT assets. Many retail stores use video monitoring cameras, which are cameras concealed in silver globes attached to ceilings. Attached to those cameras are video recorders and related components designed to capture the video feed. Electronic monitoring includes closed-circuit television systems. Some of those systems collect constant video feeds, while others sample each area of the physical environment by rotating input.

Video monitoring systems have drawbacks, however. First, they are passive and do not prevent access or prohibited activity. That, alone, speaks to the necessity to implement detection controls in combination with protective measures. Second, since there is no intelligent system capable of interpreting the video feed, human intervention becomes necessary. To determine if unauthorized activities have occurred, a security staff must be in place to constantly monitor the video in real time or perform reviews at predetermined intervals. For this reason, closed-circuit TV is used predominantly for evidence collection and forensics after an event has taken place.

Closely related to monitoring are the alarms that notify personnel or systems that an event has taken place. Alarms have the capability of detecting physical intrusion or other unexpected event. Examples of such events include a break-in, fire, flooding, or interruption of service caused by power failure. To detect intrusion, these alarms rely on sensors, including motion detectors, glass breakage detectors, or contact sensors.

Motion detectors can be either active or passive. Some emit energy beams typically in the form of laser lights, ultrasound, or sound waves. If the energy from the beam projected into the monitored area is disrupted, an alarm is sounded. Glass breakage detectors are similar to motion detectors with the exception that the sensors are embedded directly into the glass. When the glass is broken, the alarm is sounded. Contact sensors sound the alarm when a foot steps onto a pressure-sensitive pad under a rug, or when a sensor is affixed to a window and that window is unexpectedly opened.

DE.CM-3: Personnel Activity Is Monitored
to Detect Potential Cybersecurity Events

Lack of a security management process exposes an organization to risks. To help mitigate these risks, the organization needs to create a culture that raises the awareness of security and privacy among its workforce. The CSF addresses that need in the awareness and training outcome of the Protect Function. However, IT security implementation is more than just what takes place among the bits and bytes. It is also how people behave in the workplace. One employee's use of another's password probably indicates the need for a change in the overall culture. Organizations have to get all personnel to become part of an organizational culture of compliance.

Monitor personnel as well as processes. When evaluating employee response to security incidents, it is important for organizations to pay attention to employee behavior—and not just when dealing with electronic information. Who has access to the records management room?

Who can go in and out of there on a regular basis? Improperly protected paper files can be as much of a threat to organizational security as a stolen laptop.

DE.CM-4: Malicious Code Is Detected

Malicious code is software that performs unauthorized functions, causing the normal operation of an ICT system to be abnormal. According to the Committee on National Security Systems Instruction 4009 National Informational Assurance Glossary (2006), the definition states that a malicious code is "software or firmware intended to perform an unauthorized process that will have adverse impact on the confidentiality, integrity, or availability of an information system (IS)."

There are several types of malicious code such as viruses, worms, Trojan horses, and programming flaws. The programming flaws can be included with malicious intent or just be bad programming practices.

It is important to ensure that software is free of malicious code. The private and public organizations should extend more effort in preventing malicious code in their software development practices.

There are several ways that software development practices can incorporate checks for malicious code and in turn promote software that can be used with an assurance that the product is free of malicious code. Organizations should also ensure that any freeware or shareware used in the development of a product be certified to be free of malicious code. There are methods by which the freeware and shareware can be certified as being reviewed for malicious code. The user of software should be able to trust in software they are using.

Detection and prevention of malicious code during software development can be accomplished through software code inspection, through independent vulnerability assessments, and by using tools throughout the software development life cycle that identify potential area of malicious behavior.

To ensure that malicious code is not inserted during development, the internal or external developer should have processes in place that mandate software code inspections with an emphasis on reviewing the code for malicious behavior. A code compare tool, using either manual or automated processes, should be performed against all modified software units. Software security personnel who are not the original creator of the code should examine all developed units for malicious or unintended code. Moreover, the code being inspected should be controlled through a formal configuration management process.

DE.CM-5: Unauthorized Mobile Code Is Detected

Mobile code consists of programs that can be executed on one or several hosts other than the one that they were developed on. Mobility of such programs requires some built-in capability for each piece of code to travel smoothly from one host to another. Mobile code is associated with at least two parties: its producer and its consumer—the consumer being the host that runs the code.

Mobile code applications range from Java applets to intelligent software agents. These applications offer several advantages over the more traditional distributed computing approaches: flexibility in software design beyond the well-established object oriented development approach and bandwidth optimization, just to name two of them.

As usual, increased flexibility comes with the cost of increased vulnerability to malicious intrusion, often via the Internet. Possible vulnerabilities with mobile code fall in one of two categories: attacks performed by a mobile program against the remote host on which the program is executed as with malicious applets or ActiveX programs and the less classical category of attacks caused by the installation of the mobile code and its data by the remote environment.

When protecting a host from potentially malicious code or employing the appropriate detection mechanisms, code mobility imposes the following security features:

- Host and mobile code have separate identities; therefore, the mobile code's origin must be authenticated.
- Mobile code is exposed through the network; therefore, the host must verify the integrity of the mobile code it just received.
- The host does not generate the mobile code, but another party does. Consequently, the actions it performs must be limited through access control and/or checked through verification controls.

DE.CM-6: External Service Provider Activity Is Monitored
to Detect Potential Cybersecurity Events

Not surprisingly, this is the third time that we have seen the CSF address external entities. We encountered the discussion in Chapter 3 while discussing the outcome requiring cataloging external information systems in the asset management category of the Identify Function. And in Chapter 4, they are addressed in terms of third parties understanding responsibilities and roles as an outcome of the awareness and training category of the Protect Function. In this and those two other outcomes, the CSF maps to the NIST SP 800-53 SA-9 control which states that "the organization:

1. Requires that providers of external information system services comply with organizational information security requirements and employ (Assignment: organization-defined security controls) in accordance with applicable federal laws, Executive Orders, directives, policies, regulations, standards, and guidance;
2. Defines and documents government oversight and user roles and responsibilities with regard to external information system services; and
3. Employs (Assignment: organization-defined processes, methods, and techniques) to monitor security control compliance by external service providers on an ongoing basis" (National Institute for Standards and Technology Apr. 2014).

In that regard, it makes sense to discuss that control in more detail.

SA-9 requires that contracts and agreements with providers of external information system services include the following details: services comply with organizational information security requirements and services employ appropriate security controls in accordance with federal laws, executive orders, directives, policies, regulations, standards, and guidance. Documentation provided by providers of Energy Industry Super Scheme (EISS) includes the following: security roles and responsibilities for government, service provider, and end users and service level agreements. The control continues by requiring an organizational risk assessment be conducted prior to the acquisition or outsourcing. Lastly, external providers and systems are regularly monitored for compliance with security controls.

To monitor the risks associated with the use of external providers effectively, the organization should evaluate the adequacy of a provider's internal and security controls. Management should ensure that the provider develops and adheres to appropriate policies, procedures, and standards. When conducting its evaluation, the organization should consider the results of internal audits conducted by institution staff or a user group, as well as external audits and control reviews conducted by qualified sources.

The organizations review of the audit should include an assessment of the following factors in order to determine the adequacy of a service provider's internal and security controls:

1. The practicality of the service provider having an internal auditor, and the auditor's level of training and experience;
2. The service provider's external auditors' training and background; and
3. Internal IT audit techniques of the service provider.

DE.CM-7: Monitoring for Unauthorized Personnel,
Connections, Devices, and Software Is Performed

There are a number of tools available that provide monitoring of computer traffic, unauthorized actions, the connection of portable disks, and the legality of the installed software. They provide security not only of the ICT resources but also of the reputation of the company, employees' intellectual property, and customer privacy. Most employers see monitoring as a method to improve productiveness. On the other hand, employees fear control and consider it as a method of invigilation. That is why monitoring software is commonly called the software for spying on employees. However, is spying really the point of it all? Thorough control of employees' actions and improvement of the usage index of their equipment does not always give better results and attain goals and the success of the company. Sometimes relationships, mutual trust, the atmosphere, or creativeness gets hurt in the process. Everything depends on how the employees are informed about the issues related to the monitoring of devices they are using.

Employee monitoring software can help to improve work productivity, but will never replace effective goal-oriented management nor the time that the employees are to spend actively using a computer device. From the perspective of ICT departments, employee productivity is not so important. For people responsible for telecommunications and ICT infrastructure in the company, the most important aspect of such monitoring is ICT security and the opportunity to limit those, often inadvertent, employees' actions, which might harm it.

DE.CM-8: Vulnerability Scans Are Performed

Similar to other security tools, vulnerability scanning can help an organization secure their network or it can be used by the attackers to identify weaknesses in a system to mount an attack against. The idea is for organizations to use these tools to identify and fix these weaknesses before the attackers use them on the organization. The goal of running a vulnerability scanner is to identify devices on the network that are open to known vulnerabilities. Different scanners accomplish this goal through a variety of means. Some work better than others. Some may look for signs such as registry entries to identify that a specific patch or update has been implemented. Others actually attempt to exploit the vulnerability on each target device rather than relying on registry information. One issue with vulnerability scanners is their impact on the devices they are scanning. On the one hand, it is desirable for the scan to be able to be performed in the background without affecting the device. On the other hand, it is important to be sure that the scan is thorough. Often, in the interest of being thorough and depending on how the scanner gathers its information or verifies that the device is vulnerable, the scan can be intrusive and cause adverse effects and even system crashes on the device being scanned.

In most cases, there will be patches or updates available to cure the problem. Sometimes, though, there may be operational or business reasons why the patch should not be applied or the vendor of vulnerability scanner may not yet have released an update or patch. In those cases, organizations need to consider alternative means to mitigate the threat. Above and beyond performing regular updates of antivirus software and applying the necessary patches for any new critical vulnerabilities, it is wise to implement a schedule for periodic vulnerability scans to make sure nothing has been missed. Quarterly or semiannual vulnerability scanning can go a long way to helping you make sure you catch any weaknesses in your network before the attackers do.

Detection Processes Category

The number of high profile incidents of malicious software threats and attacks that have dominated media reporting for the past several years has raised awareness and forced most organizations to invest time and resources into defending against this ubiquitous security issue. However, the greatest threat to critical infrastructure may not be in the form of an attack from the outside, such as from a virus, but may well reside within the internal network itself.

Attacks launched from inside a business network have a very high potential for damage, especially if performed by personnel who hold trusted positions and who have access to all the network resources within a company. When the risks posed by both external and internal threats are carefully examined, many businesses decide to research systems that can monitor networks and detect attacks wherever they may originate.

Organizations understand that cybersecurity monitoring processes are not open for discussion; they are a requirement. As such, many industries have enacted regulations related to cybersecurity monitoring. The ever-changing regulatory environment and continually increasing demands placed on regulated organizations to secure their networks, track the identification of people who access resources, and protect private information place greater demands on organizations around the world to institute effective cybersecurity monitoring processes.

There are several reasons why security monitoring and attack detection should also be an important issue to organizations not necessarily obligated to comply with any regulatory requirements. These reasons include the consequences any organization could face if an attack on their critical infrastructure were to succeed. Not only could business operations be disrupted, resulting in productivity losses and even monetary loss, an organization could even suffer from a loss of reputation, which often takes longer to recover from than any other loss incurred due to an attack.

A cybersecurity detection process is really a continual series of activities related to planning, implementing, managing, and testing, because that is the very nature of cybersecurity detection. Because the threats to networks are always changing, the system that monitors the security in a network must also change.

Application of this process to security monitoring fits with the CSF, which you have learned seeks to accomplish the following:

- Assess organizational exposure and identify which assets to secure.
- Identify ways to reduce risk to acceptable levels.
- Design a plan to mitigate security risks.
- Monitor the efficiency of security mechanisms.
- Reevaluate effectiveness and security requirements regularly.

Many organizations agree that there are numerous challenges when attempting to construct effective cybersecurity detection processes and institute policies that support that effort. These challenges include

- Understanding the need and the benefits of securing the entire network environment from internal and external threats;
- Designing an effective security monitoring and attack detection process that includes methods that detect and prevent efforts to work around established policies;
- Implementing comprehensive and effective monitoring polices that not only detect attacks but also provide an overall picture of an environment's security level for remediation efforts;
- Maintaining policies and processes that efficiently correlate security reports with established policies to ease administrative efforts in detecting suspicious activities;
- Implementing and enforcing efficient business practices and policies that support security monitoring efforts while balancing business needs; and
- Determining acceptable risk thresholds to balance usability and risk mitigation.

A comprehensive cybersecurity detection process not only assists with the need to perform forensic analysis but can also be a proactive security measure capable of supplying information prior to, during, and after an attack. By providing a centralized repository for security reports, an attack can be detected during the probing phase, as the

Table 5.3   Framework Core Detection Processes Category

CATEGORY	SUBCATEGORY	INFORMATION RESOURCES
Detection Processes (DE.DP): Detection processes and procedures are maintained and tested to ensure timely and adequate awareness of anomalous events.	DE.DP-1: Roles and responsibilities for detection are well defined to ensure accountability.	• CCS CSC 5 • COBIT 5 DSS05.01 • ISA 62443-2-1:2009 4.4.3.1 • ISO/IEC 27001:2013 A.6.1.1 • NIST SP 800-53 Rev. 4 CA-2, CA-7, PM-14
	DE.DP-2: Detection activities comply with all applicable requirements.	• ISA 62443-2-1:2009 4.4.3.2 • ISO/IEC 27001:2013 A.18.1.4 • NIST SP 800-53 Rev. 4 CA-2, CA-7, PM-14, SI-4
	DE.DP-3: Detection processes are tested.	• COBIT 5 APO13.02 • ISA 62443-2-1:2009 4.4.3.2 • ISA 62443-3-3:2013 SR 3.3 • ISO/IEC 27001:2013 A.14.2.8 • NIST SP 800-53 Rev. 4 CA-2, CA-7, PE-3, PM-14, SI-3, SI-4
	DE.DP-4: Event detection information is communicated to appropriate parties.	• COBIT 5 APO12.06 • ISA 62443-2-1:2009 4.3.4.5.9 • ISA 62443-3-3:2013 SR 6.1 • ISO/IEC 27001:2013 A.16.1.2 • NIST SP 800-53 Rev. 4 AU-6, CA-2, CA-7, RA-5, SI-4
	DE.DP-5: Detection processes are continuously improved.	• COBIT 5 APO11.06, DSS04.05 • ISA 62443-2-1:2009 4.4.3.4 • ISO/IEC 27001:2013 A.16.1.6 • NIST SP 800-53 Rev. 4, CA-2, CA-7, PL-2, RA-5, SI-4, PM-14

Source: National Institute of Standards and Technology, *Framework for Improving Critical Infrastructure Cybersecurity.* Gaithersburg, February 12, 2014.

attack occurs, or immediately following the attack to supply responders with the information they need to react to an attack effectively, which can reduce the impact of intrusion attempts. The CSF breaks down the detection process category into five subcategory outcomes. The outcomes are identified in Table 5.3.

DE.DP-1: Roles and Responsibilities for Detection
Are Well Defined to Ensure Accountability

Most organizations cannot afford to separate network and security obligations. However, if it is large enough to split up networking, laboratory, and security detection functions, then do not share duties. There needs to be a clear delineation between networking and security detection because the group's focuses and goals are different. Networking's responsibilities mainly involve keeping resources up and available. Security detection is about monitoring the system for abnormalities and events, and compared to networking, this is sometimes unfortunately considered a less important business priority.

Not only should the networking group and security group have distinct and clearly defined tasks and responsibilities, but also they should have separate chains of command. The security group should not report to the networking group (i.e., network administrator or chief information officer [CIO]). Many organizations do have their security departments reporting to the CIO, but this is only because they do not have a chief security officer (CISSO). Problems can occur when sharing the same chain of command. For instance, let us say someone in security informs a network administrator that there is an unsafe rule set on the firewall. This traffic setting, though, may have been implemented by the network administrator to support a business need or a user's particular preference. There is a chance then that the administrator may rank the network concerns more of a priority than the security issue and ignore the information.

A security officer can delegate some tasks, but this is often done incorrectly. The process is usually sloppy, and clear lines of responsibility are frequently not laid out. If a security officer delegates some security tasks to another individual, the decision should be approved by someone in a higher position and the change in responsibilities should be documented.

The arrangement of responsibilities depends on the type of organization. In a privately held organization, there will not be any auditors or regulators forcing any form of compliance. If the organization is privately held, it should still follow the best practices stated earlier. That way, the organization is better protected and better able to mitigate potential anomalies and threatening events.

If the organization is public or a government agency, auditors (internal and external) will be detecting whether segregation of duties (introduced in Chapter 4) is in place and whether boundaries are being crossed.

DE.DP-2: Detection Activities Comply with All Applicable Requirements

The assurance of detection activities alignment with business, regulatory, and contractual requirements is generally the same as what is necessary of any other ICT life cycle process. The solution is oversight and control.

Five steps are required to create a formal detection oversight and control management function. The first step is initiation, which requires the organization to define the leadership for security review, operational roles, and a formal organizational plan. The next step requires identification of relevant review issues, which is usually done in conjunction with acquisition and line project managers. In this process, the review manager and staff must identify and prioritize the key review issues.

Then, the organization creates a generic review plan in which all pertinent audit and control activities are defined. Required standards and practices are also identified and the review plan is integrated with the project management plan. Once the review plan has been developed, the organization deploys the procedures to guide the review process. This process normally involves training reviewers to perform reviews correctly. When the review personnel are prepared, the organization implements the review process. This involves assigning roles and responsibilities, development of a schedule, defining and performing monitoring activities, and reporting and resolving problems. The review program must be evaluated periodically to determine whether it is performing effectively and as intended.

Reviews must be able to provide sufficient, documented proof that the detection processes conform to the requirements of the contract and any other regulatory requirements. In addition, the review must warrant that the outcomes of those processes comply with established requirements and adhere to plans. If problems are identified during the review process, they must be documented and resolved before the review moves forward.

Because the outcomes of review processes provide critical information that documents the history of the detection process, the results must be recorded and stored. Also, because the results of reviews are important to the business functions throughout the organization, records of their outcomes must be easily accessible to all managers.

DE.DP-3: Detection Processes Are Tested

Once a detection process is established, the organization should test each activity for conformance to risk requirements documented in the risk management plan. The ultimate goal of a test is to determine if a control is implemented properly to support or enforce a security requirement established by policy. Mapping test procedures to policy is necessary to manage the testing process. One way to do this is to create a process requirements testing matrix. The matrix is a management tool that has two parts. The first part is used to manage the life cycle of the process requirement. As tests change, it is helpful to know the history of a particular requirement or procedure. The second part is used to manage process activities, each activity in a similar manner as requirements.

The tests are conducted through manual or automated methods. Manual methods imply that a given test is performed by an evaluator in a step-by-step process. For example, a test scenario may be presented to the evaluator that requires the detection of a declined credit card transaction similar to what was described in the opening section of this chapter. The evaluator would test the process by deliberately forcing the decline of a transaction while noting the process response to the anomaly using the matrix. Automated methods are performed in much the same way with the exception being that the test is performed through an automated process. An advantage to the automated method is the ability to repeat the identical steps each time the test is performed. However, while the steps of a manual test may vary slightly each time, human knowledge of a peculiar circumstance within one of the process activities during the test will provide the means for quicker corrective action to that particular activity.

DE.DP-4: Event Detection Information
Is Communicated to Appropriate Parties

The importance of effective event detection reporting for organizations cannot be understated. Information is the lifeblood of any organization. All organizations store and use sensitive data related to their functions, employees, clients, financial information, or trade secrets. The only way to protect these critical data is to produce a useful security report that clearly shows where vulnerabilities to security exist so that they may be remediated, thus preventing breaches that might potentially be disastrous.

Effective detection reporting is necessary to stay informed about security issues on all levels of an organization. Data security and the networks that provide communication and processing functions affect everyone. Anyone in the organization that must use data or network security information needs to stay on top of what is happening, whether through a bird's-eye view needed by executives or through a more detailed view needed by analysts and members of ICT teams.

Another aspect of effective detection reporting is that it allows for quick remediation of vulnerabilities, which is vital to any organization. Vulnerabilities should be remediated as soon as they are discovered. If a vulnerability is not fixed and is allowed to languish, a breach of security could occur through that vulnerability, causing major problems for the organization. When security-reporting methodology is truly effective, it not only pinpoints trouble spots but also detects patterns inherent to similar vulnerabilities, giving analysts fast and accurate means of remediation.

Effective detection reporting also facilitates organizational communication. Organizations must be able to smoothly communicate about any kind of issue, and security certainly is one of the most important of these. Interdepartmental communication about vulnerabilities is enhanced by detection reporting that makes use of a methodology by which information about security may be easily distributed in an understandable, actionable way to all people who need to make use of the information. When communication is seamless, security is greatly improved.

DE.DP-5: Detection Processes Are Continuously Improved

When a cybersecurity event takes place, most organizations focus only on getting back to normal after an attack, with actions such as reimaging of systems, changing firewall rules, and updating intrusion detection system software. While these steps are important, they do not sufficiently reduce future risks. However, risk can be reduced by defining high-level objectives and detailed processes and procedures for detecting events. In turn, an organization can gain clearer and more detailed insights into the event. This helps them detect, investigate, and remediate attacks more rapidly and effectively and reduce the risk of damage.

In ICT security, as in many other areas, nonvigilant efforts lead to poor quality results, which can leave dangerous gaps in an organization's defenses. Predefined, monitored, and enforced process activities help assure accountability and consistency and can be more easily tracked to improve an organization's security detection posture over time. When it comes to critical events, most organizations take a reactive approach and are generally good at fighting fires and containing an event before anything really bad happens.

An organization is on its way to continuous improved detection processes if it prioritizes events to focus the most attention, staff, and budget on its highest-value ICT components, as well as those platforms that are most vulnerable to an attack. The organization has reached an even higher level of maturity if its event detection is guided by clear governance rules and understandable guidelines.

Effective event detection improves the organization's security posture over time. This requires thorough and complete documentation of the process for detecting the event, both during and after the investigation. That data should be used to improve the organization's processes and systems for detecting, investigating, and limiting the damage from future incidents. The data should address metrics such as mean time to incident detection and resolution, as well as indicate the general level of effectiveness of existing countermeasures. This enables the organization to determine whether budget is being allocated optimally.

To achieve continued improvement, detection processes must be repeatable and measurable through key performance indicators (KPIs) that are relevant to the business. If one KPI is time-to-resolution, the organization's performance against it can help identify what people, processes, or technology helped or stood in the way of reaching that goal. An incident management system can help identify the root cause, set a measurable goal to learn from the past, and measure whether and how the response is improving.

More mature organizations also document use cases in knowledge management systems that describe actual situations and threat scenarios specific to them. This helps assure that the rest of the team can learn from past incidents and improve their response.

Chapter Summary

- One of the biggest challenges faced by organizations is that cybersecurity attacks are constantly changing. As quickly as mechanisms are in place to detect existing attacks, new ways of exploiting ICT systems surface. An evolving detection process will help organizations minimize the effect of the ever-changing scope of cybersecurity attacks.
- The Detect Function supports an organization's immediate awareness of anomalies and events, allowing them to quickly change their tactics in limiting or containing the impact of the event. Examples of outcomes include detecting anomalies and events; continuous monitoring of information systems and assets; and maintaining, testing, and continually improving detection processes.
- A risk-based approach to continuous security monitoring and assessing critical devices is suggested. That means what the organization considers as its most critical assets are continuously monitored. Most organizations will use tools called IDSs for that purpose.
- Similar to other ICT system life cycle processes, a cybersecurity detection process is really a continual series of activities related to planning, implementing, managing, and testing. As is the case with other life cycle processes, detection processes must be maintained, tested, and organizational policies in place that promotes continuous improvement.

Case Project

Suny Corporation would like you to continue the work you have been doing on the plan for implementing the Framework for Improving Critical Infrastructure Cybersecurity. Now that you are familiar with the outcomes of the Detect Function, they would like you to update your plan with more specific criteria related to detection process continuous improvement. Within the plan only major steps of implementation need to be organized. In other words, focus on steps that the framework recommends for establishing and improving their cybersecurity program. The plan should continue to take the form of a project timeline that describes when each part of every step is performed. Besides providing a customized timeline and plan, include the business justification for each step.

6
RESPOND FUNCTION

After reading this chapter and completing the case project, you will

- Understand the steps that an organization should follow in the aftermath of a cybersecurity event;
- Understand the conceptual pieces of an incident response plan;
- Understand the roles and responsibilities of the computer security incident response team;
- Understand the importance of communication throughout the incident response process; and
- Understand varying strategies of incident response and need for improving on those strategies through lessons learned.

Cybersecurity response, more commonly referred to as incident response, is an organized approach to addressing and managing the negative effects created by a security breach or attack. The goal is to handle the situation in a way that limits damage and reduces recovery time and costs. An incident response plan includes a policy that defines, in specific terms, what constitutes an incident and provides a step-by-step process that should be followed when an incident occurs.

In this chapter, we begin addressing organizational needs to deal with the aftermath of an event. Many believe that the work of response and recovery (introduced in the next chapter) is entirely the responsibility of management. To the contrary, an organization's incident response is conducted by the computer incident response team, a carefully selected group that, in addition to security and general IT staff, may include representatives from legal, human resources, and public relations departments. As is the case with all other aspects of cybersecurity, an organization can prevent and react to security events much more effectively if everyone involved in developing and using the ICT assets participate in the security process, and management provides the appropriate oversight.

Respond Function Overview

Cybercriminals are successfully targeting organizations of all sizes across all industry sectors. Recent analyst and media reports suggest that attacks are becoming increasingly sophisticated and more frequent and their impact more severe. One global company that suffered a large breach spent over $100 million on investigating the incident and on other direct remediation activities. But those costs are small compared to the subsequent multibillion-dollar loss in market capitalization, which was largely attributed to investors' loss of confidence in the company's ability to respond.

That is why it is not enough to focus, as many enterprises do, on defending their ICT system with cybertechnologies such as intrusion detection and data-loss prevention. When determined attackers set their minds on finding a way inside, every organization with valuable digitized information is at risk of having its system breached and its critical assets compromised.

Moreover, most organizations today would do well to expand their efforts to mitigate the consequences of security breaches, which likely affect infrastructure systems and compromise key data such as personally identifiable information. The CSF prescribes outcomes requiring the enforcement of procedures defined in incident response/business continuity plan (created and managed through the controls that satisfy the PR.IP-9 outcome of the Protect Function) which guides the response to such breaches. Recall that the primary objective of this plan is to manage a cybersecurity event or incident in a way that limits damage, increases the confidence of external stakeholders, and reduces recovery time and costs.

When an incident response (IR) team is faced with a potential security breach or data loss, there are many concerns to address. Many incident management plans address technical issues such as investigation, containment, and recovery. But it is essential that each phase of the plan also covers communication, which is a key requirement for effective IR.

The incident communication strategy must cover compliance-related issues, media communications, and internal communications. And it must strike a balance between openness and protection. Revealing more information than necessary could result in undue escalation or exposure of an exploitable weakness that has not yet been remedied. However, withholding information can cast your organization in a negative light and create the impression that you have something to hide. Recognizing the importance of communication, the CSF outcomes go beyond the scope of addressing communication just within the IR plan, by defining outcomes that address voluntary communication between the organization and its stakeholder in order to achieve greater cybersecurity awareness.

Two other areas of IR addressed by the CSF are analysis and mitigation. Essentially, incident analysis is an examination of all available information and supporting evidence or artifacts related to an incident or event. Mitigation is the practice of preventing the incident from happening again in the future.

The purpose of the analysis is to identify the scope of the incident, the extent of damage caused by the incident, the nature of the incident, and available response strategies or work-arounds. The computer security incident response team (CSIRT) may use the results of vulnerability and forensic analysis to understand and provide the most complete and up-to-date analysis of what has happened on a specific system. The CSIRT compares activities across incidents to determine any interrelations, trends, patterns, or intruder signatures.

There are two types of analysis that organizations can choose to employ depending on the mission, goals, and processes of the CSIRT. The first one being forensic evidence collection, which is the collection, preservation, documentation, and analysis of evidence from a compromised computer system to determine changes to the system and to assist in the reconstruction of events leading to the compromise. This gathering of information and evidence must be done in a way that documents a provable chain of custody that is admissible in a court of law under the rules of evidence.

The second type of analysis is tracking or tracing, which is the tracing of the origins of an intruder or identifying systems to which the intruder had access. This activity might involve tracking or tracing how the intruder entered the affected systems and related networks, which systems were used to gain that access, where the attack originated, and what other systems and networks were used as part of the attack. It might also involve trying to determine the identity of the intruder.

As has been the case in all of the CSF functions we have discussed so far, there needs to be mechanisms in place to implement lessons learned into the IR processes. Such lessons may consist of attacks that took place that necessitate changes to the IR plan, changes to the existing communication channels that facilitate knowledge of active or past incidents. Perhaps most importantly, the lessons may trigger the need for changes in the management oversight of the overall process. In that regard, organizations should not approach IR as a one-time planning activity. Consistent with the life cycle processes that exist throughout the ICT industry, the knowledge gained from experience promotes a continuous improvement pattern, and in this case greater support for cybersecurity.

INSIGHT   FROM CYBER INCIDENT RESPONSE TO CYBER RESILIENCE

Despite having witnessed and, in some cases, experienced high-profile breaches over the past 14 months, many executives express concerns about their existing cyber incident response plans. Specifically, they believe their organizations need to do additional work to shore them up and confirm they can properly execute them in the event of a damaging cyber incident.

The uncertainty surrounding cyber incident response presents an opportunity to educate the executive team on cyber resilience—the coordinated set of enterprise wide activities designed to help organizations respond to and recover from a variety of cyber incidents, while reducing the cost, impact to business operations and brand damage.

"CIOs who have the ear of top executives are well-positioned to lead conversations about cyber resilience because they possess the influence needed to coordinate planning and action across a broad team of business leaders," says Emily Mossburg, a principal with Deloitte & Touche LLP. "CIOs have addressed cyber security longer than any other member of the executive team, and those with a deep knowledge of the business understand the impact of these incidents from an operational, financial and reputational perspective."

In the process of educating the executive team, CIOs can send the message that effectively mitigating cyber risk and responding to cyber attacks is a shared responsibility—not one that falls on the CIO's shoulders alone. Many CEOs and other senior leaders haven't considered the coordinated response efforts required across legal, communications, HR and other functions in building cyber resilience, according to Ms. Mossburg. She notes that cyber war gaming exercises can go a long way toward illustrating the coordination needed to appropriately respond to a cyber-attack.

In some cases, CIOs have to educate themselves, as well. Effectively leading discussions of cyber resilience calls upon CIOs who have traditionally approached the topic from a technology perspective to take a markedly different tact. Those CIOs who see cyber resilience strictly as a technical function and who focus primarily on redundant infrastructure and data backup and recovery procedures may leave their organizations ill-prepared to deal with the full ramifications of a cyber-incident, cautions Damian Walch, a director with Deloitte & Touche LLP.

"Certainly, resilience requires investment in traditional technology-based redundancy and disaster recovery, but organizations that focus exclusively on technology often lack the ability in the immediate aftermath of an incident to act decisively because they haven't thought through different threat scenarios, their impact on critical assets and business processes, and the stakeholders who should be involved," he says.

For example, when an organization discovers a breach, many of the important decisions leaders have to make fundamentally center on business issues rather than technology issues, such as: When should we notify our customers? Should we take a portion of our operations offline? Do we need to involve suppliers or other third parties in an investigation?

"A lack of broad business planning can hamper an organization's ability to make critical decisions, resulting in confusion and potentially deepening a crisis," adds Mr. Walch.

The notion of resilience as an enterprise's end-to-end incident response, business continuity and disaster recovery capability demands some expansion of the CIO's role and responsibilities. Specifically, risk management becomes more important, as does awareness of business and technology risk, according to Ms. Mossburg and Mr. Walch. To that end, Mr. Walch recommends that CIOs take steps to understand their enterprises' critical processes, the financial and operational impact of not being able to execute them, and the vulnerabilities that may lead to those scenarios.

In addition, Ms. Mossburg urges CIOs to gain a deeper understanding of both the risks posed by new technologies and the extent to which their companies' business operations may become dependent on them. "Companies have placed an extreme level of trust in technology; CIOs need to articulate to the business the risk implications of their deepening dependence," she observes.

The expanded notion of resilience also demands changes to the way many CIOs have traditionally approached disaster recovery. Ms. Mossburg notes that some CIOs focus their disaster recovery plans on big, sweeping events like natural disasters or data center outages, while neglecting the operational impact of comparatively smaller, targeted events. Distributed denial of service (DDoS) attacks, for example, have grown much more common since 2011 and have proven to be quite disruptive, yet many CIOs aren't creating disaster recovery plans focused on those scenarios, Ms. Mossburg observes. She recommends CIOs consider and plan for a broader range of issues that could disrupt business operations.

"Responding to a targeted cyber attack is different from dealing with typical disaster recovery events," says Ms. Mossburg. "It requires its own set of focused business workarounds and end user training for when a specific application or set of applications goes down."

Several CIOs have lost their jobs because of cyber attacks that occurred on their watch. By making the executive team realize cyber resilience is a shared responsibility and by guiding them through the creation of a comprehensive incident response plan, CIOs may accomplish two important goals, says Mr. Walch: "They may reduce their risk of becoming the fall guy for cyber incidents, and they may better prepare their organizations to promptly recover from attacks large and small." (Deloitte 2015)

Response Planning Category

The CSF describes the outcome of the response planning category within the scope that "response processes and procedures are executed and maintained, to ensure timely response to detected cybersecurity

Table 6.1   Framework Core Response Planning Category

CATEGORY	SUBCATEGORY	INFORMATION RESOURCES
Response Planning (RS.RP): Response processes and procedures are executed and maintained, to ensure timely response to detected cybersecurity events.	RS.RP-1: Response plan is executed during or after an event.	• COBIT 5 BAI01.10 • CCS CSC 18 • ISA 62443-2-1:2009 4.3.4.5.1 • ISO/IEC 27001:2013 A.16.1.5 • NIST SP 800-53 Rev. 4 CP-2, CP-10, IR-4, IR 8

Source: National Institute of Standards and Technology, *Framework for Improving Critical Infrastructure Cybersecurity.* Gaithersburg, February 12, 2014.

events" (National Institute of Standards and Technology Feb. 2014). There is an assumption built into the outcome that an organization has already developed an IR plan and a CSIRT has been identified. This category has just one subcategory and is summarized in Table 6.1 above.

Now that cybersecurity attacks are nearly unavoidable, organizations must adopt a new attitude toward being prepared for and successfully responding to incidents right at the first sign of intrusion. The speed at which they identify the attack, halt progress of infectious malware, stop access and stealing of sensitive data, and remedy the threat will make significant difference in controlling risk, costs, and exposure during an incident.

It is a given that incidents will occur. How well those incidents are responded to is dictated to a great extent by the level of preparation of the organization through its IR plan. The detection of an incident triggers the functions that make up incident management, which ensures that adequate preparation has been done to underwrite successful incident remedy. The IR plan provides commonly accepted and properly understood statements that detail the steps necessary to respond to events. Moreover, it provides a detailed set of formal policies and practices needed to establish the structure of the organization's IR capability.

Depending upon the objectives of the organization, the procedures defined in the IR plan will vary. Therefore, the best way to understand what should be included within a structured IR process might be to think about what guidance and expectations senior management should have about how incidents are handled.

Each of the remaining 14 subcategory outcomes of the Response Function provides specific criteria for the activities that provide adequate IR, and thus should be included within the IR plan. Nevertheless, one of the first tasks of managing IR is to deploy the right resources to address the incident. In that respect, a balance has to be maintained between responding appropriately and overreaching. The manager assigned to the incident gathers initial facts, analyzes them, and determines the appropriate level of response. The CSIRT can then decide on the right level of involvement for escalating the event.

That decision is based primarily on the details of the initial investigation and guidance provided in the IR plan. There are many factors that go into making the decision to respond to an incident. Not responding could result in significant financial and data losses. Depending upon the severity of the incident, the business may also suffer an interruption of operations. Worse, they risk the loss of reputation and customer loyalty. Moreover, improper responses can put an organization in the same predicament. Errors in how the organization responds can also lead to the inability to pursue legal actions against the attacker. Implemented properly, the IR plan can assist management in answering those questions and improve the odds of satisfactory response.

Communications Category

When an organization is faced with a potential security breach or data loss, there are numerous concerns to address. Many incident management plans focus on technical issues such as investigation, containment, and recovery. But it is essential that each phase of the plan also covers communication—a key requirement for effective IR.

The strategy selected for communication of an incident must cover compliance-related issues, media communications, and internal communications. Moreover, it must strike a balance between openness and protection. Revealing more information than necessary could result in undue escalation or exposure of an exploitable weakness that has not yet been remedied. However, withholding information can cast your organization in a negative light and create the impression that you have something to hide.

Table 6.2   Framework Core Communications Category

CATEGORY	SUBCATEGORY	INFORMATION RESOURCES
Communications (RS.CO): Response activities are coordinated with internal and external stakeholders, as appropriate, to include external support from law enforcement agencies.	RS.CO-1: Personnel know their roles and order of operations when a response is needed.	• ISA 62443-2-1:2009 4.3.4.5.2, 4.3.4.5.3, 4.3.4.5.4 • ISO/IEC 27001:2013 A.6.1.1, A.16.1.1 • NIST SP 800-53 Rev. 4 CP-2, CP-3, IR-3, IR-8
	RS.CO-2: Events are reported consistent with established criteria.	• ISA 62443-2-1:2009 4.3.4.5.5 • ISO/IEC 27001:2013 A.6.1.3, A.16.1.2 • NIST SP 800-53 Rev. 4 AU-6, IR-6, IR-8
	RS.CO-3: Information is shared consistent with response plans.	• ISA 62443-2-1:2009 4.3.4.5.2 • ISO/IEC 27001:2013 A.16.1.2 • NIST SP 800-53 Rev. 4 CA-2, CA-7, CP-2, IR4, IR-8, PE-6, RA-5, SI-4
	RS.CO-4: Coordination with stakeholders occurs consistent with response plans.	• ISA 62443-2-1:2009 4.3.4.5.5 • NIST SP 800-53 Rev. 4 CP-2, IR-4, IR-8
	RS.CO-5: Voluntary information sharing occurs with external stakeholders to achieve broader cybersecurity situational awareness.	• NIST SP 800-53 Rev. 4 PM-15, SI-5

Source: National Institute of Standards and Technology, *Framework for Improving Critical Infrastructure Cybersecurity.* Gaithersburg, February 12, 2014.

The CSF breaks down the communication into five subcategory outcomes. The outcomes are identified in Table 6.2.

RS.CO-1: Personnel Know Their Roles and Order of Operations When a Response Is Needed

If you have read each of the previous three chapters, you may recall similar discussions about communication of roles and responsibilities. Truth be told, each facet of cybersecurity requires involvement from numerous individuals throughout the organization. Effective mechanisms must be in place to communicate the *who's*, *what's*, *when's*, *where's*, and *why's* of each process task in order to provide assurance that function is completed and in a timely manner. Equally important is the communication of changes to process activities. It is inevitable that processes will change based on business requirements, changes in technology, and identification of new cybersecurity risk. Such changes must be documented and communicated to affected individuals.

Roles and responsibilities related to IR are normally documented within the organization's IR plan. IR plans should specify team structures, individual roles and responsibilities, escalation processes, and war room protocols. The operating models tie back to the data-classification framework. For example, it is important to specify exactly when to involve executive leadership in the decision processes, when to activate a war room, and at what threshold executives should take decisive measures, such as isolating sections of the network or shutting down core applications. Operating models also document decision rights, for instance, who authorizes contacting law enforcement.

The caveat is that the culture of many organizations is such that employees do not even know that an IR plan exists, let alone know their response roles and responsibilities, causing chaos throughout the organization as a result. Organizations must institute training and awareness programs that provide all affected personnel the knowledge they need of established plans and the contents of those plans that will provide them direction in providing security of the organizations ICT assets.

RS.CO-2: Events Are Reported Consistent with Established Criteria

A fundamental component of organizational training and awareness programs provided to personnel should be instruction on how to identify a security attack and the procedures for reporting verified events. Every organization should have a policy defined within their IR plan that provides details about the type of security attacks that could take place and the procedures for notifying the appropriate individuals. Normally, the reporting structure will follow the same path of established roles of authority. However, the reporting procedures may vary significantly depending upon the severity of the attack.

Many organizations now use automated reporting systems and knowledge management to appropriately document such criteria as the source of attack, nature of incident, and how the situation was resolved. Automated and knowledge management systems provide immediate access to event information by incident response team and management responsible for responding to the event.

One aspect of incident reporting worthy of mention is the degree by which third-party organizations within the supply chain are notified of an incident. Such protocols should also be included within the IR plan. Nevertheless, the organization must consider the effect that the incident has on the information flows between the organizations. Those incidents found to have affected or could potentially affect vital system linkages beyond organizational boundaries should be reported.

RS.CO-3: Information Is Shared Consistent with Response Plans

When the CSF was published in early 2014, the intention of the RS.CO-3 outcome was to address the need for managerial information sharing, related to cybersecurity attacks, across the organization. Further and consistent with our discussion of the RS.CO-2 outcome, information sharing should be consistent with response plans of all organizations within the supply chain. However, cybersecurity breaches of large corporations in 2014 influenced President Barack Obama to issue an executive order in early 2015 for Congress to enact a bill requiring private sector organizations to share cybersecurity attack information not only internally and within the supply chain but also to the federal government.

At the time of this writing, the Senate Intelligence Committee had drafted a bill called the Cybersecurity Information Sharing Act (CISA) and was soon to be voted on by the Senate. The CISA is intended to help anticipate cyberattacks like the one that crippled many of the large organizations in 2014, but concerns about government surveillance remains an issue. The legislation creates a voluntary framework for the private sector to share more computer data with the government by offering companies expanded legal liability if they choose to participate. While information sharing between private sector organizations and the government is the focal point of the bill, it also includes language defining an information sharing mechanism between private sector organizations using the Department of Homeland Security as an intermediary in the exchange.

This discussion may be putting the cart before the horse, in terms of what will be required of private sector organizations. Nevertheless, such government intervention will put organizations in the position to modify their existing IR plans to provide the necessary policies and procedures to conform to the new federal regulations.

RS.CO-4: Coordination with Stakeholders Occurs Consistent with Response Plans

While cybersecurity IR has historically been viewed as an ICT function issue, effective planning must incorporate coordination across all organizational business functions, for example, corporate communications, regulatory affairs, legal, compliance and audit, and business operations. Coordination, combined with easily accessible documentation of IR plans, ensures that all levels of an organization can react with greater agility during an incident. Moreover, effective IR plans should help maintain relationships with important third parties, such as law enforcement agencies and breach remediation and forensics experts. Failure to maintain these relationships can have catastrophic consequences.

RS.CO-5: Voluntary Information Sharing Occurs with External Stakeholders to Achieve Broader Cybersecurity Situational Awareness

At the federal level, voluntary information sharing occurs as the "United States Computer Emergency Readiness Team (US-CERT) generates security alerts and advisories to maintain situational awareness across the federal government. Security directives are issued by the Office of Management and Budget (OMB) or other designated organizations with the responsibility and authority to issue such directives" (National Institute for Standards and Technology Apr. 2014). Similar alerts and advisories must also be in place to provide situational awareness of incidents affecting organizations within the private sector. Just as important is the awareness necessary of the customers of those organizations.

The issue faced by organizations is the extent to which the incident awareness will affect the relationship with third-party providers or customers. We argue that the damage incurred by not providing the necessary awareness may be much more severe, even leading to legal ramifications. In the case of identity theft, for example, organizations now have procedures in place to contract with privacy protection agencies and contacting affected customers to register with those agencies. Such actions are more likely to generate a positive response from customers than if the organization chose not to do anything. Of course, such information sharing must be presented delicately in order not to create chaos and panic.

Analysis Category

Once an incident has been reported, management turns to the CSIRT to perform analysis of the incident and report back. In general, analysis attempts to answer the following questions:

- How did this incident occur in the first place?
- What systems were compromised, and what is the extent of the damage?
- What did they take? What did they change?
- How do we prevent this incident from occurring in the future?

Depending upon the extent of the incident, the analysis process can take a day, weeks, or even months to complete. For example, investigation into the extent of a malware attack through e-mail attachment may be handled by the ICT department with CSIRT oversight. On the other hand, response to identity theft potential caused by database tampering can take much longer.

The processes can be analogized to the work that law enforcement do in a criminal investigation. After a reported incident is made, that report is interpreted by individuals with expertise in that area of crime. Evidence is collected, interviews are conducted, additional security is sometimes provided, leads are chased, and hopefully a resolution is discovered. The same holds true in cases of computer crime. The difference is that instead of police detectives conducting the investigation, computer forensics experts with knowledge of technical investigative techniques typically lead the process.

The CSF breaks down the analysis category into four subcategory outcomes. The outcomes are identified in Table 6.3.

RS.AN-1: Notifications from Detection Systems Are Investigated

If you read the Chapter 5 discussion of the CSF Detection Function, you may recall that intrusion detection systems have the capability

Table 6.3   Framework Core Analysis Category

CATEGORY	SUBCATEGORY	INFORMATION RESOURCES
Analysis (RS.AN): Analysis is conducted to ensure adequate response and support recovery activities.	RS.AN-1: Notifications from detection systems are investigated.	• COBIT 5 DSS02.07 • ISA 62443-2-1:2009 4.3.4.5.6, 4.3.4.5.7, 4.3.4.5.8 • ISA 62443-3-3:2013 SR 6.1 • ISO/IEC 27001:2013 A.12.4.1, A.12.4.3, A.16.1.5 • NIST SP 800-53 Rev. 4 AU-6, CA-7, IR-4, IR 5, PE-6, SI-4
	RS.AN-2: The impact of the incident is understood.	• ISA 62443-2-1:2009 4.3.4.5.6, 4.3.4.5.7, 4.3.4.5.8 • ISO/IEC 27001:2013 A.16.1.6 • NIST SP 800-53 Rev. 4 CP-2, IR-4
	RS.AN-3: Forensics are performed.	• ISA 62443-3-3:2013 SR 2.8, SR 2.9, SR 2.10, SR 2.11, SR 2.12, SR 3.9, SR 6.1 • ISO/IEC 27001:2013 A.16.1.7 • NIST SP 800-53 Rev. 4 AU-7, IR-4
	RS.AN-4: Incidents are categorized consistent with response plans.	• ISA 62443-2-1:2009 4.3.4.5.6 • ISO/IEC 27001:2013 A.16.1.4 • NIST SP 800-53 Rev. 4 CP-2, IR-4, IR-5, IR-8

Source: National Institute of Standards and Technology, *Framework for Improving Critical Infrastructure Cybersecurity.* Gaithersburg, February 12, 2014.

of monitoring system activity and notifying responsible individuals when activities warrant investigation. The systems can detect attack signatures and also changes in files, configurations, and activity. Many analogize IDS systems similar to a fire alarm. Although it is an alarm, it is an alarm with brains. Imagine a fire detection system that had the capability of detecting a smoke or a substantial fire; distinguish the extent of the situation; pinpoint the source; alert the occupants in the area, law enforcement, and fire department; and forward intelligence to the fire department prior to their response. All these are functions of a fire detection system, with even the capability of distinguishing normal activity such as bad cooking. A properly configured intrusion detection system is such a device—an alarm with brains.

The CSF RS.AN-1 outcome recommends that one of the first response activities of the CSIRT is to "pick the brain" of the intrusion detection system. In most cases, the results of this investigation become the first source of evidence in route to incident resolution. Some of the questions requiring answer through this investigation include the following:

- Did the IDS provide the expected notifications? If not, why?
- What information was provided by the IDS through the notification function, and was that information accurate?
- Is there value of the information provided by the notification function in tracing to the root cause of the incident?
- Was the notification provided in a timely matter?

RS.AN-2: Impact of the Incident Is Understood

When an incident occurs, the procedure in which it is reported should include information about the initial account of the impact to the organization. Such information may consist simply of the inability to access a function of the ICT system, or as severe as the compromise of customer data. This information is useful to the CSIRT in prioritizing the investigation and ensuring that the proper procedures defined by the IR plan are performed.

Throughout the investigation, the CSIRT is likely to discover details of the incident impacting the organization that were not disclosed at the outset. Those details should be communicated to the management of the functional areas impacted for further review and possible recovery procedure implementation. As you will see in our discussion in a later section of this chapter, the more information available about the impact of the incident, the easier it will be for the organization to mitigate its affects.

RS.AN-3: Forensics Are Performed

Forensics is almost always associated with law enforcement. So the most fundamental purpose of the digital forensic process is to assist in gathering and preserving evidence that is used in the prosecution of computer crimes. In doing this, the forensic examiner collects and analyzes any evidence that is generated by the actual cyberexploit. That might include such artifacts as source code, malware, and Trojans. One aspect of that activity is to support criminal investigation. However, another important aspect is the potential use of forensic data to support the organizations own organized cyberdefense operations.

The evidence itself is digital and so its footprint is found in electronic sources such as computer log files, reference monitor files, and other hidden sources of information. The subsequent analysis supports decisions about the best means of identifying the source and reasons for an unauthorized access. That can include such evidence gathering methods as dynamic and static analyses.

Dynamic analysis tests a program by executing it in real time using a data set explicitly designed to identify the type and sources of a cyberattack or intrusion. The other primary methodology is static analysis. In that processes, the examiner directly reviews the code without executing it. Because such techniques require tool support, the forensic examiner also has to know how to utilize a forensic tool kit.

The process itself mainly involves evidence gathering. Once there is an indication of a breach or other form of cyberexploit, the examiner creates a forensically sound duplicate of the target of the attack. This duplicate is called a forensic image. The purpose of the image is to protect the integrity of the original crime scene by creating a duplicate to use for the subsequent data recovery and analysis procedures.

Artifacts that might be imaged include, but are not limited to, hard drives, floppy diskettes, compact discs, personal digital assistants, mobile phones, global positioning satellite devices, and all tape formats. If any of the data that is part of the examination is encrypted, the forensic examiner also decrypts it using tools. The examiner then provides a technical summary of the findings in accordance with the organization's established IR plan.

RS.AN-4: Incidents Are Categorized Consistent with Response Plans

Categorization of an incident relates to how it gets prioritized by the organization. Prioritizing the treatment of an incident is one of the most critical decisions management makes related to IR. The worst thing an organization can do is handle incidents as they happen. Rather, they should be prioritized based on a number of factors. The

NIST "Computer Security Incident Handling Guide: SP 800-61 Rev. 2" recommends prioritizing based on the following:

- "Functional Impact of the Incident—Incidents targeting IT systems typically impact the business functionality that those systems provide, resulting in some type of negative impact to the users of those systems. Incident handlers should consider how the incident will impact the existing functionality of the affected systems. Incident handlers should consider not only the current functional impact of the incident, but also the likely future functional impact of the incident if it is not immediately contained.
- Information Impact of the Incident—Incidents may affect the confidentiality, integrity, and availability of the organization's information. For example, a malicious agent may exfiltrate sensitive information. Incident handlers should consider how this information exfiltration will impact the organization's overall mission. An incident that results in the exfiltration of sensitive information may also affect other organizations if any of the data pertained to a partner organization.
- Recoverability from the Incident—The size of the incident and the type of resources it affects will determine the amount of time and resources that must be spent on recovering from that incident. In some instances it is not possible to recover from an incident (e.g., if the confidentiality of sensitive information has been compromised) and it would not make sense to spend limited resources on an elongated incident handling cycle, unless that effort was directed at ensuring that a similar incident did not occur in the future. In other cases, an incident may require far more resources to handle than what an organization has available. Incident handlers should consider the effort necessary to actually recover from an incident and carefully weigh that against the value the recovery effort will create and any requirements related to incident handling" (Cichonski et al. 2012).

The organization should also put into place an escalation process to be initiated if there is no response to an incident during a predetermined period. Again, the escalation could be based on the classification of incident or elapse of after the incident occurred. Such criteria should be communicated to anyone involved in reporting and responding to incidents, and procedures clearly defined in the IR plan.

Mitigation Category

How an organization responds to an incident can make the difference between protecting customers and the perception of their product line, with clear implications for the bottom line on the one hand and a public opinion and possible lawsuits on the other.

The reality is that incidents happen, and they happen to everyone. It is not considered a crime to experience an attack or technical issue. However, how an organization responds to these incidents may find it answering tough questions of customers or in courtrooms facing regulators, particularly if the organization does not take steps to protect valuable information or respond promptly and effectively to efforts to compromise that information. Organizations tend to react differently to incidents, and it is interesting to see public reaction to their different approaches.

As incidents continue to increase in frequency and complexity, it is no longer enough to simply monitor firewalls and install intrusion prevention or detection. Organizations must to be ready with efficient and effective response mechanisms.

Once an incident has been reported and its impact to the organization understood, the instinctive next step is to quickly implement the mechanisms necessary to prevent the impact of the incident from spreading any further through the organization or supply chain than it already has. At the same time, the organization implements procedures aimed at lessening the effect of the incident. As incidents are investigated, the organization begins to gain understanding of the root cause and, in turn, realizes risk vulnerabilities yet to be identified. Those vulnerabilities are then assessed, prioritized, and documented in the risk management plan.

This series of activities can easily be analogized to the physical world. When a fire is reported and firefighters arrive on the scene, they first identify what parts of the building are affected. Given that knowledge, they make a valiant effort to contain the fire to the smallest area of the building possible. Once the fire has been extinguished,

Table 6.4 Framework Core Mitigation Category

CATEGORY	SUBCATEGORY	INFORMATION RESOURCES
Mitigation (RS.MI): Activities are performed to prevent expansion of an event, mitigate its effects, and eradicate the incident.	RS.MI-1: Incidents are contained.	• ISA 62443-2-1:2009 4.3.4.5.6 • ISA 62443-3-3:2013 SR 5.1, SR 5.2, SR 5.4 • ISO/IEC 27001:2013 A.16.1.5 • NIST SP 800-53 Rev. 4 IR-4
	RS.MI-2: Incidents are mitigated.	• ISA 62443-2-1:2009 4.3.4.5.6, 4.3.4.5.10 • ISO/IEC 27001:2013 A.12.2.1, A.16.1.5 • NIST SP 800-53 Rev. 4 IR-4
	RS.MI-3: Newly identified vulnerabilities are mitigated or documented as accepted risks.	• ISO/IEC 27001:2013 A.12.6.1 • NIST SP 800-53 Rev. 4 CA-7, RA-3, RA-5

Source: National Institute of Standards and Technology, *Framework for Improving Critical Infrastructure Cybersecurity.* Gaithersburg, February 12, 2014.

an investigation usually takes place as to the cause. In many cases, there are lessons learned that come out of that investigation that can be communicated to the community to prevent similar events in the future.

What we are discussing here is a common practice within cybersecurity called risk mitigation. The CSF suggests that through mitigation "activities are performed to prevent expansion of an event, mitigate its effects, and eradicate the incident" (National Institute of Standards and Technology Feb. 2014). This category is broken down into three subcategory outcomes. The outcomes are identified in Table 6.4.

RS.MI-1: Incidents Are Contained

The goal of containment is to limit the scope and magnitude of an incident in order to keep it from getting worse. Organizations should have established procedures that eliminate the spread of the effects of an incident:

• Deploy the on-site team to survey the situation.
• Keep a low profile.
• Avoid looking for the attacker with obvious methods.
• Avoid potentially compromised code. Intruders may install Trojan horses and similar malicious code in system binaries.

- Back up the system. It is important to obtain a full back up of the system in order to acquire evidence of illegal activity. Back up to new (unused) media. Store backup tapes in a secure location.
- Determine the risk of continuing operations.
- Change passwords on compromised systems and on all systems that regularly interact with the compromised systems.

RS.MI-2: Incidents Are Mitigated

Given a specific incident, there are three strategies available to management and the CSIRT to mitigate the incident:

- Acceptance does not reduce the effects of the incident. However, it is still considered a strategy. This strategy is a common option when the cost of other risk management options such as avoidance or reduction may outweigh the cost of the incident itself. A company that does not want to spend a lot of money on avoiding risks that do not have a high possibility of occurring will use the acceptance strategy.
- Avoidance is just the opposite of acceptance. It is the action that avoids any further exposure to the risk imposed by the incident. Avoidance is usually the most expensive of all mitigation options.
- Limitation is the most common risk management strategy used by organizations. This strategy limits a company's exposure to the incident by taking some action. It is a strategy employing a bit of acceptance along with a bit of avoidance or an average of both.

The goal is to reduce the impact of the incident. Mitigation is accomplished by decreasing the threat level by eliminating or intercepting the adversary as soon as the incident occurs, blocking opportunities through enhanced security, or reducing the consequences of an attack. Without question, the best strategy for mitigating incidents is a combination of all three elements, decreasing threats, blocking opportunities, and reducing consequences.

A logical mitigation strategy ties assets to threats and vulnerabilities in order to identify risks. Solutions for the identified risks typically enhance three facets of security: policies, procedures, and training; physical/electronic security systems; and security personnel. A sound mitigation strategy maximizes existing security resources (optimization) and prioritizes policies first, systems second, and personnel third.

RS.MI-3: Newly Identified Vulnerabilities Are Mitigated or Documented as Accepted Risks

Risk assessment is not a one-time process done once as a security program is established and not repeated. Rather, each incident that is encountered reveals new vulnerabilities or perhaps threats that were not categorized at an appropriate priority. The RS.MI-3 outcome addresses the need for organizations to learn from experience by implementing controls to understand the vulnerabilities that made the incident possible, and implement mechanisms that eradicate the vulnerabilities. That information should then be included within an organization's risk management plan. In rare cases, the organization will choose the do nothing approach to addressing the vulnerability. In those instances, the risk management plan should be updated with indication that the risk had been identified and is considered acceptable.

Improvement Category

Most organizations focus only on getting back to normal after an attack, with actions such as reimaging of systems, changing firewall rules, and updating the incident detection system. These do not, however, sufficiently reduce future risks. By defining both high-level objectives and detailed processes and procedures for detecting, responding to, and analyzing incidents, an organization can gain clearer and more detailed insights into the incident. This helps them detect, investigate, and remediate attacks more rapidly and effectively, and reduce the risk of damage.

An organization is on the road to improved response if it prioritizes incidents to focus the most attention, staff, and budget on its highest-value applications and data, as well as those platforms that are most vulnerable to an exploit. The organization has reached an even higher level of maturity if its IRs are guided by clear governance rules and investigative run books.

Table 6.5 Framework Core Improvements Category

CATEGORY	SUBCATEGORY	INFORMATION RESOURCES
Improvements (RS.IM): Organizational response activities are improved by incorporating lessons learned from current and previous detection/ response activities.	RS.IM-1: Response plans incorporate lessons learned.	• COBIT 5 BAI01.13 • ISA 62443-2-1:2009 4.3.4.5.10, 4.4.3.4 • ISO/IEC 27001:2013 A.16.1.6 • NIST SP 800-53 Rev. 4 CP-2, IR-4, IR-8
	RS.IM-2: Response strategies are updated.	• NIST SP 800-53 Rev. 4 CP-2, IR-4, IR-8

Source: National Institute of Standards and Technology, *Framework for Improving Critical Infrastructure Cybersecurity.* Gaithersburg, February 12, 2014.

The CSF states that "organizational response activities are improved by incorporating lessons learned from current and previous detection/ response activities" (National Institute of Standards and Technology Feb. 2014). The improvements category is broken down into two subcategory outcomes as identified in Table 6.5 and described in the following sections.

RS.IM-1: Response Plans Incorporate Lessons Learned

Effective IR improves the organization's security process over time. This requires thorough and complete documentation of the IR both during and after the investigation, based on lessons learned. That information should be incorporated into the IR plan and used to improve the organization's processes and systems for detecting, investigating, and limiting the damage from future incidents. The data that lead to the inclusion of updated response processes should address metrics such as mean time to incident detection and resolution, as well as indicate the general level of effectiveness of existing countermeasures. This allows the organization to better determine whether budget is being allocated to each process activity optimally.

To achieve continued improvement, response processes must be repeatable and contain measurable process artifacts through KPIs that are relevant to the business. For example, if a KPI is time-to-resolution, the organization's performance against it can help identify what people, processes, or technology helped or stood in the way of reaching that goal.

More mature organizations also include in their response plan use cases that describe actual response situations and threat scenarios specific to them. This helps assure that all organizational personnel can learn from past incidents and improve their response.

RS.IM-2: Response Strategies Are Updated

The ability of an organization to respond to cybersecurity incidents is only as effective as the strategies adopted. The scope and severity of cybersecurity attacks are changing almost on a daily basis. Industries and government organizations (such as NIST) continuously publish guidelines recommending strategies and best practices for responding to incidents. Organizations should incorporate into their risk management framework policies requiring regular review of such guidelines and best practices, and update existing strategies in alignment with established priorities and business objectives.

Chapter Summary

- IR is the steps an organization takes to negate or minimize the effects of a cybersecurity attack. The IR plan is necessary because it provides the policies that specifically define an incident and documents the step-by-step process individuals within the organization should follow when an incident occurs.
- Effective communication is vital for successful IR. To control the validity of the communication, it should be filtered through organization management and be consistent with the communication policies defined in the IR plan. Communication between the system users, management, CSIRT, supply chain, and media need to be considered within the plan in order to minimize the negative effects resulting from incident information retrieved by alternative mechanisms.
- Computer forensics is performed during the analysis phase of IR. The goal is to collect, document, and preserve evidence of the incident. The organization may conduct informal proceedings when dealing with internal violations of security policy and standards. The evidence may also be needed

in formal administrative or legal proceeding. Above all else, the evidence will help the CSIRT draw conclusions about the root cause of the incident, and bring the event to a reasonable resolution.

• When an incident has been reported, one of the first courses of action is to contain sustained affects after which steps are taken to eliminate or lesson the repercussions. This process is called risk mitigation. A final step in the mitigation process is to understand the newly identified vulnerabilities and make determinations as to whether further mitigation is required or the risk is documented as an accepted risk.

Case Project

Suny Corporation would like you to continue the work you have been doing on the plan for implementing the Framework for Improving Critical Infrastructure Cybersecurity. Now that you are familiar with the outcomes of the Response Function, they would like you to develop an IR plan for the organization. You may need to begin by creating a business continuity plan, or building assumptions as to what that plan would include. Within the IR plan, only major steps of implementation need to be organized. In other words, focus on steps that the framework recommends for establishing and improving their cybersecurity program. The plan should continue to take the form of a project timeline that describes when each part of every step is performed. Besides providing a customized timeline and plan, include the business justification for each step.

7

RECOVER FUNCTION

After reading this chapter and completing the case project, you will

- Understand the difference between business continuity and disaster recovery;
- Understand the phases of cybersecurity disaster recovery;
- Be able to articulate the importance of continuous improvement within the phases of disaster recovery; and
- Understand the importance of communication between management, the recovery team, affected business functions, media, and external stakeholders during and after the recovery process.

In the aftermath of a cybersecurity incident, it can take an organization weeks or even months to overcome the damage done to the system and affected data. The negative impact to the organization's reputation can take even longer. An organization's investment in risk management means investing in business sustainability—designing a comprehensive business continuity and disaster recovery plan is about analyzing the impact of a business interruption on revenue.

Taking the time to map out the organizational business model, while identifying key components essential to operations and developing and testing a strategy to efficiently recover and restore data and systems, is an involved long-term project that takes a substantial amount of time depending on the complexity of the organization.

Addressing high-level business objectives for designing, implementing, and testing a business continuity and disaster recovery plan, this final chapter covering the Cybersecurity Framework emphasizes the weight that NIST puts on making the investment while discussing the inherent challenges, benefits, and detriments of different solutions.

Distinguishing between Business Continuity and Disaster Recovery

There is quite a difference between business continuity and disaster recovery processes and the plans that support them. It is important that an organization clearly understands what sort of planning each requires.

Business continuity planning (BCP) is best described as the definition and documentation of processes and procedures that are carried out by an organization to ensure that essential business functions continue to operate during and after a disaster. By having a BCP, organizations attempt to protect their critical infrastructures and make their best effort for business survival. This type of planning enables the organization to reestablish operations to a fully functional level as quickly and smoothly as possible. BCPs generally cover most or all of an organization's critical business processes and operations. The decisions that management face related to business continuity can be characterized such as "if we lost valuable ICT assets that our business depends upon, how would we recommence our operations?" Significant to our discussion here, the CSF addresses BCP as part of incident response. The PR.IP-9 outcome of the information protection processes and procedures category of the Protect Function ensures that the BCP is in place.

As part of the business continuity process, an organization will typically develop a series of disaster recovery plans (DRPs) and incident recovery plans (IRPs). The biggest difference between these two types of plans is the scope at which the plan defines the processes, procedures, and timelines. IRPs can be characterized in similarity to the scope at which project plans are developed for an individual ICT project. Once a cybersecurity incident is reported, an IRP is created to guide the organization through the process of recouping the losses suffered from that incident. On the other hand, DRPs have a scope more global in nature. In addition to providing guidelines enabling organizations to recoup from cybersecurity incidents, these plans also address the steps the organizations should take in the event of fire, flood, electrical outage, and other forms of disasters. The DRP also addresses business functions beyond the impact that the disaster has on ICT. The outcomes of the CSF focus on disaster recovery from the ICT cybersecurity perspective; therefore, we will stay within that scope in the discussions we have in this chapter. Both types of plans (IRP and DRP) are more technical in nature than most other risk management plans, and are developed for specific groups within an organization to allow them to recover a particular business application or ICT component. The decisions that management face related to disaster recovery can be characterized as "if we lost our ICT services how would recover them?"

ICT DRPs only deliver technology process guidelines to the desk of employees. It is then up to the business units to have plans for the subsequent functions. A mistake often made by organizations is to make a statement such as "we have an ICT DRP; we are all OK." That is not the case. Organizations need to have a business continuity plan in place for critical personnel, key business processes, recovery of vital records, critical supplier's identification, contacting of key vendors and clients, etc.

INSIGHT   SURVEY ROUNDUP: UNPREPARED FOR DISASTER

Not So Ready: A survey of C-suite-level IT pros at mid-sized companies in finance, life sciences manufacturing and technology sectors by data recovery and protection firm NTT Communications found half the businesses don't have a documented business continuity/disaster recovery (BCDR) plan—and of the half that do, 23% said their organizations have never tested those plans. Ninety percent of respondents said their companies spend 5% or less of their annual IT budget on disaster recovery planning.

The survey found 30% said disaster preparedness was both a business and regulatory requirement, with 10% saying their efforts were driven solely by regulatory concerns. Twenty percent said they were "not sure" if they are under any regulatory mandate to have a disaster recovery plan. "For organizations that do have plans, there is often a one-dimensional approach favoring a single technology rather than a mix of BCDR techniques," the report said. "This reliance on a one-size-fits-all strategy highlights a substantial disconnect between budgets allocated to the planning and technology of BCDR and the areas of the business at greatest risk of downtime and data loss during a disaster."

Whole Lotta Cybercrime: A review of more than 1.75 million website addresses by security firm Menlo Security found 21% of the sites were running software with known vulnerabilities.

Responsible Chains: A report from the World Economic Forum found companies that adopt socially responsible polices for how they manage their supply chains will increase revenue, lower supply chain costs, boost brand value and reduce operational risk.

Countering Counterfeiting: A report from the International Chamber of Commerce and the Business Action to Stop Counterfeiting and Piracy initiative says intermediaries in the supply chain can and need to do more to combat vulnerabilities that allow counterfeit and pirated goods to be sold.

Shipping Cybersecurity: A report by insurer Allianz Global Corporate & Specialty SE found rising concern within the industry for a cyberattack that could cripple a port or terminal, or send a ship to its doom by hacking into its electronic navigation system.

Unhealthy Hack: A report from health data security firm Redspin found 8.9 million patient health records were breached in 164 incidents in 2014—a 25.5% increase from 2013. The report said 53.4% of those breaches resulted from hacking attacks.

Feeling Insecure: A survey of 728 IT decision-makers by cybersecurity company BeyondTrust found 79% of respondents said employees are somewhat likely to very likely to access sensitive or confidential data out of curiosity. Almost 60% can circumvent whatever controls are in place.

Cloud Concerns: A survey of mid-sized and Fortune 500 companies around the world by security company CipherCloud found 64% of respondents said their biggest cloud security challenges involved audit, compliance and privacy regulations.

Cloudy Vision: A global survey of 102 C-suite-level executives and managers working in the financial services sector by the organization Cloud Security Alliance found 80% of the respondents want increased transparency and better auditing controls from cloud providers.

Ben Dipietor
Wall Street Journal, 2015

Recover Function Overview

The purpose of disaster recovery planning is to get the organization back on its feet, after a cybersecurity attack, as quickly as possible. The organization's drive toward recovery will require the efforts of many individuals carrying out a variety of predefined procedures in order to manage all aspects of the disaster, including confidentially about the incident, assessment of the damage, and recovery of facilities and ICT assets in order to regain business operations.

You learned in Chapter 6 that when an organization is victim of a security attack, incident response is largely concerned with damage assessment and salvage. Once the extent of the damage to the ICT system is known, efforts to restore business operations can begin.

Depending upon the extent of the attack, restoring business operations could be as simple as restoring a database, or in extreme situations the complete replacement of hardware or software assets. Any ICT components not affected by the attack continue to provide their support for business operations as normal. Remember that restoration and recovery operations are completely separate from business continuity efforts that focus on sustaining normality of business operations in areas of the organization not impacted, and thus not under investigation.

When the necessary repairs or replacements have been made to the system, components supporting the affected business functions need to be transitioned back into operation. This may require an interruption of service to other nonaffected business operations, and thus emphasizes the importance of a plan containing processes and procedures that address steps each individual or department should take during the transition and measures to take if something goes wrong.

The CSF characterizes the underlying objective of the Recover Function as "develop and implement the appropriate activities to maintain plans for resilience and to restore any capabilities or services that were impaired due to a cybersecurity even." It continues describing the function by saying that "the Recover Function supports timely recovery to normal operations to reduce the impact from a cybersecurity event" (National Institute of Standards and Technology Feb. 2014). Care should be taken in the interpretation of this objective, however. Recall from our previous discussion that the PR.IP-9 outcome of the information protection processes and procedures category of the Protect Function ensures that a business continuity plan is in place. That outcome also ensures that a disaster recovery plan is developed and in place.

You will notice parallels to most of the category outcomes the framework defines for the categories within Response Function and our discussion of the category outcomes of the Recover Function. This function focuses on executing the DRP, identifying lessons learned through recovery processes and updating strategies accordingly, and ensuring that the proper recovery communication protocols are established and executed.

Recovery Planning Category

The CSF describes the outcome of the recovery planning category within the scope that as "recovery processes and procedures are executed and maintained to ensure timely restoration of systems or assets affected by cybersecurity events" (National Institute of Standards and Technology Feb. 2014). This category has just one subcategory and is summarized in Table 7.1.

The processes of disaster recovery typically happen in the following sequential phases:

1. *Activation phase*: The disaster effects are assessed and announced.
2. *Execution phase*: The defined procedures to recover each of the disaster affected entities are executed. Business operations are restored on the recovery system.
3. *Reconstitution phase*: The system is restored and execution phase procedures are stopped.

Table 7.1 Framework Core Recovery Planning Category

CATEGORY	SUBCATEGORY	INFORMATION RESOURCES
Recovery Planning (RC. RP): Recovery processes and procedures are executed and maintained to ensure timely restoration of systems or assets affected by cybersecurity events.	RC.RP-1: Recovery plan is executed during or after an event.	• CCS CSC 8 • COBIT 5 DSS02.05, DSS03.04 • ISO/IEC 27001:2013 A.16.1.5 • NIST SP 800-53 Rev. 4 CP-10, IR-4, IR-8

Source: National Institute of Standards and Technology, *Framework for Improving Critical Infrastructure Cybersecurity.* Gaithersburg, February 12, 2014.

Activation Phase

A cybersecurity attack generally happens without notice. Quick and precise detection of the event and having an appropriate communication plan are the key for reducing the effects of the circumstances; this differs from other disasters in which the organization, in some cases, may be given enough time to allow system personnel to implement actions gracefully, thus reducing the impact of the disaster.

Part of the DRP contains the definition of the disaster recovery committee. This group is responsible for launching the activation phase. It should be well informed about the geographical, political, social, and environmental events that may pose threats to the company's business operations. It should also have trusted information sources with capabilities to anticipate false alarms or overreactions to hoaxes.

The activation phase involves

- Notification procedures;
- Damage assessment; and
- Disaster recovery activation planning.

Notification Procedures Notification procedures define the steps taken by the organization as soon as an attack has been detected or predicted. At the end of this phase, the recovery team will be ready to execute contingency plans to restore system functions on a temporary basis. Notification procedures should contain the process to alert the recovery team during business and nonbusiness hours. After the attack detection, a notification should be sent to the CSIRT, so that they can assess the damage that occurred and implement the IRP.

There are numerous ways in which notification can take place (i.e., by telephone, pager, e-mail, or cell phone). A notification policy should be established that describes procedures to be followed when pertinent individuals cannot be contacted. Such notification procedures should be clearly defined and documented in the contingency plans.

One very popular notification technique is a call tree. With this technique, each individual has the responsibility of calling two or more individuals. Normally, the branches are broken down into functional areas or chain of command. It is important to note that the call tree should document primary and alternate contact methods and should include procedures to be followed if an individual cannot be contacted.

Individuals to be alerted should be unmistakably identified in the contact list in the plan. This list should classify personnel by their role, name, and contact information (i.e., home, work, and pager numbers; e-mail addresses; and home addresses). If disrupted systems have interconnection with external organizations, a point of contact should be identified in those organizations as well. Notification information may contain the following:

- Nature of the attack that has occurred or is imminent
- Damage estimates
- Response and recovery details
- Where and when to assemble for briefing or further response instructions
- Instructions to complete notifications using the call tree (if applicable)

Damage Assessment You may wonder why damage assessment is repeated in both the Response and Recovery Functions. This demonstrates how closely the outcomes and corresponding controls are aligned between the two functions. To establish how the contingency plan will be executed following an attack, it is crucial to evaluate the nature and degree of the damage to the system. This damage evaluation is normally done by the CSIRT and should be done as quickly as conditions permit with confidentiality, integrity, and availability of data given highest priority. Consequently, when possible, the CSIRT is the first team notified of the incident.

As we mentioned in Chapter 6, it is advisable to prepare damage assessment guidelines for investigating different types of attacks based on levels of severity. An example might be a sudden system interruption noticed in a data center facility that has an uninterrupted power supply (UPS) backup. The investigation may determine whether the system can be restored before the UPS system runs out of battery power, in which case activating the DRP is not necessary, or otherwise, in which case the plan may be activated immediately.

Damage assessment procedures vary with each particular cyberattack; nevertheless, the following may be considered in general:

- Origin of the attack or disruption
- Potential for additional disruptions or damage

- Areas of the ICT system affected by the attack
- Status of physical infrastructure
- Inventory and functional status of the most important ICT components
- Type of damage to ICT components
- Components necessitating replacement
- Estimated time to restore normal operations if disaster procedures were not in place

Activation Planning   While it is advantageous to detect an attack at its earliest stage, putting a disaster recovery process into action for a false alarm may stall normal business operations and result in undue costs. Therefore, it is very important that disaster recovery be activated only when a thorough damage assessment has been conducted.

The DRP should have one or more criteria for activation, which become the primary input for evaluating whether the plan should be activated for each affected ICT system components. Also, it should be determined whether activating disaster response will bring systems back online faster than standard procedures.

Depending on the extent of the damage from the attack, the disaster recovery committee may do the disaster activation planning. The outcome of this planning, at a minimum, should be

- Development of a list of systems and components that need to be restored;
- Identification of interdependencies between systems and components, along with sequence of restoration;
- Time estimations for each restoration (documented in the plan);
- Instructions for reporting failures to the team leads; and
- Plan for communication between teams.

Once the disaster activation is planned, the appropriate team leads will notify staff and start their respective activities in sequence as instructed.

Execution Phase
Recovery activities begin immediately after the DRP has been activated, affected staff have been notified, and appropriate teams have

been assembled. The activities of this phase focus on bringing up the disaster recovery system. Depending on the recovery strategies defined in the plan, these functions could include temporary manual processing, recovery and operation on an alternate system, or relocation and recovery at an alternate site.

Sequence of Recovery Activities The recovery procedure reflects priorities previously determined during the activation planning phase. For instance, if a server room has been recovered after a disruption, the most critical servers should be restored before other less critical servers. The procedures should also include instructions to coordinate with other teams when certain situations occur, such as

- An activity is not completed within the estimated time frame;
- A key step in the recovery process has been completed; and
- ICT components have been identified as needing to be procured.

If a system must be recovered at a different location, specific items related to that activity must be transferred or obtained. Recovery procedures should delegate a team to manage shipment of physical equipment, media, and vital data. Procedures should also explain requirements to package, transport, and purchase necessary materials required to perform recovery activities.

Recovery Procedures The DRP should provide detailed procedures to restore the ICT system or system components. Procedures for ICT service damage should address specific actions such as

- Getting authorization to access damaged physical components or data;
- Notifying users that utilize the affected system;
- Obtaining and installing required hardware components;
- Obtaining and loading backup media;
- Restoring critical operating systems and application software;
- Restoring system data;
- Testing system functionality including security controls; and
- Connecting system to network or other external systems.

To avoid confusion in an emergency, the recovery procedures should be documented in a simple step-by-step format, without assuming or omitting any procedural steps.

Reconstitution Phase

In the reconstitution phase, operations are transferred back to the original functionality once they are free from the attack aftereffects, and execution-phase activities are subsequently completed. If the original system is unrecoverable, this phase also involves rebuilding. Therefore, the reconstitution phase may last for a few days to few weeks or even months, depending on the severity of destruction and the system's fitness for restoration. As soon as the system, whether repaired or replaced, is able to support its normal operations, the services supported by that system may be moved back. The execution team should continue to be engaged until the restoration and testing are complete.

The following activities occur in this phase:

- Continuous monitoring of the system's fitness for complete recovery;
- Verifying that the system is free from aftereffects of the attack and that there are no further immediate threats;
- Ensuring that all needed infrastructure services such as power, telecommunications, and security are operational;
- Installing system hardware, software, and firmware;
- Establishing connectivity between internal and external systems;
- Testing system operations to ensure full functionality;
- Shutting down the contingency system(s); and
- Terminating contingency operations.

Improvement Category

In the same vein as what was discussed of incidence response process improvement in Chapter 6, it is interesting to note that the same managerial philosophies hold true regarding recovery process improvement. Most organizations focus only on getting back to normal after an attack, and very little ongoing thought into how they can benefit from improvements to the process, and what those improvements might be. We believe that the general "lack of importance" attitude that exists within organizations, of their response and recovery process improvement efforts is why NIST puts related outcomes into each of the corresponding functions.

An organization is moving toward continuous improvement in disaster recovery if proper documentation is collected during the activation, execution, and reconstitution phases. That documentation should contain information that can be analyzed by management in terms of what went right and what went wrong. Moreover, decisions can then be made that affect changes in the process to be better prepared for recovery when and if another cyberattack occurs. The organization has reached an even higher level of maturity and process improvement if its incident recovery efforts are guided by clear governance rules.

The CSF states that "recovery planning and processes are improved by incorporating lessons learned into future activities" (National Institute of Standards and Technology Feb. 2014). The improvements category is broken down into two subcategory outcomes as identified in Table 7.2 and described in the following sections.

RC.IM-1: Recovery Plans Incorporate Lessons Learned

Effective disaster recovery improves the organization's security process over time. This requires thorough and complete documentation within all phases of the recovery process both during and after the system restoration based on lessons learned. That information should be incorporated into the DRP and used to improve the organization's

Table 7.2 Framework Core Improvements Category

CATEGORY	SUBCATEGORY	INFORMATION RESOURCES
Improvements (RC.IM): Recovery planning and processes are improved by incorporating lessons learned into future activities.	RC.IM-1: Recovery plans incorporate lessons learned.	• COBIT 5 BAI05.07 • ISA 62443-2-1:2009 4.4.3.4 • NIST SP 800-53 Rev. 4 CP-2, IR-4, IR-8
	RC.IM-2: Recovery strategies are updated.	• COBIT 5 BAI07.08 • NIST SP 800-53 Rev. 4 CP-2, IR-4, IR-8

Source: National Institute of Standards and Technology, *Framework for Improving Critical Infrastructure Cybersecurity.* Gaithersburg, February 12, 2014.

processes and systems for initiating recovery, performing recovery activities, and procedures for recovery conclusion. As is the case in response, the data that lead to the inclusion of updated recovery processes should address metrics such as mean time to activation and reconstitution, as well as indicate the general level of effectiveness of existing countermeasures. Again, this allows the organization to better determine whether budget is being allocated to each process activity optimally. To achieve continued improvement of any ICT process, it must be repeatable and contain measurable process artifacts through KPIs that are relevant to the business.

More mature organizations also include in their recovery plan use cases that describe actual recovery situations and threat scenarios specific to them. This helps assure that all organizational personnel can learn from past incidents and improve their recovery.

RC.IM-2: Recovery Strategies Are Updated

The ability for an organization to recover from cybersecurity incidents is only as effective as the strategies adopted. The scope and the severity of cybersecurity attacks are changing on almost a daily basis. Industries and government organizations (such as NIST) continuously publish guidelines recommending strategies and best practices for recovering from incidents. Organizations should incorporate into their risk management framework policies requiring regular review of such guidelines and best practices, and update existing strategies in alignment with established priorities and business objectives.

Communications Category

There is no doubt that the period of time in which an organization recovers from a cybersecurity attack is stressful and requires very timely and precise decisions made on the part of management and the team performing the recovery activities. One of the vital decisions faced by management is what, how, when, and to whom communication about the progress of recovery should be performed. Just about every management related book you read emphasizes that successful outcomes can be achieved only through trustworthy and timely communication filtered down from management to the individuals working directly within the process. Likewise, communication channels should be open for staff to provide management the information they need to help make decisions that affect the outcomes of the processes being performed. Imagine a cybersecurity recovery process without that type of communication. The catch is that part of the communication must provide related to cybersecurity recovery goes beyond the boundaries of the organization to stakeholders and media. The question becomes—How much information is too much, to the extent that panic is created and reputations are damaged?

The CSF breaks down the communications into three subcategory outcomes. The outcomes are identified in Table 7.3.

RC.CO-1: Public Relations Are Managed

When it comes to the role of public relations in cybersecurity, we suggest that organizations should invest resources in proactive media relations not only to establish a solid reputation for the company but also to leverage the current media attention on cybersecurity to stake a claim in a given industry. If organizations do not already do so, they should start combing the Internet for media that cover these issues and build relationships with them by discussing their content with them and, eventually, offering the company as a source for content. Cybersecurity is a hot topic right now and any company can benefit greatly from being a part of the dialogue.

Table 7.3 Framework Core Communications Category

CATEGORY	SUBCATEGORY	INFORMATION RESOURCES
Communications (RC.CO): Restoration activities are coordinated with internal and external parties, such as coordinating centers, Internet service providers, owners of attacking systems, victims, other CSIRTs, and vendors.	RC.CO-1: Public relations are managed.	• COBIT 5 EDM03.02
	RC.CO-2: Reputation after an event is repaired.	• COBIT 5 MEA03.02
	RC.CO-3: Recovery activities are communicated to internal stakeholders and executive and management teams.	• NIST SP 800-53 Rev. 4 CP-2, IR-4

Source: National Institute of Standards and Technology, *Framework for Improving Critical Infrastructure Cybersecurity.* Gaithersburg, February 12, 2014.

RC.CO-2: Reputation after an Event Is Repaired

If the organization does not already have one, they should put time into creating a crisis communication plan to help them and their customers manage their reputation in the event of a cyberattack. While media may not care to write about how your stellar technology solution helped one of your customers successfully ward off a cyberattack, they definitely will be more than excited to write about how your product failed to secure sensitive data from being compromised. A crisis communication plan will help respond to the media, customers, and the public by outlining the organization's response ahead of the crisis. As the organization is working through the recovery processes, detailed processes from within the crisis communication plan can be employed to prevent negative reactions from spinning out of control.

RC.CO-3: Recovery Activities Are Communicated to Internal
Stakeholders and Executive and Management Teams

There are several critical elements for ensuring successful communication. The first of these is planning. Recall from our previous discussion that organizations should develop a crisis communication plan. While that plan addresses communication external to the organization, it should also include defined processes for recovery communication between internal stakeholders, executives, and management teams.

The plan must include the formal provisions for communicating the results of recovery and actions taken during each phase of the recovery process to decision makers as well as any attorneys. In operational terms, this means that any procedures for communication have to ensure that all parties can understand and work with each other. The expectations of management must be clearly provided, and mechanisms are in place for constructive feedback from individuals performing process activities.

Chapter Summary

- There is often confusion between the activities that take place in business continuity and disaster recovery. Business continuity focuses on maintaining some degree of normal business operation in the face of an attack. Disaster recovery focuses on recuperating ICT assets that have been compromised as a result of a cybersecurity attack.

- Depending upon the severity of a cyberattack, recovery could be as simple as restoring a database or as complex as acquiring replacement ICT assets. Regardless of the extent of restoration, the organization should develop a plan that outlines all of the applicable activities and policies necessary to effectively manage the recovery process.

- As important as continuous process improvement is to all ICT processes, the same is true of cybersecurity recovery. Organizations should use lessons learned and feedback from recovery team members to develop matrices that can be used to evaluate and update recovery strategies used within the recovery process.

- Communication is vital for the successful accomplishment of any organizational objectives. Cybersecurity attacks often threaten the reputation and customer loyalty of the organization if not communicated properly. To provide the organization a baseline for how the recovery process is communicated externally and internally, a crisis communication plan should be developed that defines communication channels, procedures, and the individuals that should take part in the communication of attack recovery.

Case Project

Suny Corporation has suffered a tremendous reputation degrading as a result of the 2014 cyberattack. Management realizes that most of that reputation sacrifice they have encountered is due to the lack of a crisis communication plan that could have followed immediately after the cyberattack occurred. Management would like you to continue the work you have been doing on the plan for implementing the Framework for Improving Critical Infrastructure Cybersecurity. Now that you are familiar with the outcomes of the Recover Function, they would like you to develop a crisis communication plan for the organization. The best place to begin is to identify the organization's internal and external stakeholders. Next, identify the communication that is needed of those stakeholders during each phase of the recovery process. Within the incident response plan, only major steps of implementation need to be organized. In other words, focus on steps that the framework recommends for establishing and improving their cybersecurity program. The plan should continue to take the form of a project timeline that describes when each part of every step is performed. Besides providing a customized timeline and plan, include the business justification for each step.

PART II

Cybersecurity Governance, Audit, and the COBIT 5 Framework

8

THE COBIT FRAMEWORK

After reading this chapter and completing the case project, you will

- Accurately differentiate the COBIT Framework from other frameworks and methodologies that exist in the market;
- Understand IT enterprise scenarios based on the Pinpointing–Acclimating–Delegating/Driving–Synthesizing (PAD²S) approach;
- Understand the role that IT governance plays when implementing the COBIT Framework;
- Understand the COBIT Framework's audit guidelines;
- Understand the principles of the COBIT Framework; and
- Understand the various components of the COBIT Framework Model.

Assumptions

The second part of this book focuses on the COBIT Framework. The framework will be decomposed and comparatively analyzed to give the reader a thorough perspective that has been derived from IT governance leaders, practitioners, technical professionals, and other stakeholders.

One consistent assumption that you will find when considering COBIT as a framework for best practices is that the receiving enterprise must have naturally grouped processes in which IT managers and essential stakeholders can control those processes. In organizations where managers function in the capacity of solely administrators, implementing COBIT would be a challenge. IT managers and essential stakeholders must have the leeway to exercise accountability for every aspect of each business process.

In some organizations, high percentages of the technical direction come from higher levels and managers may not be as technical nor in tune with the business aspects of the work that their employees execute. The expectations of successfully implementing COBIT are that the enterprise and business will value creation from those IT personnel who are essential players in implementing COBIT's principles and processes. COBIT also assists in bringing an enterprise to be compliant with internal and external policies as well as legal regulatory parameters. The last expectation is that COBIT will satisfy the business users and stakeholders through IT engagement and services. Far too often, IT suborganizations are not valued in the highest levels of the organization. COBIT enables IT personnel at all levels to achieve and promote a better understanding and mastery of the business.

IT Governance

It is important to make the distinction among all three of these perspectives and how important each of their roles is during the framework's execution. This applies to COBIT, as well as other frameworks in the industry. For example, a chief technology officer may have a high-level perspective of the benefits of COBIT. This perspective will be discussed in the later chapters, but this book will also share scenarios which demonstrate how IT employees at the grass root levels must be on board to successfully ensure that COBIT's components and principles are properly filtered to everyday practices within the organization. Examples of these roles could be, but not limited to, chief executive officer, chief financial officer, chief information officer, chief technology officer, executive vice president of information technology, IT program manager, IT project manager, information systems security officer, IT security specialist, IT specialist (system administrator, database administrators, programmer/developer, storage/backup administrator, ERP system administrator [SAP, Oracle, or others], computer operators, LAN support technicians, network systems engineers, and several others), and, of course, the customer.

As an IT enterprise leader, it is important to relay the benefits of COBIT, and the positive potential contributions that it makes to the enterprise, to the most technical and operational levels of the enterprise. Working as a system administrator and an IT security specialist, many years ago, I always took a proactive approach in understanding the Capability Maturity Model (CMM) and how my everyday practices helps to improve the organization's maturity ratings. In some compartmentalized organizations with strong cultures of protocol, this can be a challenge; however, I have found it to work better for the organization when such ideas are communicated to the most technical levels. This approach only enhances a culture of information sharing, which results in the organization moving away from ad hoc communications and toward optimization when using the CMM as a metric. Figure 8.1 shows the CMM maturity levels and how those levels play out within the enterprise and the typical dialogue that you will hear with IT personnel.

In 1996, ISACA created COBIT as a means to unite the division that exists within organizations, when managing technical challenges and mitigating business-oriented risks. In 2012, ISACA released COBIT 5, which consists of 37 optimal practices which are assembled under five domains: (1) Evaluate, Direct, and Monitor; (2) Align, Plan, and Organize; (3) Build, Acquire, and Implement; (4) Deliver, Service, and Support; and (5) Monitor, Evaluate, and Assess. There are 17 enterprise goals that are generic and geared around the dimensions of the balanced score card (BSC) which was adapted from Robert Kaplan and David Norton's 1996 Harvard Business Review article entitled "The Balanced Scorecard: Translating Business into Action." The four BSC dimensions are financial, customer, internal, and learning and growth. To better understand how these dimensions map to the enterprise goals, Figure 8.2 offers a conceptualization.

Framework Model

It is important to specify what distinguishes the COBIT Framework as a framework and model of best practices. Oftentimes, organizations confuse COBIT with various subcomponents of the framework. If an organization has an internal group that specifically conducts audits throughout the fiscal year as an effort to mitigate IT security policy violations, this does not equate to that organization following the COBIT Framework. When I worked in an IT security role, a large part of my job was to manage and administer our UNIX systems through compliance checks with an internal audit group, which would conduct audits once per year. The internal audit group's purpose was to prevent violations that may arise during external audits, which

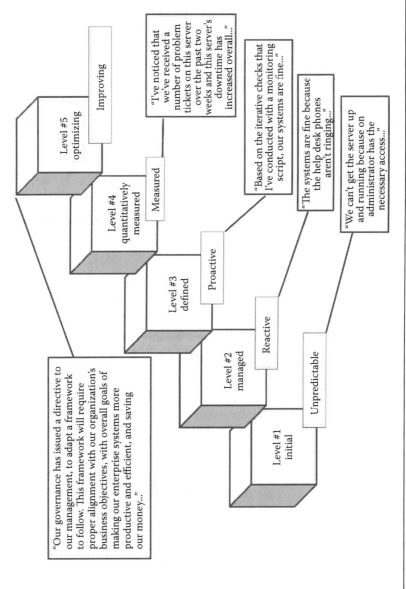

Figure 8.1   Practical enterprise dialogue of various CMMI levels.

Motivational factors			
BIG software America	Organization consultants	Local consulting	Internal IT personnel (IIP)
The engineers from BIG software America (BSA and BSA2) are trying to get the project complete with minimal conflicts. They want to get away before the political aspects of the software development life cycle begin.	The consultants from OC are trying to get the contract extended so it is in their best interest to train the internal IT personnel but in doing so, they sometimes hold back, so that higher level management will feel like they are needed, and that their contracts should be extended. They tend to also criticize BIG, as consultants, but this is due to them not knowing the historical foundation of the project and how/why things are technically set up.	These consultants also want their contracts to be extended but they are local to the Midwest office. They tend to be critical of the need for OC being around. They believe that OC is a threat to their contract's livelihood. There also tends to be a "Teach them, but don't teach them too much–type attitude," when it comes to training the internal IT personnel. Also, within the Midwest office, there is a "Contractor versus internal IT personnel" attitude around the organization.	The internal IT personnel have a number of different perpectives when it comes to the knowledge transfer process. One, they are skeptical about taking it over because they overhear all of the negative commentary that OC relays about the technical layout. The second perspective is that there is a competitiveness between the OC contractors and the IIP who are acquiring the technical skill sets rapidly.

Figure 8.2 Examples of varying goals and motivational factors within an enterprise.

were conducted every 2 years from an external auditing organization. This external group was oftentimes referred to as a watchdog over several organizations. Formulating audit scripts, which were specifically geared toward checking that certain security policies were being followed, was one of my everyday tasks. Additionally, installing and maintaining audit software on our UNIX servers to strengthen the security policies was also required. Neither of these examples distinguished our organization as one that followed the COBIT Framework. IT audit plans would have to be developed to try to simulate what the internal and external groups would be auditing for. This proactive strategy was often beneficial because it helped us to avoid violations. However, developing and following audit plans does not distinguish an organization as one that follows the COBIT Framework. These are all examples of contributing components to the COBIT Framework. Several individuals from the examples were involved in the IT audit discipline. The UNIX system administrators were involved because they were the technical professionals who would have to make changes to the scripts in order to extract the most accurate reporting data from the UNIX servers for compliance purposes. The managers which resided over the UNIX system administrators at various levels also had an interest in what would result from the IT audits. Violations often would be reported up to the director level, which was a few levels above those first line managers. IT auditors from both the internal and external audit organizations were involved in the audit work although their interests were different. Internal auditors worked toward avoiding violations through enforcing the policies and settings on the servers. External Auditors worked toward gaining an accurate picture of the "IS" state of the servers so that they could have a baseline to measure from. This is a strategy that has origins in IT research. The Action Research Design approach parallels this strategy. One must document the current state of an environment and after they have documented all of the essential aspects, they would freeze the state and document it as the IS perspective. Keep in mind that most of the aspects must be measurable. It is only at this point when an intervention can be injected into the environment itself and once that change has been executed at some point, the optimal projected view must also be conceptualized and documented. What would be considered a success with this intervention? The answer to this question feeds the "SHOULD" perspective. After a few iterations of porting the changes into the environment, the various aspects of measurable points are measured again to determine if the change brought the organization any closer to the optimal SHOULD state. These roles and process improvement IT research strategies are all similar to the roles that follow the COBIT Framework and all help to feed the internal audit discipline. Also, roles such as the IT auditor, the business process auditor, and the IT inspection team all play distinctive parts in the internal audit discipline.

The common uses of COBIT within the internal audit discipline are initiating and regulating standards, constructing and promoting measuring tools and processes to conduct risk assessments, formulating the audit plan, managing the audit itself, mitigating lingering risks, and dispatching findings and notifications to audited groups either when violations occur or when there are pending potential risks if the interventions are not made.

Practical Technical Scenarios (PTSs)

To facilitate a smoother transition of knowledge, throughout the later chapters of this book, it was decided that an approach should be created to properly express technical scenarios to readers in terms that are understandable. Since this book focuses on IT organizations and the focal points of the different security frameworks, it is important to show various perspectives within the practical real-world examples which are shared. First, the Context–Challenge–Action–Results (CCAR) format is recommended to assess executive core qualifications when applying for executive jobs through the office of personnel management.

The first step, the Context step, requires a description of the actors involved in the scenarios and the roles that they play within the organization as a whole. Also embedded in this step would be any additional detailed information that relates to governance within the enterprise (If they are a manager, how many employees do they manage and what are their level of a managerial authority? If they are a system administrator, how many users reside on the systems they administer?). It is also important to point out that there will be times when the Context step will change throughout the life cycle of the problems themselves. For example, if a storage/backup administrator wrote a script for a computer operator to make a spontaneous backup at 3:00 a.m., neither roles may have any outside knowledge beyond the fact that they are being directed to fulfill a request by management. At 3:00 a.m., when the operator inserts the tape into the machine and navigates to the script on the operating system to run the backup, the context is limited to simply running a backup for the Storage/Backup administrator who will be in the following morning. The context potentially changes if during the following morning, an executive has lost their data and they need that data restored due to a pending legal matter that has arisen. At that point, that backup's success takes on an entirely different meaning and context. If the backup failed, the criticality of the failure would be relayed at the highest levels of leadership. During the Challenge step, details to the challenge are shared, as well as any variables that may play a part of the constraint itself. For example, an executive decision was made to spend a large amount of the IT budget to replace all of the existing personal computer monitors in the company for this reason. This request has a turnaround expectation of 36 hours. Next, during the Action step, whatever intervention or strategy was injected into the scenario to make a difference is explained in detail. Finally, the Result step will explain how that intervention impacted the organization for the better. During the Result step, multiple perspectives may be shared which show the impact from the executive level, as well as practical levels, which may be rooted in configuration management, performance optimization, process improvement, or preventive maintenance.

In creating the approach for technical fact sharing, it is also important to show the perspectives of IT personnel and how they interact with internal IT disciplines such as configuration management, IT Security, capacity planning, and several others. For that purpose, the IDAO approach was identified as a grass root approach that is used for identifying and properly assigning IT stakeholders to different IT problem resolution tracking roles. The IDAO acronym represents the process that is executed to gain the necessary background information about the stakeholders. It represents the following sequence of actions:

- **I**dentify the problem tracking stakeholders.
- **D**etermine how each of the problem tracking stakeholders interact with problem resolution tracking.
- **A**ssign each problem tracking stakeholder to one of the four Problem Resolution & Tracking—Process Improvement Model (PR&T-PIM)* roles.
- **O**rchestrate execution of the PR&T-PIM.

When merging the two approaches as a customized methodology for technical IT scenarios, throughout this book you will find the PAD²S Approach. This approach consists of pinpointing all aspects of the problem or technical obstacle, acclimating to the political climate and properly assessing who is responsible for what, delegating or driving the intervention that will be injected into the technical or political environment, and synthesizing all of the findings into a conclusion, which preferably would be documented in some format for future reference.

This format will be used throughout the final eight chapters of this book when sharing PTSs. Readers who currently work in IT or manage IT personnel will certainly be able to relate to many of these scenarios.

---

* PR&T-PIM which was developed, validated and tested during my dissertation. It requires the interaction of the four roles: (1) security role, (2) manager, (3) system administrator, and (4) technical leader. These four roles interact iteratively within the process model with a configuration management system or database bringing more efficiency and accuracy to data centers and enterprise environments.

What Drives COBIT 5

There are several drivers that serve as essential factors to implementing COBIT 5. The drivers come from IT communities that have focused on business, IT risk, and security and assurance. It should also be mentioned that user communities have also been contributors in formulating these drivers. When implementing COBIT 5 driving factors include the following:

- Ensuring that the stakeholders are aware of the benefits and the level of risk and costs associated with implementing COBIT 5—The stakeholders must be given a say in determining what their expectations are from the information and related technology. This also applies to stakeholders defining if their expectations are short term or long term and how soon they are anticipating the results. The stakeholders must be involved and the IT organization must be transparent in they how go about achieving the expected results. The following PTS illustrates this from the perspective of a stakeholder who is the IT customer.

PTS 8.1 WHAT ARE THE DEVELOPERS DOING?

- Pinpoint—A group of software programmers have been directed to build a system that will track internal and external awards and certificates for all personnel in the company. As the group has progressed through the SDLC, they have found that the customer has voiced complaints about not being adequately informed of what development work is going on. The programming group has been working diligently to get the code done, and according to SCRUM meeting notes, the programmers are ahead of schedule as far as when they are projected to turn over the code to the customer for external testing. What is a strategy that can be used to make the work that they are doing more transparent to the customer?
- Acclimate—The programming group consists of five Visual Basic programmers. There is one lead programmer, and all of the group reports to one branch level manager, who in turn reports to a vice president. The lead developer also serves the role of the project manager managing the overall schedule.

Since this is a newly formed group, there is less precedent accountability practices in place. The lead programmer holds daily SCRUM meetings with the group to assess where each programmer stands with their deliverables and also to determine if anyone needs help. Typically, no managers are involved in these meeting because they are very technical in nature.

- D^2—First, the SCRUM meetings would have to change its logistics to focus on some of the business aspects of the project and the overall project schedule. In order to change these focus, the lead programmer would start to share with the team about where they stand as far as the project's schedule during the daily SCRUM meetings. The lead would also notify the team that the customer would have the option of joining the daily SCRUM meeting in a couple of weeks. The technical aspects of the meeting would continue as always, but the change would be only to ensure that the customer was able to hear firsthand what work was going on daily. If the customer had any questions, during the meetings, they would be addressed when asked.

- Synthesize—The programmers and the lead became comfortable with communicating about the project and this also fostered more transparency between the work that was being done and the customer. Another result was that the developers were able to see beyond the code that they were writing and look at the bigger picture, and how that code was being measured and monitored in the schedule and what the customer's expectations were.

PTS 8.1 demonstrates the importance of stakeholders being included in implementing the components of a framework. It also leads us to the next driver. There must be an understanding that the success of the enterprise heavily relies on external business and IT stakeholders, such as outsourcing groups, IT management consultants, IT vendors, and service providers. The success also relies on internal employees from various IT organizations and internally developed tools and processes. This can be a challenge at times, because there are instances with different groups that are tasked to work on the same project have different political motives.

- Promoting IT as an essential part of business also serves as a driver of COBIT 5—The framework states that it needs to be an integral part of business projects, organization structures, risk management, policies, skills, processes, etc. (ISACA 2012, pp. 1–5).

  Since the access to and storage of information has significantly increased, the most relevant data must be determined. This approach optimizes the business. Whatever data are agreed upon as being important should be managed through COBIT 5 and the framework will assist in facilitating this driver. It may also be a wise strategy not to be close-minded to models that may have been developed by technical internal personnel who have developed their technical expertise within the environment and infrastructure itself.

Framework Principles

There are five major principles for governance and management of IT within the COBIT 5 Framework. They are as follows:

- Principle 1 (P1)—Meeting stakeholder needs
- Principle 2 (P2)—Covering the enterprise end to end
- Principle 3 (P3)—Applying a single, integrated framework
- Principle 4 (P4)—Enabling a holistic approach
- Principle 5 (P5)—Separating governance from management

P1: Meeting Stakeholder Needs

In many IT organizations, there are different subgroups that consistently maintain different sets of objectives. In fact, you will find many IT organizations to also have varying cultures that have derived informal drivers or precedented perspectives of how certain IT work has been executed in the past. For example, a group of system administrators may find themselves being more reaction oriented as opposed to proactive. As an IT manager, you may hear statements such as "The systems are fine because the help desk is not calling me and there are no problem tickets in my e-mail inbox." On the other hand, a software development group may be more methodical in how they spec out the requirements that will eventually lead to the programming work. Both perspectives are extremely important and many times, the way each group prioritizes is based on sheer circumstance. As a UNIX systems administrator, I was promoted to a role of SAP Basis Administrator. SAP is middleware, Enterprise Software which interacts with the database, the operating system and the module of SAP which is being used to strategically manage business operations and customer interaction and satisfaction. Parts of this role include enterprise administration and manageability of; System Availability, Operating System Administration, Database Administration, SAP Application Administration, System Configuration, User Administration, Desktop Management and Corporate Networking and Support Package Application. This required an expertise of several operating systems, the database, and the SAP module that I was administering. After I gained this expertise as a basis administrator, higher-level management delegated me with the responsibility of powering down the ERP system in multiple data centers. This required me to technically coordinate all ERP powerdowns. All of our systems had different components and applications that were housed in multiple data centers. This expertise led to a further promotion as an infrastructure architect. Being the infrastructure architect was the most technical assignment that I had. It was my job to know every UNIX command, every SAP transaction code, every cluster takedown code or process, every configuration management report format, and many additional highly technical processes. While I worked as the infrastructure architect on the ERP project, it was one of my duties to manage the knowledge transfer phase of the project. This was a high-profile project for the government agency, and it required a great deal of diplomacy when it came to dealing with the various contractors and higher-level government managers. One of these duties required the coordination of all training efforts between all of the engineers and the government IT personnel. For the purposes of confidentiality, I have applied hypothetical names to the following groups. BIG America (BIG), was the software company that implemented the ERP system at the government agency. The consultants from BIG were engineers by discipline and they were responsible for the implementation and testing phases of the SDLC. Once those engineers came close to successful testing of the environment and the ERP system, an additional group of consultants was sent in to transition the body of knowledge about the environment from BIG to the government agency. These consultants are called Organization Consulting (OC) and by nature, they were analyst types, as opposed to engineers. These contractors resided in the headquarters with the BIG engineers. There was an additional group of contractors that resided at the Midwestern data center, where I was working at the time. This group was from a consulting firm, called Local Consulting (LC). With all of these consultants from all of these different firms, there was plenty of room for controversy. Everyone had his or her own motives.

Overall, as you see above, this environment fosters a complexity of controversy and technical/management perspectives. I had to manage all of these aspects of the knowledge transition process. Making this environment harmonious was often a challenging task. My approach was to foster an environment that was more receptive to diplomacy rather than silo-type functional units. Instead of allowing SAP to handle efforts where one of the other units could be involved, I required participation from all four teams. Meetings were held that required participation from everyone. Whenever there was a need to handle an issue that affected system administrators nationally, I would invite all of the teams to the emergency meeting, encouraging all participants to participate. The following PTS illustrates this from the perspective of an IT manager.

PTS 8.2   BLACKOUT, DATA CENTERS, ALL HANDS ON DECK

- Pinpoint—Unexpected change and pressure is the best way to gauge how one will react to it. In 2003, there was a blackout that hit from New York throughout the Midwest where the data center was located. The challenge was how we were to bring down over 100 servers and multiple platforms in a half an hour, which was only given to us because of our backup generators. Preservation of the data and all our hardware was the objective to this challenge.
- Acclimate—Mission-critical applications and systems are housed in a data center located in the Midwest, and users and IT personnel log on to the systems from all over the country.

- D^2—Since I had gathered documentation for takedown procedures for all of our systems, I immediately started to distribute copies of the standard operating procedures (SOPs) to all of the system administrators. Since I was a manager at the time, this was one of those times where I had to roll up my sleeves and bring down multiple systems myself. Armed with our SOP documents, our system administrators attacked taking down our systems floor by floor as quickly as we could.
- Synthesize—All systems were brought down on time. No loss of data came about. There were no hardware failures in the entire data center.

COBIT 5 has several enablers and processes which are defined as principles. The first principle requires the promotion of business value creation through the use of IT. An important part of this perspective is that the utilization of IT must feed and lead to creating business value. It is important to emphasize that in organizations where IT is viewed as nothing more than a subgroup of professionals with the toys, implementing this framework and this principle will be challenging. IT leadership must have a governance that resides in the upper levels of leadership. In many instances, the criticality of data and the systems themselves dictate how IT is perceived throughout the organization. The following PTS has ties to this as it shares a perspective from an IT manager.

PTS 8.3 WHICH SYSTEMS WARRANT THE HIGHEST PRIORITY LEVELS WITH MONITORING?

- Pinpoint—Mission-critical applications as defined by the highest levels of an organization's leadership were running in a data center located in the Midwest. As the manager of the IT specialist group of the data center during the midnight shift, it was the job of my team to ensure that those systems were up by 5:00 a.m. during times when there were problems.
- Acclimate—This involved several teams of IT specialists, computer operators, and many different managers. There were several platforms and applications that operated throughout the night and 100% of the applications running in this Midwest

city's data center were 24-hour operations. The criticality of the systems being up and running when morning came was so important that if some of these systems were down for an hour, an executive would be on the phone, and if those systems were down for more than a day, that executive would fly to the data center. There were also systems that were so critical that if they were down for more than a week, the highest executive leadership would be informed and involved.

- D²—Establishing a solid preventive maintenance and monitoring strategy was my approach to resolving this issue. Being able to foresee issues before they happen and being proactive with those systems were strategies that were difficult and tedious to build and execute but they were worth it.

- Synthesize—Although the systems that resided in this Midwest data center were mission critical and had direct ties to executive leadership, it was more important to encourage my employees to understand the ties of our systems to our customers. When I packaged the initiative in that way, our personnel took pride in making the difficult decisions.

P2: Covering the Enterprise End to End

Everything that is considered IT related and any IT personnel who works with these IT components are all considered assets when following the COBIT 5 Framework. During the blackout–data center–all hands-on-deck scenario, it did not matter if a server's host name was embedded in an SOP or written in a text file that is saved on one's laptop as long as it was accurate and could be used to bring down a server. Likewise, the SOP documents themselves had to be accessible and distributable to qualified trained technical personnel in order to facilitate expedient successful emergency server takedowns. This principle in COBIT 5 is challenged during these sorts of situations. However, this principle can also be used in more of a proactive sense. The following PTS speaks from the perspective of an IT researcher that worked in an enterprise. It also speaks to how tracking an organization's assets can be used in a proactive sense to determine what path to take in resolving enterprise-wide technical issues.

PTS 8.4   **WHAT TYPES OF PROBLEMS CAN BE POTENTIALLY RESOLVED THROUGH USING AN IT ENTERPRISE ARCHITECTURAL FRAMEWORK?**

- Pinpoint—This challenge was directly articulated and posed by IT's leadership in an organization's data center. The leadership asked for ideas of best practices or a strategic intervention that could be executed which could enhance the data center's reputation among the various other data centers in the organization.

- Acclimate—The problem was rooted in redundancy in all of the data center's configuration management processes. Another component of the overall challenge was that communication processes were either nonexistent or unreliable between management, executive management, IT personnel, IT security personnel, and the users. Since the challenge involved all multiple data centers, one data center became the guinea pig of all three for the intervention prototype run. There were also thousands of technical stakeholders that held an interest in correcting this technical problem.

- D^2—The preliminary research to determine whether an IT architectural framework was a feasible solution was achieved by populating a Perks Beveridge IT Architecture Health Matrix. Following this strategy, five IT assets are required to be tracked. They were security assets, data assets, software assets, hardware assets, and networking. Each of these assets is essential to an organization's IT infrastructure. The IT researcher had to hold several meetings with several subject matter experts from respective domains to ask a set of questions that focused around procurement, integration, security, and a few additional topics. Once those answers were acquired, they then had to migrate the data into numeric form. Once those numbers were analyzed, they were able to prove that it was a feasible approach. The IT researcher then had to do extensive research on the enterprise manageability subview of the Open Group Architectural Framework (TOGAF—a European IT Enterprise Architectural Framework) and this part of TOGAF focused on configuration management, preventive

maintenance, and performance optimization. Once they established an expertise in TOGAF, they then had to build a functional prototype of the process improvement model that could
be followed and injected into the technical environment.
- Synthesize—Communications between management, executive
  management, IT personnel, and security personnel increased in
  quality. System downtime was decreased based on the usage of
  archived data, which was an embedded component of the process improvement model's functional prototype. Overall configuration management ticket numbers decreased.

One of my first IT jobs was when I worked for a municipal public
school system in a major city. My post of duty was in one of the largest
high schools in this city. During my first week of working in that job as
a computer education technician, I was exposed to multiple operating
system platforms and technologies and it was one of the most challenging yet rewarding jobs I have ever experienced. In this role, I dealt
directly with system administration functions such as the following:

- Administering early generations of Apple's operating system
- Administering IBM's AS/400 platform and administering
  networking which dealt with either Appletalk or Ethertalk
- Administering early versions of security software (Macintosh's
  At Ease)
- Building, maintaining, and administering databases in Microsoft
  Access or Macintosh Claris Works

Many of these daily tasks dealt directly with tracking inventory
assets. The AS/400 system was being used to track student records and
textbooks. A database that I built would eventually lead to decreases
in truancy amongst the high school's students. Teachers and students
would feel more comfortable with saving their work and sensitive files
such as a student's grades to our Macintosh servers which I admin-
istered protection through Macintosh's security software, At Ease.
Needless to say, it would have been great if we had the knowledge
back then to understand the importance of enterprise architectural
frameworks and how they can be used to optimize managing an
enterprise which in this case was a high school's IT infrastructure.
Ironically enough, I had a solid understanding during this time of the

CMM, and I worked toward defining processes to make the infrastructure and organization more efficient.

P3: Applying a Single, Integrated Framework

There are several best practices that fall under various IT subdisciplines. Project managers follow Project Management Body of Knowledge (PMBOK), and some use Six Sigma as a measuring tool to optimization. Enterprise architects may follow TOGAF to accurately manage an enterprise's infrastructure. Every day, IT professionals strive to improve and further define processes within IT organizations through using the CMMI Maturity levels as a guide to improvement. The Supply-Chain Operations Reference model is used by supply chain managers to communicate best practices amongst each other. COBIT 5 enables all of these methodologies to tie into it, serving as an overarching avenue to best practices and IT governance management. In enterprises that have several different technologies and technologists, every subgroup has their own set of best practices, which oftentimes are followed without communicating to each other. COBIT 5 enables the leadership in the enterprise to orchestrate communication between all of these subgroups more effectively.

P4: Enabling a Holistic Approach

There are seven enablers that COBIT 5 defines as promoting the achievement the objectives of an enterprise. The enablers must work cohesively in order to achieve governance. The seven enablers are Enabler 1: Principles, Policies, and Frameworks; Enabler 2: Processes; Enabler 3: Organizational Structures; Enabler 4: Culture, Ethics, and Behavior; Enabler 5: Information; Enabler 6: Services, Infrastructure, and Applications; and Enabler 7: People, Skills, and Competencies.

Enabler 1: Principles, Policies, and Frameworks
The governance in any IT organization's attitudes are asserted through the principles that it relays to its personnel, which in turn define the direction that the enterprise is moving in and why they have decided to navigate in that direction. Through an enterprise's set of principles, governance relays transparency of assets all of the stakeholders

who reside both within the enterprise and outside of it. An enterprise's mission, many times, is further decomposed and elaborated upon through its principles. Governance documents which outline an enterprise's ethical expectations as well as their social responsibilities to its stakeholders both fall under this principle. An example of this comes to mind from when I worked in an IT UNIX system's role. There were IT security policies that were written at a very high level in which I was asked to contribute to authoring. Additionally, there was a relationship between what was actually stated in the high-level IT security policies and the actual UNIX scripts which I authored and executed to run on the servers which insured that the high-level policies were adequately reflected in the most technical settings on our servers. Many times, I would inject comments within the shell script itself which would reflect the high-level policy numbers which the script was reflective of. At the most technical levels IT system's personnel have an direct interest in understanding what it expected because it is documented in the comments of the code itself, whether that be a UNIX shell script or a C++ or Java program. This traceability is important and enhances the relationship between what leadership conveys as policy and what is expected of the enterprise's technical IT personnel.

Enabler 2: Processes

There are 37 processes associated with the COBIT 5 Framework. Although implementing these processes gives leadership a firm grasp of the enterprise, there are several enablers which are not embedded in those processes. When one thinks of an enterprise, you cannot ignore culture. COBIT 5 specifically defines 26 practical roles that are categorized under either business or IT. Keep in mind that depending on the organization, various process stakeholders as listed in Figure 8.3 could be broken up into different roles and subroles. For example, some organizations have equity and diversity executive officers, which may serve in the same function as the head of human resources' capacity, which is listed in Figure 8.3.

There are direct potential challenges that arise when leadership fails to address the culture in the enterprise before they try to streamline the processes throughout IT personnel as far as best practices. Summaries of the 37 processes are shown in COBIT 5's Process

COBIT5 process stakeholders	
Business	IT
Board	CIO
CEO	Head architect
CFO	Head of development
COO	Head of IT operations
Business executives	Head of IT administration
Business process owners	Service manager
Strategy executives commitee	Information security manager
Steering (program/project) committee	Business continuity manager
Project management office	Privacy officer
Value management office	
Chief risk officer	
Chief information security officer	
Architecture board	
Enterprise risk committee	
Head human resources	
Compliance	
Equity and/or diversity executive (and their organization can reside in either column in many goverment agencies)	

Figure 8.3 Stakeholders of COBIT 5 from both IT and the business.

Reference Model (PRM). The PRM groups the processes into five domains. They are (1) Evaluate, Direct, and Monitor; (2) Align, Plan, and Organize; (3) Build, Acquire, and Implement; (4) Deliver, Service, and Support; and (5) Monitor, Evaluate, and Assess. Goals are associated with each process that allow the practitioner to gauge how close they are to achieving optimization toward those goals. This process serves as an embedded metric.

Enabler 3: Organizational Structures
There are few common characteristics that COBIT 5 requires the practitioner to consider when planning organizational units. Those are as follows:

1. The various well-defined roles of different staff members, and the scheduling frequency of meetings along with how those meetings will be documented.
2. From the perspective of a complete structured unit, how many of the stakeholders are internal verses external?
3. Who makes the decisions and what authority does each manager have when it comes to the IT personnel that they are responsible for?

4. What parts of the enterprise are controllable by a person?
5. Delegation practices must be well defined as to what is permitted and what is not.
6. Escalation practices must be well defined as to how the practitioner and stakeholders elevate matters that cannot come to resolution through normal avenues.

Enabler 4: Culture, Ethics, and Behavior
The key stakeholders who facilitate this enabler typically will be rooted in human resources management, lawyers, Equal Employment Opportunity Commission (EEOC) counselors and managers, compliance personnel, and individuals who serve in the role of ranking promotion packages for promotions and hiring initiatives. These people focus on optimizing an organization's behaviors when it comes to cultural characteristics such as fairness, equality, and properly promoting the rules of behavior in the enterprise. Practices that openly promote fairness and cultural enrichment must be routinely communicated in all levels of the enterprise to ensure that certain behaviors are consistent among the stakeholders and the values expressed from leadership. Leadership must lead by example and encourage stakeholders by providing examples. There must also be an emphasis placed on how misrepresentations and deviations from these expected behaviors will be handled by the enterprise.

Enabler 5: Information
Since information will always have an important role in business, COBIT 5 emphasizes this and categorizes it as an enabler. The information which is stored on computers may not be recognizable in its most decomposed context. That information is migrated to an understandable asset, after which it is ported into meaningful knowledge for the enterprise. Another result are business processes which require IT and business stakeholders to work together in formulating and maturing the data into meaningful business knowledge. There are several stakeholders who are involved with this enabler. COBIT 5 categorizes these stakeholders into three categories. Information producers are involved in the creation of the information. Information custodians deal with the storage and maintenance of the information. Information consumers utilize the information.

COBIT 5 emphasizes and defines certain optimal qualities for the information. The framework strives to ensure that it is accurate and reliable (intrinsic quality). COBIT 5 also measures the relevance of the information (contextual quality). The third and final emphasis for quality of information focuses around availability and adequate restrictions of access to the agreed upon stakeholders (security and accessibility qualities). As part of the COBIT 5's Information Model, the Semiotic Framework is executed to determine which information will be the most helpful in driving certain business decisions. The Semiotic Framework sets out to conceptualize the four perspectives (and various subcomponents), which reside between what is viewed as the social world and the physical world. The four major perspectives are pragmatic, semantic, syntactic, and empiric. They deal directly with the following three groups: people activities, information systems, and IT systems.

Enabler 6: Services, Infrastructure, and Applications
COBIT 5 informally defines service capabilities as a merger of infrastructure and applications. The best way to understand this is to envision the typical roles that reside in a data center. Multiple operating systems may employ teams of system administrators to properly maintain each operating system platform and vast numbers of servers. Desktop and hardware IT personnel who work on maintaining the personal computers and their connectivity to the network are included. Database administrators who plan the capacity of large databases and who formulate complex queries to extract data in order to build meaningful reports are included. Telecommunications IT personnel who work with the cables and maintaining the physical aspects of the network are included. Storage area network IT personnel who work with backing up data and applying the strategies to capacity planning for backups are included. Each of these groups and many more must work cohesively when delivering results to the stakeholders, customers, and businesses. Employing solid enterprise architecture is the only way to bring about manageability to all of the complexity. COBIT 5 serves as a framework that several best practices can plug into (e.g., TOGAF, PMBOK and Information Technology Infrastructure Library [ITIL]).

Enabler 7: People, Skills, and Competencies

Skill sets are essential in order to facilitate any and all of the seven enablers for COBIT 5. Proper skills must be in place for both internal and external stakeholders. Most roles will have specific requirements for skill set competencies.

P5: Separating Governance from Management

COBIT 5 specifically distinguishes between the roles of management and governance. Roles that fall under these two categories have a set of distinct activities and responsibilities associated with them. The differences are shown next.

Management

Management deals directly with facilitating concurrence with the employees that they manage and the direction that an enterprise's governance provides. The manager will therefore promote, frame, conduct, and administer policies that come from governance.

Governance

Governance deals directly with safeguarding stakeholder commitments and privileges through proper analysis. This analysis will result in the defining the following:

1. Enterprise objectives that the enterprise sets out to accomplish
2. Prioritizing the direction to assist in strategic decision making
3. Tracking concurrence and attainment of those objectives

Other Governance Frameworks and Best Practices

It is also important to discuss additional frameworks that may either serve as potential architectural plug-ins to COBIT 5 and a general understanding of others that exist in the industry. For the purpose of maintaining our focus on enterprise governance, we will discuss three frameworks, namely, the U.S. Committee of Sponsoring Organizations (COSO) Internal Controls, ITIL, and COSO Enterprise Risk Management (COSO ERM).

COSO Internal Controls

IT managers in the enterprise must ensure that certain controls are being followed consistently. This attention to detail is oftentimes a balancing act because it sometimes causes conflicts between IT security personnel and IT systems personnel. For example, when an enterprise is subjected to random audits, an enterprise IT security team may be responsible for checking various security and capacity settings on servers to make sure that they are compliant before external auditors come into the picture. IT security personnel may not have enough access to change or manipulate the configuration settings on the servers themselves. In many cases, they can only report their findings to IT systems personnel who then log on and make the necessary changes. IT systems personnel, therefore, are placed in a difficult situation, because making some of the recommended configuration changes, often times, depletes the server's resources, which they are responsible for. Each role reports to an enterprise manager, but in many cases, these managers work for different suborganizations. When following COSO Internal Controls, all of the internal stakeholders of an enterprise hold an obligation to follow the internal controls in wherever suborganizations they reside in. Therefore, in the earlier example, both the IT security group and IT systems group must work toward executing and maintaining the controls that are defined by enterprise governance. An organization has a set of good internal controls if it (1) accomplishes its stated mission in an ethical manner, (2) produces accurate and reliable data, (3) complies with applicable laws and enterprise policies, (4) provides for the economical and efficient uses of its resources, and (5) provides for appropriate safeguarding of assets (Moeller 2013).

COSO Internal Controls primarily focus on accounting and financial matters and enterprise processes.

Information Technology Infrastructure Library

Many of the PTSs lend themselves to the ITIL Framework because they come directly from IT operations (or enterprise operations, as it is called many times in the industry). The ITIL 2011 edition includes a series of five publications that focus on the various IT Service Management (ITSM) life cycle stages. The five publications are

(1) ITIL Service Strategy, (2) ITIL Service Design, (3) ITIL Service Transition, (4) ITIL Service Operation, and (5) ITIL Continuous Service Improvement. There are several decomposed parts that apply to each of these five publications. Since this book is not focusing on ITIL, let us summarize the ITIL Framework. The framework outlines a generic set of processes. This set of processes is adaptable to most organizations and, therefore, can be practiced in various IT enterprises. It requires the framework to be consolidated with the objectives that are formulated by the organization's governance. Outputs of the framework include an informal criterion from which the organization can begin measuring ITIL's practices.

Committee of Sponsoring Organizations Enterprise Risk Management

The COSO ERM Framework consists of eight segments and four objectives categories. The eight segments are (1) Internal Environment, (2) Objective Setting, (3) Event Identification, (4) Risk Assessment, (5) Risk Response, (6) Control Activities, (7) Information and Communication, and (8) Monitoring. Next are the four objectives categories: (1) Strategy, (2) Operations, (3) Financial Reporting, and (4) Compliance.

Chapter Summary

- The outcomes of understanding the practical perspective of what it takes to feed CMMI maturity levels provide IT managers with a solid foundational understanding of how to evaluate what enterprise systems personnel are working on at the front lines of ICT, and many of the obstacles which they're confronted with day in and day out.
- The PAD^{2}S model feeds the perspective understanding of IT managers and they're most technically granular job functions. The model can be used as a tool to better understand a technical challenge within the enterprise. It can also be promoted and streamlined to ICT employees as a way of attacking and managing ICT issues. Practical technical scenarios are introduced to also support and better facilitate a practical understanding of ICT issues.

- A solid understanding of how the framework ties into ICT governance is also essential and a byproduct of this chapter. Enterprise environments are complex, and this in itself hosts several day-to-day challenges and proper management of those challenges during the life cycle of each technical enterprise issue.
- Varying motivations exist in the ICT enterprises, and it's important for ICT managers to have a good understanding of factors that may motivate different subgroups and the cultures and subcultures that exist in the enterprise.
- ICT managers must also have a solid understanding of how to learn about the stakeholders. This chapter offers the IDAO process as a way to acquiring and fostering this knowledge base.
- ICT Enterprise Architectural Frameworks and Project Management best practices are also touched upon at a high level in this chapter (TOGAF, PMBOK, ITIL, COSO, and COBIT 5).

Case Project

An organization's data center will have to conduct a semiannual powerdown a week from now and it is the middle of the summer in Phoenix, Arizona. All involved IT personnel are to report to the Thursday-morning configuration management meeting. This is called the Change Board Meeting because it also included IT enterprise managers from various domains (Telecommunications, Programming and Development, Windows System Administration, UNIX Systems Administration, Mainframe Systems Administration, Windows Security Administration, UNIX Security Administration, Mainframe Security Administration, Database Administration, Storage Area Network [SAN] Backup Administration, and several other groups). Keep in mind that each of the subgroups that were mentioned has multiple managers and IT personnel. For example, the UNIX Systems Administration categorization covers three different IT enterprise managers, who have three teams that focus on three different flavors of UNIX and who administer different servers (Solaris, Red Hat Linux, and SCO Unix). During the powerdown, all electricity will be shut down in the building; however, there are backup generators which 100% of the servers, SANs, and tape libraries are connected to. The sales vendors from the various hardware and software companies all have assured us that 100% of the equipment can run comfortably in varying temperatures. Some of their technical representatives will also be present during the Change Board Meeting. The powerdown will occur on a Friday evening and all power will be restored to the data center on Sunday night to allow for extra time for issues that may arise when the power is brought back up. Some IT managers have opted for their system administrators to bring their servers down during the weekend window. Others are taking the advice of the sales vendors and entrusting the fact that the hardware will continue to run properly throughout the time that the air conditioning units are down. One hundred percent of the hardware has warranties and contractual agreements for support from the hardware and software companies. Adequate data backups will be needed prior to the powerdown. Some network managers have decided to make some changes to the cabling during the downtime. One of the PC support groups, which report to the Windows Systems Administration senior manager, has decided that they will install 150 new flat-screen monitors during the downtime window. Following all sets of SOPs will be mandatory during this event.

Taking some of the knowledge that you have acquired about COBIT 5 and other frameworks from this chapter, can you determine why you would opt to follow either COBIT 5 or one of the other frameworks? What are some of the questions you would raise during the change board meeting?

9

DECOMPOSITION
OF FRAMEWORK

After reading this chapter and completing the case project, you will

- Understand the creation of framework principles;
- Understand the definition of categories and seven enablers;
- Understand the control issue; and
- Understand navigation overview.

Framework Principles: Creation

COBIT 5 primarily used existing reference models to establish the following generic business requirements: quality requirements, security requirements, and fiduciary requirements. Decomposing these further, COBIT 5 focuses on quality confidentiality, cost integrity, delivery availability, effectiveness and efficiency of operations, reliability of information, and compliance with laws and regulations.

Definition of Categories and Seven Enablers

These various metarequirements can be factored into the seven distinct end qualities: effective, available, efficient, compliant, confidential, reliable, and having integrity. These are the universally desirable characteristics that information should exhibit.

Government systems tend to lean toward each of these end qualities when it comes to the various regulations that govern how data are formulated, stored, and regurgitated in reports for legal reasons or regulatory compliance. Availability is certainly subjected to intense scrutiny when it comes to who can monitor or administer what data. When it comes to fiduciary requirements, the organization must have the highest levels of reliability because requirements may be subjected to future audits. The auditors will have to know what those requirements were, what was actually agreed upon by the system's builders and administrators, and what falls beyond the scope of those requirements. It is also important that traceability is distinct and clear between the requirements themselves and the most granular technical components (often computer code or functional deceptive use cases). The following PTS illustrates this from the perspective of a stakeholder who is the project manager over a modernization project.

PTS 9.1   Do You Have a Signed Set of Requirements?

- Pinpoint—A group of software programmers has been directed to modernize a system from an older programming language into Java. This will increase the functionality and scalability of the newer version of the system. Since the older system had no formalized enterprise life cycle nor project management documentation, those developers have been forced to rely on the expertise of one subject matter expert who worked on the building of the first system. It is, therefore, the job of the group of developers to reverse engineer the requirements from scratch. The issue became how to acquire agreement from the customer on what we would build for them without allowing the customer to continuously add functional requirements to the developer's tasks. Additionally, another factor contributed to this problem. No project management plan (PMP) nor a project tailoring plan (PTP) were endorsed from leadership. Since there was not budget to fund the project, it was brought forth by leadership as a project which could be executive through shared resources. Since these documents are essential to moving a project forward through the project management enterprise life cycle, it was difficult to acquire the necessary support at higher levels, which would facilitate cooperation from the customer.
- Acclimate—The group of developers consists of one subject matter expert who has the most understanding of the older system two expert Java developers who understand the newer programming language, and seven junior-level Java developers who have been through an intense 10-week Java technical

training program (but who have minimal programming experience). There are three other team members who are responsible for managing the development tasks and the project management aspects of the project, as well as the required project management life cycle. For the purposes of project tracking and the project's life cycle, this project will follow an iterative path; however, there will be agile components that feed the development phase. SCRUM meetings will be held daily to track the developers and documentation progress and efforts.

- D^2—There was a three-legged stool approach when it came delegating and driving the development activities along with the enterprise life cycle documentation. One project lead would facilitate daily SCRUM meetings and document the findings daily. Another project lead was responsible delivering and logistically managing all of the sign-offs of the documentation. A manager would manage the managerial aspects of personnel and two other subdevelopment leads would manage and participate in the development activities.

- Synthesize—Without a signed PMP or PTP, there was no evidence of a set of fiduciary requirements which the customer had relayed to the developers and agreed upon. The workaround was to develop a simple spreadsheet that consisted of each and every detailed functional requirement and have the customer endorse that spreadsheet by way of a digital signature. Once this was achieved, both the PMP and eventually the PTP were updated to reflect this agreement and deviation from the normal development path. In the future, that signed portable document format spreadsheet with the digital signature from the customer would be able to stand up to future internal and external audits.

The COBIT 5 framework emphasizes seven enablers. The first enabler emphasizes the principles, policies, and frameworks. This enabler derives the behaviors that are desired for IT employees and the practical guiding aspects of manageability for daily progressive optimal performance. The next enabler focuses on processes. This enabler defines a group of practical behaviors and tasks that ultimately result in successfully upholding, supporting, and maintaining IT goals.

Organizational structures is the enabler that feeds the most important decision-making components in the enterprise. Traditionally the next enabler was not keyed in when it came to progression of the enterprise but culture, ethics, and behavior of how IT employees and stakeholders are managed is important in how it serves as a catalyst in fostering success in governance. The final three enablers make up the resources of COBIT 5. Any information which is formulated, utilized, stored, or retrieved by the enterprise is a fierce enabler and puts IT organizations at an advantage. This enabler also ties to the everyday operations because embedded within this component, there is high probability that the information itself is one of the most important factors. IT is often composed of employees who provide services in maintaining an enterprise's infrastructure. Falling under this umbrella is the everyday preventive maintenance and performance optimization duties that come along with administering processing within the enterprise. This enabler is services, infrastructure, and applications. The final enabler of COBIT 5, people, skills, and competencies, is one of the most important. IT personnel's skill sets and consistently building upon their expertise will eventually foster more strategic and accurate decisions when resolving technical issues and taking action with resolving issues. Figure 9.1 shows a conceptualization of the seven enablers of

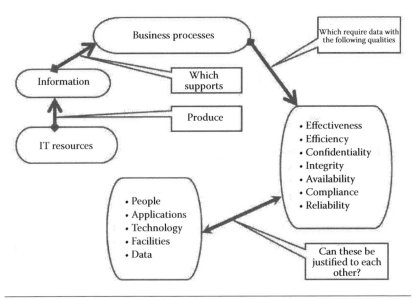

Figure 9.1   Process flow for COBIT 5.

COBIT 5 and was adapted from Chapter 5 of *COBIT 5: A Business Framework for the Governance and Management.*

Control Issue

Figure 9.2 shows a simplified conceptualization of the control issue. IT resources reside at the beginning of most project's success. IT resources formulate, administer, archive, and recall information. Valuable information should always support business processes and the business strategy and direction should always be reflected in IT initiatives. Business processes require data which contain the following characteristics: effectiveness, efficiency, confidentiality, integrity, availability, compliance, and reliability. Likewise, there is justifiable parallelism between those qualities and the various aspects of IT (people, applications, technology, facilities, and data).

In government agencies, there are several checks and balances in place when it comes to ensuring that a new build of a system is compliant when it comes to confidentiality, integrity, and compliance. Typically, there will be an internal security-oriented organization that is responsible for auditing newly built systems, during the time that they are being built and after the system goes into production and maintenance. The user population and maintainers of the system will determine that system's effectiveness, efficiency, availability, and reliability.

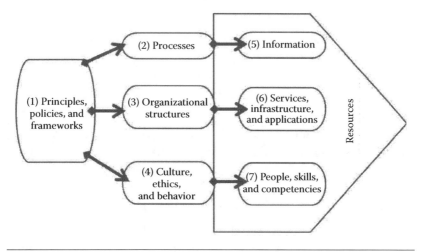

Figure 9.2 Seven enablers of COBIT 5, working as a cohesive unit.

Navigation Issue

There is a reliance that exists between IT processes and business requirements. This relationship ensures that business is the focal point of processes that govern and drive IT. When formulating a set of requirements to build a new system, it is important to have the business stakeholders present to assure that each requirement matches what that business stakeholder or customer is looking to achieve. IT processes, therefore, satisfy business requirements. In organizations, there is a consistent tendency for managers and leaders that manage these types of work (IT processes and business requirements) to have disagreements on which is most important. IT process managers that are closer to the development work, often times, express frustration when it comes to business requirements holding up development work, and therefore hindering an expedient go-live date. IT managers who are aligned with the business aspects of building a new system tend to continuously search to assure that their business objectives are embedded in the technical functional requirements. A challenging part of the SDLC is acquiring the sign-off from the business customer on the technical functional requirements, which will be followed when building a system or writing a Design Specification Report (DSR). In fact, when one analyzes what makes up a thorough DSR, they find technical sections such as Application Design, Application Architecture, Integration Design, Security, and Data Design. As you can see, there is nothing in this documentation that specifically targets the business side nor the business objectives. However, that is why it is so important to make sure that the business objectives are reflected in the requirements that are agreed upon. The project document that focuses more around the business expectations of building a new system is the Business System Report (BSR). In this document, one would see subsections that focus heavily on the business such as business system concept descriptions, business drivers and objectives, current state, future state, conceptualized solution, and stakeholders. The documents become a little more technical as you get to the later parts of it when you would see subsections such as Business Architecture, Business Process Architecture, Business Rule Sets, System Architecture, Infrastructure Architecture, Application Architecture, and finally there would be a traceability subsection that speaks about relationships between what

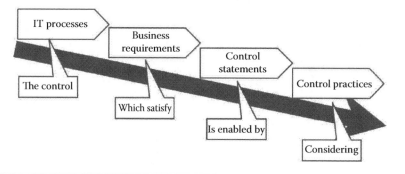

Figure 9.3 The navigation issue.

the customer and builders agreed to in the functional requirements and what the expectations are for insuring that those requirements are reflected in the finalized system. Figure 9.3 shows a simplified conceptualization of how the navigation issue flows.

Chapter Summary

- The seven end qualities and enablers of COBIT 5 are introduced to provide ICT managers with a high-level foundation of what COBIT 5 sets out to accomplish.
- The process flow of COBIT 5 shows actionable tasks and questions that further explain what COBIT 5 manages the enterprise.
- Cohesive work is required when executing any ICT Enterprise Architectural Framework, and this is properly facilitated through defining the resources and stakeholders.
- The navigation issue is one that exists between stakeholders that build enterprise systems and the customers for which those systems are built. This concept is further decomposed for better understanding by ICT managers.
- The extensive documentation requirements of managing a project through planning and execution are essential to enhancing CMMI maturity levels. The case study in this chapter attempts to relay that complexity to the reader and demonstrate some of the everyday constraints that ICT managers and project managers will be faced with when using COBIT 5.

Case Project

As a senior IT manager who manages a group of UNIX system administrators, you are enjoying your new promotion. This potentially makes large technical change efforts a little easier for the enterprise because of your experience as a former technical UNIX systems administrator and project manager. An initiative has come down from an executive from the internal IT security organization requiring a group of files on every UNIX server to be edited to reflect new security settings and monitoring information, which will have to be scripted, on the various servers. Since this initiative is coming from the executive level, it has been determined that a scaled-down version of the iterative process will be followed to properly document the project through the various life cycle stages. This will require several documents to be formulated before the technical work is initiated. Those documents are as follows: PTP (with a Milestone 4B Exit that specifies all of the remaining documents, including the PTP), PMP, Configuration Management Plan, Disaster Recovery Document, and a Computer Operators Handbook. Formulating these documents will assist in cases where future audits may arise, so executive endorsements from the technical side, the IT security side, and the customer side of the enterprise will be mandatory on each document's endorsement page. The change itself is supposed to align the UNIX side of the enterprise with the external auditor's expectations that conduct audits on the enterprise every two years. Since you are ultimately responsible for maintaining the UNIX systems (and the UNIX system administrators who administer these servers), this requires your team to conduct these changes on 54 UNIX servers over a 24-hour period. You delegate the work to your team members. As an IT manager, express how you would approach this effort based on what you know about the navigation overview and the control issue. With the time constraint approaching rapidly, would you push back to executive leadership and ask for more time (which is absolutely necessary to formulate the required documentation in time)? Or would you push forward with the technical work, and take the risk of being subjected to an audit before the documentation is complete? What are some critical points that you will make to your UNIX system administrators before they get started with this work (on both the documentation and the technical work itself)?

10

FRAMEWORK STRUCTURE'S GENERIC DOMAINS

After reading this chapter and completing the case project, you will

- Understand planning and organization;
- Understand acquisition and implementation;
- Understand delivery and support; and
- Understand monitoring.

COBIT's Framework Structure

Evaluating the framework from operational level, there are activities that are composed of the day-to-day tasks that the business carries out to produce measurable outcomes. Activities within this domain have a life cycle orientation, while tasks are more discrete. The life cycle view has control requirements different from those of discrete activities.

Taking responsibility and ensuring accountability are essential to COBIT 5's success. "In all cases (of various sized and structured organizations), appropriate governance organizational structures, roles and responsibilities are required to be mandated from the governing body, providing clear ownership and accountability for important decisions and tasks. This should include relationships with key third-party IT service providers" (ISACA 2012, p. 57). Management level processes are then defined one layer up. These can be viewed as a series of logically related functions with natural divisions in responsibility and control. In essence, this provides the functional definition of IT work from which information requirements can be derived. At the organization level, processes are naturally grouped together into generic domains. That natural grouping is often defined as the things that an organization has to do in order to be effective. It is the presence or absence of these generic features at any level of functioning that dictate the relative performance of the organization (or organizational unit). Control can be dictated from three vantage points:

- Operational—with discrete information requirements/criteria
- Managerial—functions deployed to perform IT work
- Organizational—logically related IT processes

Four generic domains can be identified for the organizational level:

- Planning and organization
- Acquisition and implementation
- Delivery and support
- Monitoring

Planning and Organization

Strategic planning is such an essential part of the COBIT 5 Framework. It can be generically defined as a well–thought out initiative that results in which direction drives what the organization is, its stakeholders, and its customers and why the organization is moving in a certain direction. One of the following questions or a combination of two or all three should be asked when strategically planning an IT enterprise project. Generally, strategic planning deals with at least one of three key questions:

1. What direction are we going in?
2. Who is the stakeholder or customer we are working for?
3. How can we improve our performance and efficiency to make it there?

Planning and organization has four distinct elements, all of which need to be established in order to successfully follow the COBIT 5 Framework. Those elements are vision, mission, values, and goals. Figure 10.1 shows a general conceptualization of these elements along with the questions that must be asked in order to acquire and define these elements.

Planning and organization is the domain that is focused on strategy and tactics. It centers on the identification of the way IT can best contribute to the achievement of business objectives. When working on modernization efforts where IT developers are porting systems

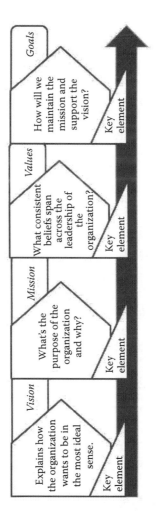

Figure 10.1   Conceptualization of COBIT 5 elements and supporting questions.

which are programmed in older programming languages to newer programming languages and more scalable platforms, oftentimes development teams and managers will meet with the customer and brainstorm and document what they are setting out to achieve with the newer modernized system. In some organizations, these meetings are referred to as business requirement harvesting meetings. Once those requirements are established and agreed upon by the appropriate stakeholders and the concurrence signatures are received, then the project manager will work to formulate the work breakdown schedule and finalized project schedule.

In walking through COBIT 5's practical aspects associated with planning and organization and its control objectives, next you will see a high level of the decomposition of the expectations of COBIT 5 (in Chapter 11, the purposes, employment, and structures of COBIT 5's control objectives will be discussed):

- Define a strategic IT plan
  - IT as part of the organization's long-/short-range plan
  - IT long-range plan
  - IT long-range planning—approach
  - IT long-range planning—structure
  - IT long-range plan changes
  - Short-range planning for the IT function
  - Communication of IT plans
  - Monitoring and evaluating of IT plans
  - Assessment of existing systems
- Define the information architecture
  - Information architecture model
  - Corporate data dictionary and data syntax rules
  - Data classification scheme
  - Security levels
- Determine technological direction
  - Technological infrastructure planning
  - Monitor future trends and regulations
  - Technological infrastructure contingency
  - Hardware and software acquisition plans
  - Technology standards

- Define the IT organization and relationships
  - IT planning or steering committee
  - Organizational placement of the IT function
  - Review of organizational achievements
  - Roles and responsibilities
  - Responsibility for quality assurance
  - Responsibility for logical and physical security
  - Ownership and custodianship
  - Data and system ownership
  - Supervision
  - Segregation of duties
  - Staffing
  - Job or position descriptions for IT staff
  - Key IT personnel
  - Contracted staff policies and procedures
  - Relationships
- Manage the IT investment
  - Annual IT operating budget
  - Cost and benefit monitoring
  - Cost and benefit justification
- Communicate management aims and direction
  - Positive information control environment
  - Management's responsibility for policies
  - Communication of organization policies
  - Policy implementation resources
  - Maintenance of policies
  - Compliance with policies, procedures, and standards
  - Quality commitment
  - Security and internal control framework policy
  - Intellectual property rights
  - Issue-specific policies
  - Communication of IT security awareness
- Manage human resources
  - Personnel recruitment and promotion
  - Personnel qualifications
  - Roles and responsibilities
  - Personnel training

- Cross training or staff backup
- Personnel clearance procedures
- Employee job performance evaluation
- Job change and termination
- Ensure compliance with external requirements
  - External requirements review
  - Procedures for complying with external requirements
  - Safety and ergonomic compliance
  - Privacy, intellectual property, and data flow
  - Electronic commerce
  - Compliance with insurance contracts
- Assess risks
  - Business risk assessment
  - Risk assessment approach
  - Risk identification
  - Risk measurement
  - Risk action plan
  - Risk acceptance
  - Safeguard selection
  - Risk assessment commitment
- Manage projects
  - Project management framework
  - User department participation in project initiation
  - Project team membership and responsibilities
  - Project definition
  - Project approval
  - Project phase approval
  - Project master plan
  - System quality assurance plan
  - Planning of assurance methods
  - Formal project risk management
  - Test plan
  - Training plan
  - Postimplementation review plan
- Manage quality
  - General quality plan
  - Quality assurance approach
  - Quality assurance planning

- Quality assurance review of adherence to IT standards
- System development life cycle methodology
- System development life cycle methodology for major changes to existing technology
- Updating of the system development life cycle methodology
- Coordination and communication
- Acquisition and maintenance framework for the technology infrastructure
- Third-party implementer relationships
- Program documentation standards
- Program testing standards
- System testing standards
- Parallel/Pilot testing
- System testing documentation
- Quality assurance evaluation of adherence to development standards
- Quality assurance review of the achievement of IT objectives
- Quality metrics
- Reports of quality assurance reviews

Acquisition and Implementation

There is a great deal of preplanning which goes along with executing acquisition and implementation. Since the documentation during this stage are all living documents which more than likely will be updated as the project migrates through the life cycle, many of the same documents will be repeated throughout the delivery and support part of the project. Early in the project's life cycle, finalized versions of both the Business Systems Document and the Design Specification Document should be completed. Other documents will be written in their first drafts enabling technical personnel, project managers, and IT managers to revise them as the project moves forward including

- Business Systems Document (finalized draft);
- Design Specification Document (finalized draft);
- Interface Control Document (first draft, living document);
- System Deployment Document (first draft, living document);
- Transition Management Document (first draft, living document);

- User Training Documentation (first draft, living document); and
- Computer Operator's Handbook (first draft, living document)

Delivery and Support

When looking at acquisition and implementation, both of these components of IT management are also extremely important to properly feed the COBIT 5 Framework. In software development, the organization that is responsible for building a system typically holds the responsibility of formulating the documents which will drive the project through the implementation phase of the SDLC. Some of those documents are listed below:

- Business Systems Document
- Design Specification Document
- Interface Control Document (finalized draft)
- System Deployment Document (finalized draft)
- Transition Management Document
- User Training Documentation (finalized draft)
- Computer Operator's Handbook (finalized draft)

Some of these documents can be written in their entirety by project managers who consult with technical personnel; however, the Design Specification Document should be written by some of the most technical resources involved in the project. Depending on your company or agency, in some instances, the Business Systems Document may be written by the customer stakeholders in order to insure that every aspect of the business their business expectations are properly documented.

One of the issues that consistently arise when executing these tasks is that technical personnel will be asked to step away from their technical job functions to either add input to a technical document or scrutinize what a project manager or less technical team member has written. This is why it is important for team members and managers who are involved in both the documentation and the technical aspects of the project to understand at a high level what both groups are working on. This also holds true beyond the development of new systems. The following PTS gives an example of how redundancy can have a potential issue if groups are not on the same page when dealing with configuration management.

PTS 10.1 GETTING ON THE SAME PAGE

- Pinpoint—There was a great deal of miscommunication between the contractors and internal IT personnel when it came to configuration management processes. This miscommunication took place in all levels on both sides. The challenge, therefore, was to decrease miscommunication and increase the accuracy of information on both sides.
- Acclimate—Contractual employees in the organization were called *prime*. In several consistent instances, there were times when system and policy changes were initiated by one side or the other, and those deviations were tracked on two separate tracking systems. In fact, there were different problem ticket numbers at times tracking these changes where the other side would not be aware of the progress to various resolution efforts.
- D^2—Someone developed the "handshake process" and sold the idea to executive leadership on both the internal side and the prime side. What it basically involved was every time a problem ticket or policy change was opened on either side, whatever ticket number was created on one of the two systems that ticket number would be embedded into the history of the other ticket on the opposite tracking system.
- Synthesize—This simple yet innovative intervention enabled both contractors and internal personnel to query one system (whichever that chose) on a ticket number and get accurate feedback as to the progression of the resolution and/or policy changes.

Transition management is also a focal point of delivery support. This is the subprocess that promotes organizational acceptance to own, administer, and maintain the new systems. It is sort of a watchdog that gives the OK for the builders to hand over the keys to the newly built system. Figure 10.2 shows how the transition management process works and the various aspects of this subprocess must be documented in formal transition management document. In many organizations, there are internal transition management suborganizations that are responsible for analyzing whether the customer/stakeholder's organization is ready to receive the system and technically maintain it.

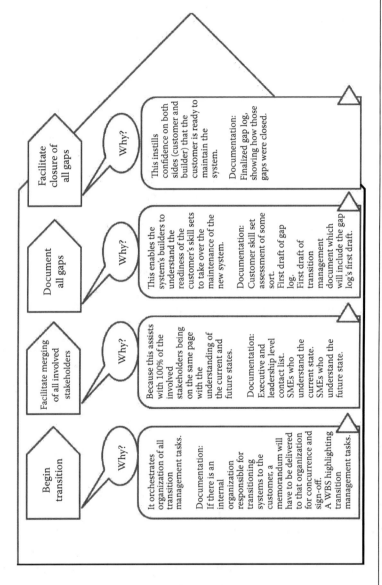

Figure 10.2 Transitioning a newly built system, essential documentation and questions.

Two critical documents must be finalized that will assist in elevating an internal transition management organization's confidence in concurring with the system's handover. Those are (1) Adequate User Training Documentation and (2) a thorough Computer Operator's Handbook (COH). The building organization should also offer at least a few informal training sessions to walk through these documents so that the customer will understand how to use the documents as tools.

Monitoring

Preventive maintenance and performance optimization are IT disciplines that are usually mastered by system administrators and database administrators as opposed to developers. When building a new system, a developer will have minimal background in understanding how the system's performance will be without being there to monitor it for a few months after it has been in production. Therefore, the COH will ultimately have an addendum attached to it to increase the customer's understanding of how to properly maintain the system. This will be used only for reference purposes for those customer stakeholders who would be responsible for maintaining the system. No additional signatures will be required for the concurrence pages of the COH itself and this in no way would prevent the project from exiting the final milestone of the project's life cycle.

When it comes to monitoring a new system whether it is an application or an operating system where the application resides (or a database's capacity), it cannot be acceptable to have a reactive mindset among those who are conducting iterative monitoring tasks. This was touched upon in Figure 8.1 from Chapter 8 of this book. As an IT manager, when you approach IT personnel to inquire about a new system's performance, an unacceptable answer would be, "There are no problem tickets opened for the system, so things are looking good." That is the answer that a reactive mind-set promotes. On the other hand, an acceptable answer would be, "Based on iterative checks which we have run during these cycles, the systems are looking good based on the analysis which we have conducted."

COBIT 5 has two levels of monitoring. The first level is relevant in a governance context. The process EDM05 Ensure stakeholder transparency explains the director's role in monitoring and evaluating IT governance and IT performance with a generic method for establishing goals and objectives and related metrics (ISACA 2012, p. 57).

Chapter Summary

- There are essential questions that leadership must ask when approaching the implementation of COBIT 5, and those questions were discussed in this chapter, including the four elements of planning and organization.
- It is very important for leadership to understand how COBIT 5 feeds the enterprise's vision, mission, values, and goals. Supporting questions should be asked at the highest levels of ICT leadership, as they pertain to each of these key elements of the enterprise.
- Many times in large ICT organizations, there is a consistent riff between contractors and internal ICT personnel. The practical scenario (PTS) in this chapter provides an example to learn from.
- Pre- and post-transition planning are an essential factor when building a new system, and following COBIT 5. An approach to managing this process was provided in this chapter.
- Many ICT frameworks don't put a great deal of emphasis on preventive maintenance and performance optimization and monitoring. This chapter explains how COBIT 5 can be used to focus on monitoring.
- Because of the amount of stakeholders that are involved in implementing COBIT 5 (or any other ICT Enterprise Architectural Framework), the case study sets out to confront the reader with an example of one of the most difficult challenges of ICT leadership, promoting transparency.

Case Project

You are an IT executive over a group of IT managers who manage various operating system IT specialists. There will be a massive push-out of patch updates that will be applied to every personal computer that is connected to the network on Thursday night. These patches are being applied to strengthen the security settings on all of the MS Outlook e-mail servers. When users log on to the network on Friday morning, as they are logging on and after the operating system stabilizes (fully boots up), they will receive a message from one of the operating system's groups, which reside in your organization. The message will read as follows: "Select *OK* for the updated configuration patch to be applied to the MS Outlook Application. Select *Cancel* if you want to wait until a later time." The CIO's office has sent out an info alert, via e-mail, telling everyone in the entire organization that this is a mandatory security patch. He/She also has stated that an internal audit group will be spontaneously checking for individuals who have not completed this task by Monday morning. As for everything else, it is business as usual. Data backups will also be run on Thursday night on all Wintel and UNIX servers for an upcoming external IT audit (on Friday morning). This requires computer operation's personnel (from outside of your organization, but also under the CIO) to physically place tapes into the servers and execute the *dumpallimportantDATA forBACKUP.sh* UNIX script and this will dump all data to the tape so that it can be utilized to restore the data if an emergency was occur and to hand it over to the internal auditors on Friday morning. Two options are available for the personnel conducting the backup. They can execute the script from the console, or they can connect from their personal computers in their cubes on a different floor, which in both cases must allow for the backup run for 8 hours. The second approach allows the IT personnel to be able to be engaged in other work. Midnight IT personnel will have to execute the backups. An enterprise-level change board meeting on Wednesday meeting will take place where multiple executives will be involved. Knowing what you have learned about COBIT 5 as it pertains to roles and also the levels of monitoring, how would you approach this as a participating IT manager? In this case, the users of the organization who use e-mail are the customers. What additional steps can you take to ensure that this effort is transparent to the stakeholders? It has been determined that a Session Description Protocol (must be written to properly document this effort. Who will you choose to write this document and why? Also, when should this document be finalized in relation to the patch pushout effort?

11

Decomposition
of COBIT 5 Principles

After reading this chapter and completing the case project, you will

- Understand Principle 1: installing the integrated IT architectural framework;
- Understand Principle 2: what do stakeholders value?
- Understand Principle 3: the business context focus;
- Understand Principle 4: managing risk; and
- Understand Principle 5: measuring performance.

Purpose of COBIT Control Objectives and Principles

The five principles that streamline COBIT 5 coupled with seven enablers promote governance through practical actionable management approaches and identifying everyday tasks which can be generically followed. Those in turn become a set of optimal management approaches that impact managerial governance throughout and above-enterprise IT. Many of the identified management approaches and tasks serve as an initial execution of control above the process that leads to acquiring the desired outcome.

In 2011, Erik Guldentops, a professor from University of Antwerp, Belgium, authored an article in the *ISACA Journal* that brought up some great points about control objectives. He makes the distinction between the objectives and actions. These two components of the various releases of the COBIT Framework throughout the years have oftentimes become mistakenly meshed together. This is due to the dilemmas that often arise between both audit and management. This conflict also exists at times between auditors and IT systems personnel. For example, while working as a UNIX systems administrator, there were internal audits that would require audit logs to be turned on to their full capacity. This translated to every keystroke being tracked and stored away in a log file for a duration. To satisfy the auditors, system administrators would turn on those log files. However, they would voice frustration about it because having those audit logs turned on took away from the system's performance because it was using the system's resources.

The older term of *control objective* used in earlier versions of the framework offered a precise and clear definition of activities to ensure effectiveness, efficiency, and economy of resource utilization. Thus, the control objectives allowed the control framework concepts to be translated into specific actions applicable for each IT process. Detailed control objectives were identified for each process defined by the framework. These were, by definition, the minimum controls required.

It is important for a relationship to exist between the framework's intent and the actions that are being documented and executed at the most granular levels. Since these written actions are essentially tools that produce results and increase efficiency and effectiveness in various IT processes, they must be authored in a concise detail with commotion also tied into the actual management practice. Some practitioners argue that this is one of the main reasons for IT enterprise architectural frameworks because the frameworks themselves make the most enterprises and infrastructures more manageable. Through observation and practice, this is evident when surveying the vast amounts of technology platforms that exist within an enterprise. There are times when platforms do not apply only to categorizing technology or operating systems but instead goes beyond this. The following Practical Technical Scenario (PTS) is an example I was confronted with early on in my IT career.

PTS 11.1   INTERNATIONAL SYSTEM ON THE WAVES

- Pinpoint—Tracking inventory payments on shipping vessels as they travel through foreign waters was a huge task that was set before a government agency. This directly dealt with the ever-changing global environment.
- Acclimate—There were potentially 500+ agency and stakeholder end users of this system, in addition to external authorities which would need access to various reports. The scale of this system was therefore enormous.

- D^2—We developed a system that could track all of the taxes in real time, 24 hours a day, 7 days a week. This involved purchasing the SUN E-XX hardware and the Solaris Operating System, building the accounts for 100% of the users, and building and maintaining the application itself. We will refer to the system for confidentiality purposes as the Ocean Inventory Tracker (OIN) system. This system comprised a set of production applications/activities that provide inventory information and support processes to assess the health and direction of the inventor-tracking program. Multiple applications support excise business processes and internal/external stakeholder activities.
- Synthesize—The system has been a success since its rollout and we have had minimal problems with it. Customers globally have been beyond satisfied. The long-term outlook for the system requires minimal changes.

Although this is an older example and today with Wi-Fi and satellite communication being so readily available, security has come to the forefront as a concern that must be mitigated and managed when dealing with this type of system.

COBIT 5 principles are universal in their commonalities and this enables them to be applied to varying practical functions of IT processes. Because of their adaptability, they can be used on multiple platforms.

Principle 1: Installing the Integrated IT Architectural Framework

Prior to COBIT 5, the earlier releases of COBIT's high-level control objectives were enabled by control statements (i.e., each of these control statements requires a set of potentially applicable control functions). Each control objective related to a corresponding process/activity, but navigation aids were provided to allow entry from any one vantage point and to facilitate combined or global approaches.

COBIT now enlists certain aims to adjust IT operation-oriented tasks with all the vast components of enterprise operations—setting up and strengthening partnerships between the business partners that reside in the enterprise and all of the planning which focuses on IT. This principle also directly deals with processes in how it sets out to foster and validate valued partnerships.

To further explain this principle, first, the needs of stakeholders are relayed to COBIT processes with a primary focus on value objectives and IT governance. Additionally, if there are internal or external standards or frameworks in place, COBIT seeks to work with them. Those needs are then fed through COBIT's seven enablers: (1) processes, (2) principles and policies, (3) organizational structures, (4) skills and competencies, (5) culture and behavior, (6) service capabilities, and (7) information. Once all seven enablers are calibrated to process those needs, they are utilized in a supportive way to the COBIT knowledge database. This is also inclusive of guidance materials that already exist and conceptualizations for future tasks. These become supportive catalysts to the overarching adaptation of COBIT processes. COBIT processes all have supportive reference guides.

Principle 2: What Do Stakeholders Value?

It is important to make good on the affirmations of IT delivery as they progress through the software or project's life cycle. Checks and balances should be in place to show the customer that their needs and expectations are being met at each milestone. The artifice to accomplishing this is to be able to present the how IT delivery is cost effective and beneficial to the organization because whatever is expected to be delivered is being done, ahead of schedule and within the parameters of the budget.

To accomplish this, all stakeholders must be properly defined and accounted for as well as the needs and concerns which they bring to the table. Associations between those needs and the leadership's strategic direction must be perpetuated thoroughly. Leadership in most cases will be governance and senior managerial leadership. It is important to point out that in some organizations, pinpointing the leadership is more of a challenge. Someone may not be a senior manager or executive in an organization but at the same time has the ear of their leadership when it comes to large-scale IT investments.

It is best to view stakeholders in two groups, which could be centralized and outer. Centralized will refer to internal stakeholders for the purpose of this discussion. They are individuals such as the following: the constituency of the board of directors, highest-level executives (CEO, CIO, CTO), senior management, IT security executives and management, finance executive management, HR managers, internal auditing leadership, IT operations management and personnel, IT systems management and personnel, and several other groups which are customizable and distinguishable based on the organization itself. The catalog of stakeholder's needs should serve as a single point of reference but should not be restricted to serving as the know-all-say-all because it is certain to grow. One must also take into consideration the culture in many organizations that may not openly promote the raising of issues whether those issues are with strategic direction or IT resources (which we are talking about here). This also applies to various levels of the centralized stakeholders. For example, someone who falls in the IT systems personnel group may think of an issue due to their analysis of process that is taking away from a system's performance and increasing various system downtimes. The same system person's executive may view the same issue from a varying perspective where they are looking at how many human resource hours it is taking to accomplish maintaining the issues in multiple environments per month.

The second group, the outer group, is what COBIT specifies as external stakeholders. This group may include (but are not limited to) contractors who are hired to support and strategically direct IT delivery, stockholders, external auditing authorities, and taxpayers (if dealing with a municipality/state/federal tax-collecting organization). Outer residing stakeholder's questions are more likely to focus around cybersecurity as it relates to the integrity of an enterprise and the regulatory requirements set forth by external auditing and justice-oriented policy makers. Most of this group's questions will focus around the three generic governance objectives defined in COBIT 5: (1) benefits realization, (2) risk balancing, and (3) cost optimization.

Principle 3: The Business Context Focus

This principle keys in on IT as more of an investment opportunity to save cost and increase efficiency in the organization. In most organizations, there will be a managerial structure in place to lead IT resources which are considered critical. This group will also be composed of system applications, infrastructure maintainability, and other IT personnel. These individuals are the closest to the systems.

They know the granular details of everyday performance optimization and preventive maintenance as well as the challenges which are most frequent. Capitalizing on this knowledge base of the infrastructure is an essential component of successful IT governance.

In the context of COBIT's value objectives, COBIT 5 associated each of these generic objectives to three enterprise goals: (1) financial, (2) customer related, and (3) internal (enterprise). There are either primary or secondary affiliations within each generic governance objective. *P* denotes *Primary*, and *S* stands for *Secondary*, of course. When looking at the granularity of a detailed mapping between one of the governance groups and one of the goals, it is easy to assess that the framework focuses on multiple levels of stakeholders.

Principle 4: Managing Risk

Managing risk should be prevalent in most organizations, whereas most IT management will have a good handle on how an enterprise deals with risks and also how the enterprise takes on compliance matters. There should also be a solid sensitivity to what risks are most important to the enterprise. Sometimes, this is guided in a reactive sense from something catastrophic that happens. If an organization is hacked and valuable data are stolen, of course risks of cybersecurity will be elevated to being the most important. Various operational organizations should have compartmentalized risk management duties as well as collective approaches to managing risks.

Principle 5: Measuring Performance

The measurement of projects throughout their life cycles should be evident in most organizations and processes should also be in place. To this end, there is an important distinction between governance and management. The governance in an organization is the pathway by which all stakeholders are able to relay their perspectives when it comes to direction, monitoring compliance challenges, performance optimization, and various project statuses. Although this responsibility falls upon the shoulders of the constituency of the board of directors in most enterprises, the perspectives of various levels of stakeholders execute their right to voice their concerns through this pathway. Management, on the other hand, oversees and drives various resources in pursuing the direction set forth by higher-level leadership and management.

Chapter Summary

- Control objectives and principles of COBIT's various versioned frameworks throughout the years have been the focal points of understanding for ICT leadership. These components are discussed at a high level in this chapter.
- Enterprise systems and organizations are international and have been for many years. The PTS in this chapter discusses an example that was derived from my professional experiences.
- How does leadership migrate from the idea of how an ICT Enterprise Architectural Framework would benefit their enterprise to actually implementing COBIT 5? This chapter discussed the installation of the framework from a high level.
- Understanding what the stakeholders of the enterprise value. This may assist leadership in promoting COBIT 5.
- Enterprise management requires a business focus that aids in aligning ICT and business focuses.
- Measuring performance and risk is also very important to ICT leadership and how one goes about selling the framework to other internal leadership organization.
- An inherent dilemma exists in many ICT enterprises when it comes to porting older systems, which are written in older programming languages, to newer programming languages. Managing this development process using the COBIT 5 principles is the subject of this chapter's case study.

Case Project

An IT organization's sub–Project Management Organization (PMO) was created to plan and manage the technology responsibilities in relation to the implementation of an Environmental Clean Air Act (ECAA) in 2008 and this resulted in several legislative requirements which are included under the areas of the ECAA PMO. ECAA ACA PMO is responsible for

- Defining the overall direction;
- Driving the day-to-day management and oversight;
- Formulating whatever requirements can be documented from the older system;
- Porting the essential requirements from the older system into a newer set of requirements; and
- Delivery of the new modernized IT ECAA system that will require an older system which was written in the Formula Translating System (FORTRAN) programming language to be rewritten in the newer programming language of Java.

There are several challenges that this project presents. There is an aging workforce composed of experts in the FORTRAN programming language but they are approaching retirement age. Most of these developers who were with the IT organization in the 1960s and 1970s, when the original system was built, came aboard with the organization after the system was built so they were only there for maintenance as opposed to planning and development. The tools that are currently used for requirements traceability are newer and modernized. How would you approach this problem while focusing on each of the COBIT 5 principles in this chapter?

12
COBIT Management Guidelines

After reading this chapter and completing the case project, you will

- Understand enterprise management;
- Understand risk management;
- Understand the status of IT systems; and
- Understand continuous improvement.

Enterprise Management

Senior managers in corporate and public organizations must consider expenditures to improve the control and security of their information infrastructure. While few would argue that this is not a good thing, all must occasionally ask themselves: "How far should we go, and is the cost justified by the benefit?" The answer to that question is provided in the COBIT Management Guidelines. The management guidelines also enhance and enable good enterprise management. They are intended to help the enterprise more effectively deal with the needs and requirements of IT security. In many organizations, there are extensive differences between the cultures of internal organizations who are responsible for different requirements. For example, cybersecurity may be interested in making sure that a system being built falls in alignment with the Federal Information Security Management Act requirements. Embedded in this culture, you may find IT auditing professionals who are certified information systems security professional. On the other hand, there is—a group of developers who are charged with formulating requirements for a customer and the traceability of those requirements through the requirements life cycle; these professionals are more concerned about being accurate

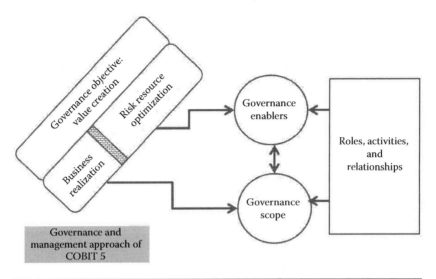

Figure 12.1   Conceptualization of COBIT 5, value creation.

with documenting what the customer/stakeholder wants so that the building organization can acquire some sort of sign-off.

Each of the COBIT 5's seven enablers has five subcomponents. They are (1) enabler stakeholders, (2) goals and measuring metrics, (3) enabler life cycles, (4) best practices, and (5) enabler attributes. Each of the seven enablers will have embedded centralized and outer stakeholders. As we stated earlier, the different cultures that exist when it comes to managing IT enterprises carries over to many of the stakeholders being internal and external. Figure 12.1 shows a conceptualized view of value creation.

Enabler goals should always be stated explicitly in a way that the aspired outcome is clear. Whether that outcome is a deliverable such as a project management artifact or a conceptualized process model, it is a very important component of the process goals. There is an inherent relationship among process goals, IT goals, and enterprise goals.

Risk Management

Risk management and security assurance depend on the ability to apply specific, repeatable management practices. The primary purpose for the development of the COBIT Management Guidelines is to provide a set of these for IT managers.

Goals can be formulated in different ways. For example, some goals are geared toward quality, whereas others may be geared toward timeliness in delivery. When following COBIT, one has to take all of these varying goals into consideration as well as the complex subcultures that exist when managing risks of different capacities.

Risk management should be proactive for the most part but when we think about disaster recovery and how this IT discipline focuses around simulating various events and the preparedness of the enterprise to handle those risks, it can be argued that it is reactive. While working as an IT specialist, every year we would conduct disaster recovery exercises to evaluate our readiness for our systems as far as data recovery, system downtime, and emergency awareness. This mandatory yearly requirement was a headache to many but because it was required, leadership can have a certain level of confidence knowing that so many people have been trained and know how to react in the wake of an emergency.

Prior to 9/11 HAZMAT, there were risk exercises that were performed by a combination of IT personnel, local fire departments, and several other groups responsible for maintaining an organization's infrastructure. When the tragedy happened, these sorts of exercises were elevated to become far more important to organizations in which they were not at first.

Status of IT Systems

Every organization has a basic need to understand the status of its own IT systems and to decide the level of security and control they should provide. Neither aspect of this issue—understanding or deciding on the required level of control—is straightforward. Furthermore, it is hard to get an objective view of what should be measured and how it should be measured.

Years ago, there was an application that ran on data center infrastructures, which would show indicator readings on a Graphical User Interface (GUI), reflecting the status of systems. If a system or application was down, it would show a red status on the GUI and the dashboard consisted of several indicator bubbles, each of which is represented on system, server, or application. Each could have thousands of users associated with them. Because of the critical applications and the amount of users, along with the money that was spent to build and maintain these systems, keeping an accurate eye on the status of every system was important.

Those same GUI status readings could be rolled up and manipulated to show executive-level dashboards, which the executives would define as mission critical. This sort of application becomes the backbone of war room efforts that may be maintained to strictly monitor problem resolution efforts.

Continuous Improvement

Besides the need to measure where an organization is at, there is the requirement to ensure continuous improvement in the areas of IT security and control. This implies the need for an executive dashboard to monitor that improvement process. One may ask why it is important for an IT executive to be involved in continuous improvement or the status of IT systems. Figure 12.2 shows the differences between governance and management.

Many times, there are efforts that are going on at the grass roots level which impact the enterprise at the highest levels. An IT leader should

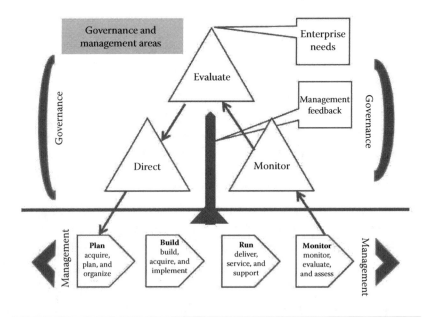

Figure 12.2   Conceptualization of COBIT 5, differences between management and governance.

not be blindsided by a catastrophic event if avoidable. Additionally, an essential component of COBIT 5 is to provide that overarching access which can key in on what is going on at the most granular levels of the enterprise. It is a matter of leadership preference.

When James taught as an adjunct professor at the University of Detroit Mercy, he always relayed to his students that it would be key in their successes to be observers as opposed to catalysts for change when they entered their first ICT jobs. In many enterprises, there are varying cultures that exist within, and many times, organizational charts do a poor job of actually relaying which personnel actually know how to get results. Working in four data centers, two in the private sector (automotive and banking) and two in the federal sector (intelligence community and administration), provided me with a unique perspective. Any mandated leadership program emphasizes the importance of culture and understanding those individuals or sub-organizations (and groups) that truly get results and are the "go to" entities in handling the most critical issues. ICT managers often have to inject change into a highly culturally diverse enterprise. PTS 12.1 gives an example of this.

PTS 12.1   CULTURAL DATA CENTER BIASES

- Pinpoint—When working in a data center, although it is the nerve center of your entire organization, at times it tends to be isolated when it comes to external policies and vision that is initiated by headquarters. This in itself fosters a culture that is skeptical when work has the potential of leaving the data center. There is somewhat of a unionized nature that is instilled in personnel in remote locations and when work leaves the location, it causes tension. My challenge was to teach my employees to become more competitive when it comes to getting new work to be directed toward the data center.

- Acclimate—The attitude of insecurity is derived from the consistent thought that the data center in the major U.S. city Detroit would be closed down one day because work and/or projects were being taken away. There were over 1000 employees at the data center in this city, and more than 50% of them had these types of insecurities when it came to projects being taken away.

- D^2—I developed a strategy to get my employees more proactive when it came to competing for work and new projects from headquarters. This involved teaching them how to research for different projects that were on the horizon. It involved teaching to how to make presentations to high-level executives and how to volunteer to the right assignments when they came up.
- Synthesize—My team was directly responsible for bringing three national projects to the data center, resulting in morale going up in the data center and insecurity decreasing. Other teams and managers began to adapt this strategy and more projects began to be directed toward the data center in this major U.S. city.

Chapter Summary

- The risk management component of COBIT 5 has several ties to governance, and these ties are elaborated upon and conceptualized in this chapter.
- "What is the status of an enterprise system (or system)"? This is a common question that is floated between leadership and ICT management. This chapter discusses this in more detail.
- Properly and accurately understanding an enterprise system's status also facilitates continuous improvement, which is a byproduct of COBIT 5 and also decomposed and conceptualized in this chapter.
- The case study in this chapter provides the reader with why it's important to focus on monitoring when using COBIT 5.

Case Project

This scenario is associated with an earlier example that was mentioned in this chapter. You are an IT manager who has been asked to fill in for another manager who works the second shift in a data center. The other manager's job is to document iterative readings of mission-critical applications that are housed in the data center. Your current managerial assignment does not deal with monitoring at all, outside of a few small monitoring processes, which you use on your team members and the projects they are involved with. Before you agree to the backfill assignment what essential information would you need from the manager you are backfilling for? At 1:23 a.m., after you have departed from the data center, you receive a call from one of your team members who relays to you that a major system is showing a red status on the Enterprise IT Status Monitoring System. How do you approach this problem and why? Based on enterprise management, risk management, status of IT systems and continuous improvement, why is this essential to COBIT 5?

13

COBIT Management Dashboard

After reading this chapter and completing the case project, you will

- Understand performance measurement;
- Understand IT control profiling;
- Understand awareness; and
- Understand benchmarking.

Performance Measurement

COBIT 5 assesses each of the enabler dimensions (stakeholders, goals, life cycle, and best practices) to manage performance. This is accomplished through asking about each the simple question of whether or not those enabler dimensions were adequately satisfied. The inherent need for continuous improvement implies the need for an executive dashboard to monitor the improvement processes.

This dashboard must address the following types of management concerns:

1. Performance measurement—What are the indicators of good performance?
2. IT control profiling
   a. What is important?
   b. What are the critical success factors for control?
3. Awareness—What are the risks of not achieving our objectives?
4. Benchmarking—What do others do? How do we measure and compare?

IT Control Profiling

When determining what is important as far as the critical success factors for control, it is important to have a full understanding of the environment and the stakeholders. Leadership aspires to have the entire enterprise understand what is considered a success and what is considered a failure so when information is relayed through the dashboard, everyone on every level has the same expectations and understanding. Also factored in must be the understanding that different levels and variations of personnel bring about varying perspectives about the same challenges. We touched on this in a prior chapter.

Awareness

COBIT 5 sets out to increase awareness from the governance in the enterprise, which is composed of several levels of technical stakeholders and throughout the enterprise. For example, when looking at software quality assurance (SQA), most of the problems encountered by SQA revolve around staffing, authority, and control issues. To do its job properly, software professionals who are specialists in quality must make up the majority of the SQA staff. The problem with SQA is that it complicates group dynamics. That is because nobody likes to be criticized, so an organization-wide awareness has to be created that minimizes that kind of stress. Because it inspects the work rather than produces it, SQA often does not attract the top-notch people who gravitate toward development. This has to be taken into account by the decision makers when they set up the SQA operation. COBIT 5 promotes promoting awareness.

Benchmarking

This is the research component to the implementing framework. It requires the organization to have an in-depth understanding of what is going on in the industry and how are other agencies or companies accomplishing the same initiatives using the COBIT 5 Framework. This leads us to another PTS.

PTS 13.1 THE PULSE OF AN ENTERPRISE

- Pinpoint—Employees had no set of processes and/or strategies to attack quantitative analysis problems and make recommendations for solutions to mission-critical issues.
- Acclimate—This was also a problem that was prevalent throughout most organizations that were in an IT specialist's location. There were no documented processes for quantitative analysis. There were over 1000 employees at a certain data center.
- D^2—I developed a set of practices that all employees could follow during these types of issues. Problem solving within the discipline of project management determines the differences between a state of affairs that is desired and a state of affairs that are actual. Problem solving executes the necessary action to resolve the difference itself to create an optimal solution. The problem-solving process consists of seven steps and they are as follows:
  1. Pinpoint the problem.
  2. Analyze the set of alternative solutions.
  3. Formulate the criterion or criteria that will be used to evaluate the alternatives.
  4. Process the alternatives through careful analysis.
  5. Pick the alternative.
  6. Implement the selected alternative.
  7. Evaluate the results to determine whether a satisfactory solution has been obtained.

The first five steps, which cover the components of this process, are rooted in decision making. The first step has the IT specialist identifying and defining the problem for what it is. The fifth step has the IT specialist picking an alternative. This step, in actuality, is when the IT specialist makes the decision.

An example could be used when we look at Ross, an IT manager, from Data Center 1. Ross would like to choose a server to back up large files to, which will lead to more efficient system performance. He has four servers to choose from, which are located in four data centers. Those are Data Center 1 (DC1), Data Center 2 (DC2), Data Center 3 (DC3), and

Data Center 4 (DC4). Thus, the alternatives for Ross's decision problem can be relayed as follows:

1. Save data to the server at DC1.
2. Save data to the server at DC3.
3. Save data to the server at DC3.
4. Save data to the server at DC4.

The next step, after Ross determines the alternatives, is for him to figure out the criteria that will be used to evaluate the four alternatives. Capacity would be one of the obvious factors that would contribute to making the decision, and this may be dictated by how many applications are running on the servers and how much current data are stored to the servers. If this was the sole criterion for Ross's decision, then the problem would be a single-criterion decision problem. On the other hand, Ross can add some additional factors to consider which may be proximity to DC4 and frequency of cyberterrorism threats. Thus, the three criteria in Ross's decision problem are capacity, proximity to home base, and frequency (of terrorism threats). These extra factors turn this problem into a multicriteria decision problem. From a quantitative perspective to IT research and methodology, Ross would use four approaches. The first approach he used is linear programming. Using this approach, he would have to determine first whether the problem is the maximization or minimization problem. Second, he would determine the set of alternative solutions. Third, he would have to determine the criterion that would be used to evaluate the alternatives. Fourth, he would evaluate the alternatives. Fifth, he would choose an alternative. Finally, he would implement the chosen alternative, and then evaluate the results.

The second approach that Ross can use is the inventory approach. This approach poses two questions to the IT manager (or personnel): (1) How much should be ordered when the inventory is replenished? (2) When should the inventory be replenished? The analyst is able to determine the answer to these questions by using the Economic Order Quantity (EOQ) model.

The third option that Ross can use is the waiting line approach. These models have formulas that determine the performance measures for a waiting line. Performance measures of interest include the following:

- The probability that no units are in the system
- The average number of units in the waiting line
- The average number of units in the system (the number of units in the waiting line plus the number of units being served)
- The average time a unit spends in the waiting line
- The average time a unit spends in the system (the waiting time plus the service time)
- The probability that an arriving unit has to wait for service

  The final approach that Ross potentially uses focuses on risk analysis. This approach involves developing what-if scenarios based on data that you have already collected over time. That data can be placed into a gap analysis of some sort to document it.
- Synthesize: Employees all became comfortable with working on quantitative problems where they actually had to utilize measurement strategies to resolve issues.

Chapter Summary

- COBIT 5 sets out to promote more awareness and transparency from leadership all the way down to the enterprise systems personnel, and this chapter expands upon this.
- The project management task of benchmarking also holds an embedded presence with COBIT 5, and this assists with keeping an accurate picture of an enterprise's systems. The COBIT Dashboard assists in facilitating this.
- The case project provides an actual scenario in which the reader can conceptualize the COBIT Dashboard into the facts of the scenario.

Case Project

A badge-issuing initiative has been brought forth from executive leadership. The system shall be capable of issuing corporate badges. The PMO estimates the work and uses archived project data on similar badge issuance systems to establish the basis of estimates. Project resources and the schedule are based on a requirement size that has been understood to consist of 30 business rules. The four highest-level processes are shown below.

- Verify that the employee has passed their background investigation.
- Evaluate corporate training test results.
- Evaluate corporate benefits enrollment completion.
- Issue new badges.

The data gathered from this system will be stored and must be retrievable at any point because an employee's badge and security access is embedded in the badge and gives them varying access throughout the corporate offices. How can this case be tied to and expanded when using the COBIT Management Dashboard?

14

WHAT COBIT SETS OUT TO ACCOMPLISH

After reading this chapter and completing the case project, you will

- Understand adaptability to other existing frameworks;
- Understand constituency of governance for finance; and
- Understand constituency of governance for IT.

Adaptability to Existing Frameworks

COBIT 5 sets out to address governance and management so when followed in its most extensive capacity, it will be able to morph to fit most frameworks and best practices which are on the market. ISO/IEC 38500:2008, Corporate Governance of Information Technology, is the international standard that focuses on the accountability of the most senior-level executive leadership. The three tasks that this standard promotes are evaluate, direct, and monitor. Also embedded in the standard are the six principles of (1) responsibility, (2) strategy, (3) acquisition, (4) performance, (5) conformance, and (6) human behavior. The three standards should sound very familiar to COBIT 5 facilitators because ISACA streamlined those into COBIT as embedded governance practices within each of the five processes in the governance domain. The evaluation, directing, and monitoring of the governance system is how each is entitled.

The ITIL 2011 edition focuses on optimally delivering IT services to business partners. The three focal components of this framework are (1) services, (2) processes, and (3) functions. ITIL 2011 keys in on facilitating a service delivery life cycle that is made up of (1) service strategy, (2) service design, (3) service transition, (4) service operation, and (5) continual service improvement. Out of the 37 processes of COBIT 5, 15 of them have guided associations from ITIL 2011.

The ISO/IEC 20000 Information Technology Service Management System framework consists of 13 processes, all of which are referenced by COBIT 5 as guidance. The 13 service processes are broken to focus on resolution, control, relationship management, and service delivery.

The Projects in Controlled Environments (PRINCE2 2009) framework's eight components also has associations with COBIT 5 by guiding two of COBIT 5's 37 processes.

PMBOK has several processes which are embedded in the five process areas: (1) Initiating, (2) Planning, (3) Executing, (4) Monitoring and Controlling, and (5) Closing. This framework also consists of 10 knowledge areas: (1) Project Integration Management, (2) Project Scope Management, (3) Project Time Management, (4) Project Cost Management, (5) Project Quality Management, (6) Project Human Resources Management, (7) Project Communications Management, (8) Project Risk Management, (9) Project Procurement Management, and (10) Project Stakeholders Management. Three of COBIT 5's 37 processes have referenced PMBOK for guidance.

Constituency of Governance for Finance

COBIT 5 distributes the responsibility for the governance of finance to through the Board. When using the term "Board" in this context, it varies from organization to organization. Some private sector companies have high level executives which report directly to the Chief Information Officer (or Chief Technology Officer). Some Boards are composed of individuals who report one level higher to the CEO, so it depends on how heavily involved Boards are in management of the enterprise. The main point which COBIT 5 points out in its executive summary is that leadership from both the business and ICT must work collaboratively to ensure that ICT is not excluded from the governance and management strategy. In the book, the term *constituency* is used to describe the Board, because when you decompose the framework, you find that stakeholders exist from all levels of the enterprise. The constituency appraises all drivers along with their current performance levels. These drivers can be internal or external. Once they appraise the drivers, they use their analysis to feed the financial decisions they make and the financial strategies that they pursue. In the end, the Board provides direction based on the most senior management teams which fall under the CFO's purview of responsibility. Those management teams acquire their direction for controlling finance from the CFO.

Constituency of Governance for IT

The constituency in IT consists of the CIO and top-management team from the enterprise. They appraise all drivers along with their current performance levels. The CIO provides oversight through policies and determines the overall objectives of the enterprise. The management teams that reside under the CIO facilitate the delivery of IT services. These groups also keep the CIO informed, via reporting, on the status of IT initiatives and if those initiatives have an impact on the business. The CIO then ports those reports back to the board for mission-critical IT initiatives and the board may have feedback on changes of direction or soliciting more details. For example, if a project has been vetted to build a new system and cost associated with this initiative is extensive, this may turn out to be an initiative that is being closely monitored by the Board. There have been many cases when overspending has become an issue when it comes to the enterprise having to build multiple releases of a system due to the requirements growing to a point that it continues to increase the cost and scope of a project. In the end, the Board provides direction based on the most senior management teams which fall under the CIO's area of responsibility. Those management teams acquire their direction for pursuing IT directives from the CIO.

Chapter Summary

- This chapter keys in on ITIL, and a light comparison is discussed with COBIT 5.
- Comparisons are also offered between COBIT 5 and ISO/IEC 2000, PMBOK, and PRINCE2 2009.
- Governance is also discussed more granularly in this chapter.
- The case study focuses on how to approach the highest levels of leadership with the proposition of implementing COBIT 5. How would you sell it to your leadership based on what you've learned from this chapter?

Case Project

Carrying over from the case study in Chapter 13, this scenario expands upon that one. The badge-issuing process has been defined and is now ready to be built. Figure 14.1 shows the process as well as the high-level functional requirement derived from statements that will contribute to driving the programming code at a high level.

During analysis of the process and further discussions with involved stakeholders, it has been discovered that the badge-issuing process is missing some key components. Employees are now entitled under new legislation to receive a copy of all corporate test results. Another change will be necessary because recent changes to the background investigation clearances will require the system to give a summary about why the employee's clearance was denied. Since this system is a high-profile build, being communicated with the governance board for IT, how do you anticipate the CIO or CFO to address these matters when using COBIT 5? Which role would the building of this system fall under, CIO or CFO, and why?

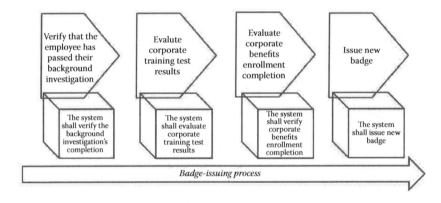

Figure 14.1 Case study—badge-issuing system with accompanying *shall* statements.

15
INTERNAL AUDITS

After reading this chapter and completing the case project, you will

- Understand the purpose of an internal audit following COBIT;
- Understand the roles that potentially use COBIT for the internal Audit Function;
- Understand the approaches to using COBIT as an internal audit;
- Understand the types of audits that can be facilitated using COBIT; and
- Understand the advantages of using COBIT in internal audits.

Purpose of Internal Audits

It is essential to have the fundamental understanding that COBIT in prior releases represented a control framework, which included a set of generally accepted control objectives, and the audit guidelines. Figure 15.1 conceptualizes the prior releases as they relate to the Audit Function.

COBIT 5 has changed its terminology and gotten away from control objectives and focuses more on best practices, governance, and the business drivers. Part of its underlying philosophy is that there is a need to holistically define and manage groups of processes, which in turn facilitates an IT enterprise's achievement of agreed-upon well-defined objectives. COBIT 5 empowers stakeholders who are close to business processes with a framework, which should enable them to go above and beyond with managing all the different activities underlying IT management and systems deployment.

"Internal auditing is an independent, objective assurance and consulting activity designed to add value and improve an organization's

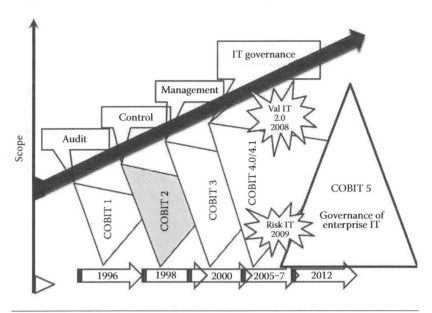

Figure 15.1   Conceptualization of COBIT 1 through COBIT 5, the framework's maturity.

operations. It helps an organization accomplish its objectives by bringing a systematic, disciplined approach to evaluate and improve the effectiveness of risk management, control, and governance processes." This definition continues to be a fair representative to defining what internal IT auditing groups do and why they do it. The only thing worth adding is that many organizations are subjected to external audits which routinely are scheduled in cycles. Internal Audit groups, therefore, strengthen the likelihood that the organization will be compliant during those audits.

One of the embedded missions of many internal audit groups is to analyze the efficiency and impacts of an organization's internal processes and procedures. Internal auditors make recommendations based on this analysis.

Roles That Potentially Use COBIT

There are various internal auditing roles that use COBIT 5. Some are as follows: the IT auditor, business process auditor, the IT inspection team, the IT control team, internal system administrator groups, managers of system administrators, and cybersecurity analysts. There are several additional roles that fall into this category because in order for an enterprise to be compliant with certain regulations, it employs full-time IT personnel who are responsible for internally enforcing or documenting compliance and noncompliance matters.

In some organizations, due to their immensity, there are more than one group of internal auditors who are responsible for checking. These groups are responsible for monitoring everything from when you log on to a system to password aging processes, which may be in place to ensure that the systems are more secure.

Approaches to Using COBIT in an Internal Audit

Internal auditors following COBIT to conduct their auditing generally approach audits when: formulating control baselines and standards, building or coordinating performance metrics for risk assessments, authoring and maintaining the audit plan, driving the audit, and mitigating risk or relaying advisements and recommendations to the IT manager and IT personnel.

Internal auditors bring with them a certain type of impact on the culture in an enterprise. While working in a bank data center years ago, while going through technical training, the entire training class was composed of computer programmers who had just finished college and were computer science or management information systems majors. However, there were 3 individuals in the class (out of about 15) who were from the internal audit group. It was essential for them to know the most technical inner workings of the bank systems since they would be monitoring what the rest of us were doing on those same systems after we completed the training.

Types of Audits That Can Be Facilitated Using COBIT

Audits can be initiated in conjunction with COBIT 5 to accomplish many monitoring capabilities in an IT enterprise. Some include analyses of requirements baselines and standards processes for IT, application and software development implementations, predevelopment planning, certification reviews, milestone entries and exits, lessons learned, postimplementation reviews, programmer's peer reviews, enterprise operation reviews, or data center reviews.

Internal entities that can result in being focal points of IT internal audits using COBIT are BCPs, organizations that are responsible for security settings on enterprise systems, IT procurement organizations, and any system that falls under the parameters of FISMA.

Advantages of Using COBIT in Internal Audits

Some of the advantages of using COBIT for internal audits are

- Control evaluations processes are standardized across the IT environment in many cases;
- Comparative analysis of system management processes spanning over different systems;
- Portability of benchmarks and standards throughout the enterprise;
- Postaudit benchmarking is easily achieved through existing COBIT enablers; and
- COBIT can easily be mapped to relevant regulatory examination components.

Figure 15.2 shows a conceptualization of roles and their interactions with activities and relationships in an enterprise.

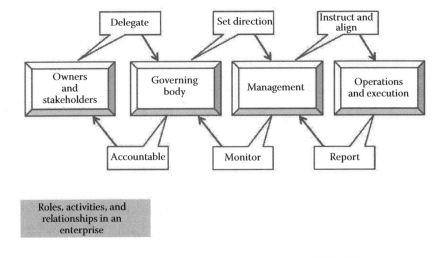

Figure 15.2   Conceptualization of COBIT 5, roles, activities, and relationships in an enterprise.

Chapter Summary

- This chapter discusses internal auditing and how COBIT 5 should be used with internal audits. It gives a foundational definition of internal auditing.
- There are auditing roles that cater to COBIT 5 and are heavily involved in the successful implantation of the framework.
- Different types of audits can be facilitated through COBIT 5, and there are distinct advantages to using COBIT 5 for auditing.
- The case study focuses on one of the grassroots practices of audits and a common dilemma that ICT managers go through when it comes to performance optimization versus compliance on enterprise systems.

Case Project

As an IT security manager, you are responsible for managing a group of IT security specialists who are responsible for monitoring the compliance of several internal systems (over 50). The security specialists that you are responsible for are well versed in the internal policy which lays out how security settings are to be set up on each system that falls under your group's jurisdiction.

In about a month, an external audit group will be coming to town to conduct a full-scale audit on your systems. You have alerted your team that they are to be fully cooperative with giving the auditors what they need. One of your team members approaches you and shares that it is their belief based on careful analysis that a few of your systems may not be compliant in time for the upcoming audit. They also share that they have evaluated these systems and spoken with the system administrators who are responsible for maintaining these systems (which do not report to you, but report instead to an IT manager). The system administrators have shared that they refuse to change the settings on their systems and they would rather take the hit during the audit. How do you handle this as an IT security manager?

16
Tying It All Together

After reading this chapter and completing the case project, you will

- Understand COBIT working hand in hand with Sarbanes–Oxley;
- Understand GETIT working hand in hand with COBIT;
- Understand the Process Assessment Model.

COBIT Works with Sarbanes–Oxley (SOx)

The part of SOx which focuses on internal control reviews (Section 404) was a challenge to implement due to there not being many guidance practices available when SOx first came on the scene. Recently many organizations have begun to follow COBIT 5 to better enable them to meeting SOx compliance requirements.

SOx Section 404, which focuses entirely on internal control assessment requirements, employs evaluative internal controls that are risk based. These controls place a great deal of attention on the COSO internal control framework. COBIT 5 is well suited for enterprises that have extensive IT processes in place. Both COSO and COBIT 5 are very complex frameworks when it comes to internal control. Either framework helps enterprises tremendously with bringing them into SOx compliance.

GETIT Working Hand in Hand with COBIT

Governance of Enterprise IT (GETIT) has no well-defined nor mandatory recommendation for how to go about implementing it. COBIT 5 does offer in-depth discussions on some of the challenges that often come up and how an organization can mitigate those challenges. Since the COBIT Framework is based on over 60 other frameworks, one would think that this framework could easily be associated as being the only framework for GETIT. There are others which potentially work with GETIT (many of which were discussed in prior chapters). Careful analysis must be placed into truly understanding the enterprise and documenting those findings through interaction with the stakeholders. This offers two unique perspectives: those stakeholders who are embedded in environments that understand the inner workings of the enterprise thoroughly and those stakeholders who are consultants that come to the enterprise for the first time to evaluate it. The second group sets out to acquire different information about the enterprise. What is the mission? What are the policies that deal directly with governance? These are questions that external stakeholders will ask and seek to acquire answers for. It is important to understand that without the support of the board membership, it is highly unlikely that using COBIT 5 for GETIT will be successful.

Process Assessment Model (PAM)

The PAM has a close relationship with ISO/IEC 15504-2, Software Engineering—Process Assessment: Performing an Assessment. The six capability levels of the PAM are 0: incomplete process; 1: performed process; 2: managed process; 3: established process; 4: predictable process; and 5: optimizing process. The levels determined through using process attributes. Each capability level consists of two process attributes.

Chapter Summary

- This chapter discusses at a high level COBIT and Sarbanes–Oxley (SOx).
- This chapter discusses at a high level governance of enterprise IT (GETIT) and how it interacts with COBIT 5.
- The chapter evaluates the process assessment model (PAM).
- The case study is very general but allows for the readers to expand upon what they've gathered from all of the approaches that were discussed in the chapter.

Case Project

As an IT manager in the private sector, you have been asked to research which framework would better facilitate SOx compliance. The company that you work for is small in size (about 35 employees), and you have an international presence with offices in Brazil, China, the United Kingdom, Canada, and Australia and four offices in the United States. Which framework will be your selection and why?

Bibliography

Ackoff, R. L. (1989). "From Data to Wisdom." *Journal of Applied Systems Analysis*, Vol. 16, pp. 3–9.

Bailey, J., Kandogan, E., Haber, E., Maglio, P. P. "Activity-Based Management of IT Service Delivery," ACM 1-59593-635-6/07/0003.

Bolinger, J., Horvath, G., Ramanathan, J., Ramnath, R. (2009). "Collaborative Workflow Assistant for Organizational Effectiveness." ACM 978-1-60558-166-8/09/03, pp. 273–280.

Brynjolfsson, E., Yang, S. (1996). "Information Technology and Productivity: A Review of Literature." *Advances in Computers*, Academic Press, Vol. 43, pp. 179–214.

Chan, W. T., Chua, D. K. H., Kannan, G. (1996, July). "Construction Resource Scheduling with Genetic Algorithms." *Journal of Construction Engineering and Management*, pp. 125–132.

Cichonski, P., Millar, T., Grance, T., Scarfone, K. (2012, August). *NIST Computer Security Incident Handling Guide: SP 800-61 Rev 2.* Gaithersburg.

Coulibaly, M. M. (2006). "A Strategy for Proactive and Predictive Services." Cisco Systems.

Council on Cybersecurity (2014). *The Critical Security Controls for Effective Cyber Defense Version 5.1.* Industry Guide, Arlington: Council on Cybersecurity.

Creswell, J. W. *Research Design, Qualitative, Quantitative, and Mixed Methods Approaches*, Second Edition.

Cross, J. (1995). "IT Outsourcing: British Petroleum's Competitive Approach." *Harvard Business Review*, Vol. 73, No. 3, pp. 94–104.

Davenport, T. H. (1994). "Saving IT's Soul: Human-Centered Information Management." *Harvard Business Review*, Vol. 72, No. 2, pp. 119–131.

Davenport, T. H. (1998, July–August). "Putting the Enterprise into the Enterprise System." *Harvard Business Review*, pp. 121–131.

De Marco, A. (2006). "Modeling Project Behavior: Dynamic Tools for Early Estimates in Construction Project Management." *Project Management Institute*, pp. 1–12.

Deloitte (2015, March 3). "From Cyber Incident Response to Cyber Resilience." *The Wall Street Journal*.

Dey, S. K., Sobhan, M. A. (2008, December). "Conceptual Framework for Introducing e-Governance in University Administration." ACM 978-1-60558-386-0/08/12.

Dietal, K. (2004, October). "Mastering IT Change Management Step Two: Moving from Ignorant Anarchy to Informed Anarchy." ACM 1-58113-869-5/04/0010.

Dipietor, B. (2015, March 27). "Risk and Compliance Journal." *Wall Street Journal*. http://blogs.wsj.com/riskandcompliance/2015/03/27/survey-roundup-unprepared-for-disaster/ (accessed May 3, 2015).

Estublier, J., Leblang, D., Van der Hoek, A., Conradi, R., Clemm, G., Tichy, W., Wiborg-Weber, D. (2005 October). "Impact of Software Engineering Research on the Practice of Software Configuration Management." *ACM Transactions on Software Engineering and Methodology*, Vol. 14, No. 4, pp. 383–430.

Ewusi-Mensah, K. (1997, September). "Critical Issues in Abandoned Information Systems Development Projects." *Communications of the ACM*, pp. 74–80.

Fenner, A. (2002, Spring). "Placing Value on Information." *Library Philosophy and Practice*, Vol. 4, No. 2.

Haeckel, S. H., Nolan, R. L. (1993, September–October). "Managing by Wire." *Harvard Business Review*, Vol. 71, No. 5, pp. 122–132.

Hales, S., Rea, D., Siegler, M. (2000, October/November). "Creating a Technology Desk in an Information Commons." ACM 1-58113-229-8/00/0010, pp. 96–101.

Hall, W. K. (1973). "Strategic Planning Models: Are Top Managers Really Finding Them Useful?" *Journal of Business Policy*, Vol. 3, No. 3, pp. 19–27.

Hiyassat, M. A. S. (2000, May/June). "Modification of Minimum Moment Method Approach in Resource Leveling." *Journal of Construction Engineering and Management*, pp. 278–284.

Hiyassat, M. A. S. (2001, May/June). "Applying Modified Minimum Moment Method to Multiple Resource Leveling." *Journal of Construction Engineering and Management*, pp. 192–198.

Homeland Security Presidential Directive 5 (2003, February 28). *Department of Homeland Security*. http://www.dhs.gov/publication/homeland-security-presidential-directive-5 (accessed January 22, 2015).

Homeland Security Presidential Directive 7 (2003, December 17). *Department of Homeland Security*. http://www.dhs.gov/homeland-security-presidential-directive-7#1 (accessed January 20, 2015).

Hoos, I. R. (1972). *Systems Analysis in Public Policy*, University of California Press, Berkeley, California.

Huber, R. L. (1993). "How Continental Bank Outsourced Its 'Crown Jewels.'" *Harvard Business Review*, Vol. 71, No. 1, pp. 121–129.

Iacovou, C. L., Dexter, A. S. (2005, April). "Surviving IT Project Cancellations." *Communications of the ACM*, pp. 83–86.

Information Systems Audit and Control Association (ISACA) (2014). *Implementing the NIST Cybersecurity Framework.* Rolling Meadows.

Information Systems Audit and Control Association (ISACA) (2012). *Control Objectives for Information and Replated Technology—Version 5.0.* Framework, Rolling Meadows: ISACA.

International Organization for Standardization/International Electrotechnical Commission (ISO/IEC) (2013). *ISO/IEC 27001 Information Technology—Security Techniques—Information Security Management System—Requirements.* Standard, Geneva: International Standards Organization.

International Society of Automation (ISA) (2009). *ISA 62443-2-1:2009 NIST Cybersecurity Framework Core: Informative Reference Standards.* Standard, Research Triangle Park: International Society of Automation.

International Standards Organization (ISO) (2008). *ISO/IEC 12207:2008 Systems and Software Engineering-Software Lifecycle Processes.* Standard, Geneva: ISO.

ISACA (2012). *COBIT 5: A Business Framework for Governance and Management of Enterprise IT*, ISACA, pp. 1–5.

Jarzabek, S., Sison, R., Hock, O. S., Rivepiboon, W., Nam Hai, N. (2006). "Software Practices in Five ASEAN Countries: An Exploratory Study." ACM 1-59593-085-X/06/0005, pp. 628–631.

Karlsson, K. (2005, November). "Triage: Performance Differentiation for Storage Systems Using Adaptive Control." *ACM Transaction on Storage*, Vol. 1, No. 4, pp. 457–480.

Keen, P. G. W. (1976, July). Managing organizational change: The role of MIS. In Proceedings of 6th and 7th Annual Conferences of the Society for Management Information Systems, White, J. D., Ed. University of Michigan, Ann Arbor, Michigan, pp. 129–134.

Kissel, R., Regenscheid, A., Scholl, M., Stine, K. (2014, December). *NIST Special Publication 800-88: Guidlines for Media Sanitation.* Gaithersburg.

Klievink, B., Janssen, M., "Improving Integrated Service Delivery: A Simulation Game." The Proceedings of the 10th International Digital Government Research Conference.

Kling, R., Gerson, E. M. (1977, Fall). "The Social Dynamics of Technical Innovation in the Computing World." *Symbolic Interaction*, Vol. 1, No. 1, pp. 132–146.

Kuhn, K. M., Joshi, K. D. (2009, August). "The Reported and Revealed Importance of Job Attributes to Aspiring Information Technology Professionals: A Policy-Capturing Study of Gender Differences." *The Database for Advances in Information Systems*, Vol. 40, No. 3, pp. 40–60.

Lacity, M. C., Willcocks, L. P., Feeny, D. F. (1995, May–June). "IT Outsourcing: Maximize Flexibility and Control." *Harvard Business Review*, pp. 84–93.

Lei, K., Rawles, P. T. (2003, October). "Strategic Decisions on Technology Selections for Facilitating a Network/Systems Laboratory Using Real Options & Total Cost of Ownership Theories." ACM 1-58113-770-2/03/0010, pp.76–92.

Madachy, R. (2006). "Simulation for Business Value and Software Process/ Product Tradeoff."

Markow, T. (2004, May). "A Knowledge Maturity Model: An Integration of Problem Framing, Software Design, and Cognitive Engineering." (Under the direction of Dr. Thomas Lynn Honeycutt). Decisions, pp. 25–30.

Marwah, M., Sharma, R., Shih, R., Patel, C., Bhatia, V., Mekanapurath, M., Velumani, R., Velayudhan, S. (2009, January 9–10). Data analysis, visualization and knowledge discovery in sustainable data centers, *Proceedings of the 2nd Bangalore Annual Compute Conference on 2nd Bangalore Annual Compute Conference*, Bangalore, India, ACM.

Miles, R.S. (1996, May/June). "Twenty-First Century Partnering and the Role of ADR." *Journal of Management in Engineering*, pp. 45–55.

Moeller, R. (2013). "Executive's Guide to IT Governance: Improving Systems Processes with Service Management, COBIT, and ITIL," John Wiley & Sons, Inc., Vol. 1, pp. 50–51.

National Institute of Standards and Technology (2014, February 12). *Framework for Improving Critical Infrastructure Cybersecurity.* Gaithersburg.

National Institute of Standards and Technology (2014, April). *NIST SP 800-53 Rev 4: Security Controls for Federal Information Systems and Organizations.* Gaithersburg.

National Institute of Standards and Technology (2012, September). *NIST SP 800-30 Guide for Conducting.* Gaithersburg.

Nolan, R. L. (1998, July–August). "Connectivity and Control in the Year 2000 and Beyond." *Harvard Business Review.*

O'Brien, J. O., Plotnick, F. L. *CPM in Construction Management*, Sixth Edition.

Paquette, M. (2015, January 23). *APTs: Minimizing losses with early detection.*

Sauer, C., Liu, L., Johnston, K. "Enterprise-Level Project Management Capabilities: A Comparison of the Construction and IT Services Industries," pp. 440–445.

Schwalbe, K. *Information Technology Project Management*, Third Edition.

Shoemaker, D., Sigler, K. (2015). *Cybersecurity: Engineering a Secure Information Technology Organization.* Stemford: Cengage Learning.

Son, J., Skibniewski, M. J. (1999, January/February). "Multiheuristic Approach for Resource Leveling Problem in Construction Engineering: Hybrid Approach." *Journal of Construction Engineering and Management*, pp. 23–31.

Steekamp, A. L., Konda, D. (2003, August). "Information Technology, the Key Enabler for Knowledge Management, A Methodological Approach." *The International Journal of Knowledge, Culture and Change Management.*

Volkov, M. (2014, December 16). *Corruption, Crime, and Compliance.* http:// blog.volkovlaw.com/2014/12/adding-cyber-security-corporate-risk -management/ (accessed January 30, 2015).

Wachob, W. "Applying the IT Service CMM Model in a University Service Delivery Environment." Educase 2005 Conference.

Wang, Y., King, G. (2000). *Software Engineering Processes, Principles and Applications*. CRC.

Xia, W. (2004, May). "Grasping the Complexity." *Communications of the ACM*, pp. 69–74.

Index

Note: Page numbers followed by "f" and "t" denotes figures and tables respectively.